CHANGES IN AMERICAN MORALITY: OF THE PEOPLE; BY THE PEOPLE; FOR THE SELF

CHANGES IN AMERICAN MORALITY: OF THE PEOPLE; BY THE PEOPLE; FOR THE SELF

Frank S. Farello, MA

Writers Club Press

San Jose New York Lincoln Shanghai

CHANGES IN AMERICAN MORALITY:
OF THE PEOPLE; BY THE PEOPLE; FOR THE SELF

Writers Club Press
an imprint of iUniverse.com, Inc.

For information address:
iUniverse.com, Inc.
5220 S 16th, Ste. 200
Lincoln, NE 68512
www.iuniverse.com

ISBN: 0-595-19213-0

Printed in the United States of America

Dedication

This book is dedicated to:
My beautiful and darling wife, my true angel, Pattie;
My wonderful children, Frank, Evamarie, Sean;
My dear parents, Frank and Rose;
Robert, JoAnn, Christa, Robert;
Kathy Ann, Peter, Peter, Alyssa;
Sal and Lee;
Mike;
Maria, James, SaraMarie;
Ben, Sue, Nadine, Eric.

(TYG)

Contents

Epigraph

"No man is an island, entire of itself; every man is a piece of the
continent, a part of the main."
John Donne, *Devotions upon Emergent Occasions*, 1624

Preface

The prevalent perception of a lack of inclusion of religious, ergo morally implicit, considerations within the political and legal codes of the United States (specifically the Constitution, the Declaration of Independence, and the Bill of Rights) as composed by the Founders, is erroneous.

Rather, the relatively homogeneous nature and ideologies of America's colonial population and the mutuality of its religious convictions led to an unofficial civic piety (a modified Protestant Christianity) which was sufficient enough to have an ethical influence upon American law, politics, and behavior. This directly resulted in an underlying moral compass which oriented the individual, as well as the society, and remained in place for most of this county's history.

However, during the twentieth century, as the population became inalterably heterogeneous, this implied civic piety no longer represented the diversity of America's inhabitants. Ultimately, that previously implicit moral field became increasingly ambiguous and unsatisfactory to many groups, resulting in a decline of its influence upon all aspects of American culture and society. In addition, as this country's mainstream religions were associated with this dissatisfaction, they similarly suffered in their influence upon American attitudes and behavior.

Since nothing as fundamentally principled has replaced this lost civic piety, nor collectively united the population under any particular moral code, the influence of the politics of liberalism and the philosophy of individualism have resulted in an alternate social concept. This alternative is the belief that one's own interpretation of a variety of religious, political, and social sources are to be utilized to produce a personally conceived moral compass with which to live by.

The result is a myriad of individual interpretations of behavior clouding the moral field, coupled with a seemingly vacillating, confusing, and oftentimes contradictory central government that rarely offers definitive definitions. Additionally, differing interpretations of theological concepts among religious institutions only adds to the turmoil.

Therefore, the satisfaction of the self has become the primary basis for the structure of our society, resulting in the deterioration of America's formerly community oriented population and those organizations associated with the same. The consequence of this is that, as each individual seeks his/her own self-fulfillment via whatever criteria he/she has selected, and an expanding heterogeneity further segments America, we have been witness to a sharp increase in the breakdown of moral order as the achievement of this unbridled personal satisfaction becomes *the* cultural norm.

As this behavior continues to dominate modern American society, a similar breakdown of our communal social order has become evident as crime and other forms of antisocial activity rise in conjunction with the need for further self-gratification. Moreover, as our society and its members move further along less the influence of a collectively conceived moral compass, much of the underlying religious considerations woven throughout America's political and legal codes are increasingly either ignored, disputed, or rendered inappropriate by today's citizens.

Propelled along in this manner, we find the thin line between individual autonomy and social order becoming increasingly problematic as the excesses of the former seemingly create the antithesis in the latter. Could this eventually result in anarchy?

At the heart of this book is the argument that, America has lost touch with the fundamental ethics of its founding principles and needs to reconsider the role of a collective morality. We need to re-explore the elemental communal concepts upon which this country was established and reexamine the philosophical and theological basis for our laws, government, and society.

Furthermore, I propose that the current confusion within modern American society with regard to morally based issues, attitudes, and behavior is the direct result of a deterioration of our formerly collectively composed moral compass in favor of one more personally conceived. Secondly, I contend that the consequence of this focus on the supremacy of personal choice has changed America from a nation of communities in cooperation toward achieving a common good for all, to a nation of competing individuals seeking to extract increasing levels of personal satisfaction and fulfillment from the larder of common goods.

The resulting scramble for this heightened self-gratification has left America floundering either in neutrality or ambivalence with regard to moral and religious issues, as the underlying locus for individual behavior finds itself based primarily on further unrestricted material acquisition.

At the onset, I must advise the reader that this is an exploratory effort, not a systematic historical analysis, nor an empirical study of American morality and religion. However, as there is an undeniable historical factor involved here which contributes greatly to my argument and which is an important foundational element to the contentions I raise, the reader will find the historical inexorably intertwined throughout the pages of this work.

In this sense, what this book attempts to expose is:

A)   that within the public sphere and private life, religion in America is perceived differently today, both in importance and performance, than it was during earlier eras in American history;

B) that since its founding, certain factors within America's sociopolitical and economic systems, both inherent and contrived, have fostered that difference, and over time have significantly diminished religion's role and influence specifically within the public arena;

C) that the effect this has had upon modern America's moral field is one where an increasingly ambiguous set of moral principles has resulted in a steady rise in the breakdown of moral order;

D) that to reverse this deleterious social tendency, religion, as is the case with all other institutions involved with achieving the common good, must be included within America's public dialogue.

Here I define religion to mean: faith-based, worship oriented organizations whereby adherence to a belief and trust in God is a fundamentally relevant condition of human existence, both for these organizations and their members, who then aspire to interpret and adhere to perceptions and conclusions gained from determinations considered to be revealed with regard to natural law/moral law principles.

In addition, for the casual reader it would be helpful to clarify a few basic points. First, throughout much of the first half of this book I often refer both directly and indirectly to the homogeneity of the colonial population. This homogeneity primarily refers to both common religious and political beliefs and ideals that the vast majority of the arriving settlers possessed. Secondly, although closely aligned to this homogeneity is the European origin of these settlers, their actual national background—be it English, Dutch, Irish, etc.—lessens the concept of homogeneity somewhat, due to cultural differences. Still, the most dominant nationality of these settlers was English, who established the American colonies, and whose political, religious, and cultural influence is considered foundational to American society.

Finally, in dealing with early American history the generic term "colonial period" needs some clarification. The true colonial period began in the early 1600s and continued well into the mid-1700s. During this time the foundation of American society was formed from the political and religious ideologies, and cultural influences of the arriving settlers—again mostly English. From the 1760s to the late 1780s "colonial" America was a well-defined area composed of the original thirteen colonies. Their ideological similarities led them to entertain the notion of independence from English domination and engage in an era of revolution which resulted in the Declaration of Independence, and later the drafting of the Constitution and the Bill of Rights. From the end of the 1700s to roughly the mid-1800s is considered the "early national" period. Here, the devotion to national interests coalesced into a consolidation of power, expansionism, and the increasing development of a distinctly American culture which further unified American society. It is here that we find a more homogeneous population, relative to that of the colonial era, in that, this increased attention to national interests produced an overall drive amongst Americans to actively produce a common good and a more defined mutual destiny. It is from within this early national period that the renowned social anthropologist and historian Alexis de Tocqueville recorded his conclusions and observations of colonial America; of the revolutionary and Constitutional eras, and the America of his day. Therefore, unless specified as "colonial," "revolutionary" etc.—the period of American history I mainly focus upon primarily within the Introduction and first two chapters, is that of the Founders, that is, the latter half of the eighteenth century—which is also referred to as the Constitutional, or Founding era.

In closing, and especially relevant to the central theme of this book is the concept Abraham Lincoln immortalized within his "Gettysburg Address," that ours is a, "government of the people, by the people, for the people." However, the conditions present in America today apparently ignore the final phrase of this dictum and replace it with the sobering realization that we have become a social conglomeration increasingly determined to reconstitute its essential elements, solely for the satisfaction of the self.

Acknowledgements

This book would not have reached fruition without the wisdom, guidance, and patience of Dr. Alan Mandell, SUNY Empire State College—Downstate. Alan, throughout the drafting of the original thesis you were always there, and it is with sincere appreciation that I thank you for everything—including responding to my "multitudinous" emails!

Also, thanks to Dr. Robert Carey, SUNY Empire State College—Downstate for his suggestions, insight, and involvement.

Introduction

The nature of our humanity is inherently imbued with an irresistible desire to seek and secure freedom. In this pursuit of freedom, the human entity intrinsically appeals to an inborn tendency to differentiate between freely conceived acts categorized as either right or wrong. This inborn tendency is recognized as reflective of a perceived structure of moral principles which is made manifest through the innate human inclination to adhere to a natural law.

As Frank Schmalleger, Distinguished Professor of Criminal Justice at Pembroke State University and Chairman of its Sociology Department, points out, "(n)atural law comes from outside the social group and is thought to be knowable through some form of revelation, intuition, or prophecy." (112).

In, *Sources of the Self: The Making of the Modern Identity*, the respected moral philosopher and political scientist Charles Taylor observed that, "(w)e are dealing here with moral intuitions which are uncommonly deep, powerful, and universal." (4). Continuing on, he further notes that although cultural influences may help define the boundaries of human interaction, the sources of the "basic reaction" is created elsewhere.

According to St. Thomas Aquinas in, *Summa Theologiae*, natural law is the active and intelligent human participation in the eternal law which directs the universe and the activity of all created things. This eternal law, or Divine plan, is perceived as existing within the mind of a Supreme Being who rules over the universe. As the contemporary author and Professor of Moral Theology, William E. May indicated, "(t)he end to which the eternal law directs all of creation is the universal common good of the entire created universe." (45).

There is a continuous legacy of ontological thought extending back over two millennia, from the ancient Greek philosophers (Plato, Aristotle, the Stoics) to those of the early and current modern era (Locke, Hobbes, Kant, Hegel) which considers the concept of natural law as universally operative and normative. This not only further involves human participation and activity, but our moral motivations and inclinations as well.

Whether this human propensity to perform morally conceived acts is personally or collectively realized, the basis for this assertion is set within the conscience of the human being. It is identified as reflective of the existence of a natural order permeating throughout the universe and the associated moral implications thereof.

That this perceived structure of moral principles is indistinguishable from natural law is further outlined by Aquinas through a series of primary and common precepts. The first of these, and upon which all other Aquinian components of natural law follow, is the identification of the "universal common good" as being desirable; that it should be performed, pursued, and that evil is to be avoided. We find similar references to this duality of moral principles and natural law reflected in the philosophical works of both classical and contemporary origin.

According to Lloyd L. Weinreb, Professor of Law at Harvard Law School, the Stoics of Hellenistic Greece concluded that, "the entire material universe is infused...with a rational creative force that orders and unifies it." (36). They further equated this "ordering principle" as the conjunction of nature and the Divine which has unavoidable influence upon human behavior via the resulting "dictate of nature" constituting right or wrong actions. Hence, although in this sense moral responsibility was "fully determined" it was, in effect, voluntary due to the inclusion of human free will.

Previous to the Aquinian tradition, several other thinkers sought to reconcile the issues of natural law and moral principles. Among them were: Cicero, whose writings were essentially repositories of Stoic thought, yet was the first to distinguish natural law as a separate philosophical doctrine; and St. Augustine of Hippo, whose merging of Divine law and that of nature was explained as being reflective of God's will.

This synthesis of natural law and moral principles is further evident in the works of several philosophers of the early modern era. John Locke, Thomas Hobbes, and Jean-Jacques Rousseau, to mention but a few, explored this natural law/moral law conjunction. Furthermore, many of their conclusions on this subject, specifically that of Locke, had profound influence upon the thinking of America's Founders. These ideas, reconsidered to be "natural rights" would eventually find their way into the drafting and ratification of America's Declaration of Independence, Constitution, and more specifically in the Bill of Rights. Incidentally, this thereby set the stage for further speculation involving natural law concepts well into our contemporary era.

Although the later influence of the nineteenth century philosophy of utilitarianism (as promoted mainly by Jeremy Bentham and John Stuart Mill) argued that human values should be based on the pursuit of pleasure and the avoidance of pain and therefore theories involving natural rights and natural law were invalid—many of the Founders deeply believed in a natural law originating with a Supreme Being. Samuel Adams, John Quincy Adams, Alexander Hamilton, and many others all referred to and recognized that, "the...natural law was given by the Sovereign of the Universe to all mankind"—John Jay, First Chief-Justice of the U. S. Supreme Court, April 15, 1818. (Barton 225).

Even modern theories of relativism (in law known as legal positivism) involving substitution of the laws of the state for the laws of nature, or the deontological ethic which maintains that the multitude of conceptions of the good leaves humanity's end unidentified and therefore subject to choice rather than being granted—ultimately fail to negate the influence of those classical concepts of natural law on the thinking of America's Founders.

We must be mindful that the current and purported clarity of our modern vision's tendency to discount the concept of natural law, or relegate it to the shelf of the quaint and outdated, cannot dispel the fact that recognition of natural law/moral law concepts was indeed a prime motivating factor behind colonial thought and structure. This is confirmed in the Declaration of Independence with the words, "to which the laws of nature and of nature's God entitles them" which refers to those grievances our American forerunners had with England over transgressions against one's "inalienable rights."

Given the well documented historical accounts of the political, economic, and religious strife endured by America's first settlers under the intolerant and monarchical regimes of seventeenth and eighteenth century Europe, and the regularity of these regimes to ignore and/or deny many of the basic rights of their citizens—there existed a fundamental desire within both America's original emigrants and their descendants to construct and maintain a society based upon natural law/moral law concepts and the securing of a citizen's natural rights. John Kekes, Professor of Philosophy and author of numerous works dealing with America's ethical and moral issues, states quite clearly that, "rights thus define areas whose violation is morally impermissible because they constitute minimum requirements of human welfare." (9).

Thomas Jefferson, Samuel Adams, John Quincy Adams, Alexander Hamilton, Noah Webster, John Jay, Thomas Paine, and so many other sources clearly indicate that the Founders' intentions were to involve a theistic-centered concept of the natural law into the foundation of American government, and to promote humanity's "inalienable" natural rights, that is, those given prior to politics. In support for this basis of the Founders' intentions, and as noted by the American historian David Barton, is the fact that the contemporaneous French notion of natural law, "excluded all Divine revelation and was man-centered not God-centered, (yet) such was *not* (author's emphasis) the case in America." (224).

It is noteworthy here and pertinent to this book's introductory discussion, to include a brief summary of the relevant thoughts of some of those philosophers who had such enormous influence upon the early American experience.

In, *Second Treatise of Government*, Locke outlined three propositions upon which the entire balance of his work rests. In essence, he acknowledges the existence of a God who ordained a natural order within the universe; that by employing reason, human beings can discern the prescribed rules of conduct as set forth by God, and that these rules can be known and understood with certainty.

In part, Hobbes' *Leviathan* discusses the notion of "prudential considerations"—which dictate the laws of nature, and "prudential principles"—a term he substituted for moral law. Both are analogous to the Aquinian conception involving that segment of natural law which Aquinas associated with the tendency of material creation to be inclined toward the good. The certainty of his conclusions led Hobbes to proclaim these concepts to be unconditionally true.

Although Rousseau dismissed the idea of natural law per se—in, *The Social Contract,* his conception of law and political obligation regarding the common good relies heavily upon the notion of an all encompassing "general will" as that factor which determines that which is just and unjust. In determining those judgments involving this general will, Rousseau acknowledges the existence of a "superior intelligence" or supernatural "legislator" who set forth the original civil laws, which according to Weinreb, "in the end is...not so different, after all, from the ultimate basis for theories of natural law that Rousseau (originally) rejected." (86).

The point I wish to make here is fourfold. First, there is that ubiquitously accepted source and long-standing deduced reality of a moral dimension of human existence that can neither be denied as having significant influence upon our behavior, nor determined to be solely acquired purely via human precedent. Secondly, there is the established intrinsic reality of an underlying, fundamental cornerstone of human conduct, distinct from the involuntary, which is influenced by natural law and is motivated by its inherent moral principles. Third, the placement of that behavioral reality lies outside the range of human construction, control, or influence, even though it has been continuously discussed, defined, explained, and refined throughout human history. Fourth, despite centuries of speculation, admittedly some to the contrary, this intangible and essential element regarding the framework upon which human moral motivation and behavior is hung, can neither be denied, ignored, nor rationally abolished. Here, Weinreb appropriately concludes, "insofar as moral responsibility is an essential characteristic of persons and at the heart of the distinction between persons and things, natural law addresses not only the moral qualification of our experience but its conceptual structure." (7).

As mentioned previously, the American Founders addressed the notion of natural law/moral à la Locke, et al. and sought to incorporate elements of the same into this country's basic political and social structure via a government based on those principles. Here, the Declaration of Independence, the Constitution, and the Bill of Rights—America's most sacred documents—address the reality of the existence of a fundamental moral compass with which to orient humankind's affairs.

However, as indicated earlier there was a twist! That is, the Founders conceived of the notion of "natural rights" emanating from the duality of natural and moral law as the direct antecedent of liberty. With regard to this concept, the contemporary philosopher Iris Murdoch recently noted the, "influential presence (and) continuing importance and value (of natural law, and its) special case (as) an intuitive axiomatic moral understanding." (360). Furthermore, Murdoch recognized that natural law and natural rights have a "special relation" with happiness and the value of liberty. Of particular interest here is her observation that, "(t)he flag of natural rights or natural law has often been that of revolutionary change." (361). In seeking to implement this natural rights concept into America's political foundation, the Founders were unique and indeed revolutionary.

According to Dr. George Chryssides, Senior Lecturer in Religious Studies at the University of Wolverhampton, England, natural rights are principally based upon John Locke's philosophies which, "created awareness that life, liberty and property were basic entitlements of human beings, and not privileges afforded only to the more fortunate of society." (84). The term "inalienable rights" as stated in the Declaration of Independence establishes the fact that these natural rights stem from a God-given natural law which Barton concludes, "were never to be violated nor abridged by any government." (220).

It would be helpful here to briefly discuss the cardinal difference between natural law and the closely related concept of natural rights.

To recapitulate, natural law essentially refers to that doctrine of ontological thought which describes humanity's free and rational participation in a definite, universal, and naturally occurring order resulting from an eternal or Divine plan as conceived by a Supreme Being.

The doctrine of natural rights construed in the mid-eighteenth century sense, and which is being addressed here, refers to that sociopolitical concept, à la the Jeffersonian conception as outlined in David Barton's book, *Original Intent: The Courts, the Constitution, & Religion*, which states that God Himself via the Scriptures has guaranteed to humankind certain liberties and freedoms that, "flowed from the 'natural laws' " (220), and which exist prior to political involvement. Incidentally, several of these rights were listed in the Declaration of Independence as: "life, liberty and the pursuit of happiness." In addition to Thomas Jefferson—James Madison and many other early American leaders also examined the concept of natural rights.

The distinction is of course between an all encompassing normative natural law, which in the ontological sense explains and regulates all existence within the material universe; and those specific and categorical rights having precedent within the natural law that are thus extended to humanity by God and which relate explicitly to human existence. Furthermore, according to the Constitutional scholar Jack N. Rakove, the Founders were quite clear with their intentions in, "distinguishing (between) the inalienable natural rights that individuals could never renounce from those alienable rights whose exercise was subject to the regulatory power of the state." (290).

It must be noted here that concerning human knowledge of natural law principles, two opposing schools of thought influenced early American thinking. Also, inherent within this contrast of opinion lies the very question of the nature of authority within civil institutions. With reference to the Founders' attempts to draft a governing system for the new nation, this question would have been of great concern to them. Indeed, their efforts did include major debates involving church v. state, where this issue of authority was thus centered. Of course, the most notable of these debates was for the drafting of the First Amendment, which will be examined in a later chapter.

The first school holds the belief that human reason alone is sufficient to discern and understand principles involving natural law; the second stresses that human reason is insufficient for this purpose and these principles become more clearly defined via the process of revelation. The former would place authority solely within the realm of human construction, that is, the state; the latter would deflect authority to the source of the revelation, that is, within the supernatural, which involves the existence of a Supreme Being, religious belief, and the ecclesiastical.

The contention I will develop later reveals that as the Founders were inherently religious men, they instinctively understood the important influence and motivating power of the supernatural upon the affairs of humankind, both historically and as it then applied to the foundations already established within the new nation. In this respect, the Founders realized the intrinsic necessity to equally protect those belief systems associated with the supernatural, i.e. religion, and to circumvent the possibility of abuse, à la the theocratic, which they themselves had knowledge of, and/or experienced not only in Europe, but even within some of America's earliest settlements.

I believe that the Founders also recognized the influence of the inevitable authority of a Supreme Being within the realm of human experience; the reality of a system of Divine revelations regarding natural law principles, and the ability of human reason to discern and employ each within our human endeavors. In fact, there are numerous references in support of these contentions spread throughout the written works of the Founders. (David Barton's, *Original Intent: The Courts, the Constitution, and Religion,* is an extremely useful compilation of most).

Here, I strongly believe that the Founders' attempts to keep religion and the state separate in no way was meant to imply any elimination whatsoever of the authority of the Supreme Being and those revelations associated with the same within the affairs of humankind. I also believe that the Founders sought to establish a governing system that developed civil order through the procedures of positive law, which were established via the ability of our human reason to conceive of a moral law and discern principles of natural law as revealed to humanity by the Supreme Being—the ultimate authority of the universe and all things within it.

My conclusions here are based on the following. Natural law is a component of the Eternal law composed within the mind of the Supreme Being. Natural law is that which orders and orients the entire physical universe. As members of the physical universe human beings, by their very existence, automatically participate in the natural law.

Since human beings are not privileged to know the thinking within the mind of the Supreme Being, our understanding of natural law is incomplete and rests mainly on suppositions arrived at through our reasoning abilities. However, to state that human reason is sufficient enough to discern natural law principles is similar to standing on a mountain at night and viewing the city below that has been struck by a blackout. The outline of the city is apparent to us, but less any illumination—the details are not. Therefore, unless the Supreme Being reveals his thinking to us, humans will continue to speculate and approximate natural law principles. In addition, human reason also involves the capacity to distinguish between concepts involving the right and wrong consequences of our actions within the structure of natural law. Our conclusions here are known as moral law.

Throughout human history, traditions have emerged based upon our speculations regarding natural law principles and out judgments involving moral law. In addition, whole systems of belief have developed employing this duality of natural law/moral law which state that the Supreme Being has indeed revealed some of his thinking and intentions to us. These systems of belief have evolved into our various religious institutions.

Still, as humanity in and of itself is inadequately able to know or understand the full mind of the Supreme Being and the laws composed by that Being, we must accept the distinct possibility that some, if not much, of what we do know of these principles has indeed been revealed to us by that Being. These known revelations are the chief raison d'être for our religious institutions. Here, our human reason is fully engaged in the initial awareness of a naturally occurring order, yet less the involvement of the Supreme Being's revelations the purpose of these principles, specifically with regard to human existence and destiny, would be meaningless. As such, religion is that link between humanity and the Supreme Being, and the reality of the revealed authority of the Supreme Being over all his created order.

Finally, within the Founders' deliberations regarding efforts to compose a governing system for this nation, in my opinion, it would have been impossible for them to avoid reaching these conclusions. As such, I believe it was extremely obvious and vitally relevant for them to include components involving the authority of the Supreme Being, natural law/moral law principles, and religious considerations within their thinking and decisions. Once again, this was made evident by various statements and sentiments contained within both the Founders' public and private writing. Here, the Founders sought to derive a system faithful to Supreme authority, natural law/moral principles, religious expression, and concepts of positive law in the governing of individual behavior and the destiny of the new nation.

It is here that we uncover the crux of the intent and basis—both historical and contemporaneous to early American society—for the underlying motivation of the Founders, as is outlined in the Preamble to the Constitution of the United States: to "establish Justice...and secure the Blessings of Liberty to ourselves and our Posterity."

Here I will continue on with a brief overview of early American inhabitation, which will introduce additional elements in support of an underlying religious orientation as fundamental and foundation to colonial society.

Settlement in the nascent United States was arduous at best. Yet, colonialization persevered spurred by the deep-seated desire to establish communities which were protected and maintained by the underlying premise and pursuit of freedom and equal treatment under the law. Despite the continued reliance on slave labor, or the subordinate status afforded to America's indigenous peoples, the nucleus for the eventual abolition of these practices was predicated with the affirmations stated in several of America's foundational documents, many dating back to its origins.

We of course are familiar with the various social and economic conditions which resulted in the mainly English migration to the New

World; in the foundation of the original thirteen colonies, and which produced a relatively uniform population. From the vantagepoint of the early nineteenth century, Tocqueville commentated on this uniformity and characterized it as, "homogeneous in all its parts." (39).

However, to the majority of scholars the prime motivation behind the emigration of thousands of English citizens to America was religiously oriented. Patricia U. Bonomi, historian and Professor of History at New York University, observed this tendency and remarked, "if there was a single determinant of the colonists' political responses more important than any other, it might have been religious." (vii). Ira Glasser, author and Executive Director of the American Civil Liberties Union, similarly noted, "(t)he English citizens who came to the new world were deeply familiar with the denials of religious freedom." (70). Granted, there were numbers of settlers who arrived for more secular reasons (e.g. business opportunities, employment, adventure) but the majority were primarily seeking religious freedom.

Puritans, Catholics, protesting Protestants, Quakers, Jews, and other religious groups suffered from widespread religious intolerance at the hands of the English State and its Anglican Church (the Church of England). In fact, Glasser further reveals that, "(i)n England in the 1680s, less than a hundred years before the American Revolution, it was a crime not to go to the Protestant Church of England." (70).

The masses that fled from England to America, the great majority being Christian denominations, sought mainly to secure their religious freedom. Although at times that freedom was a strictly enforced theocracy—as in the case of the Puritan establishment of the Massachusetts Bay Colony in 1630—the motivation was the ability to practice one's religion freely, albeit here, it was only the Puritan religion.

Regarding this observation, Barton states that, "the motivations of the colonists who came to America can be documented from an examination of their approved intentions." (76). In this respect, Barton notes that the charters for the foundation of the vast majority of the original American colonies all declared in summary and essence a deep desire to structure their governments and society based on religious faith, and as specifically stated in many of these documents, for "the glory of God."

The influx of this mainly Christian migration which was comprised mostly of Protestant sects, resulted in an underlying foundation of religious ethics (commonly known as the Protestant ethic) to permeate throughout colonial government, society, and culture. Here, I would like to pause and clarify this concept of "the Protestant ethic" and further discuss its effect upon America's development.

While we speak of a religious ethic woven throughout the fabric of early American society, there is an important distinction I wish to make, and most fail to realize, between two terms of seemingly equal value: the Protestant ethic and the Puritan ethic. Despite their interchangeability there is quite a difference between them.

The Puritan ethic—which incidentally Alexis de Tocqueville spoke of quite frequently in, *Democracy In America,* as being (up to the early nineteenth century) the basis for the evolution of mores throughout much of America's history—refers to that particular Protestant sect's religiously based community concepts of tolerance, equality and freedom under the law. The Puritans were one of the first groups to flee religious persecution in England. By 1640 their Massachusetts Bay Colony numbered 20,000 inhabitants. As a result, their influence was significant to the structure of American society and government via the foundational laws they drafted.

However, the Protestant ethic has a completely different origin. Though also religiously based, it is quite dissimilar to the Puritan ethic, in that, it is essentially a generic term coined to refer to a certain ethical practice regarding one's occupational performance. The Protestant ethic is traditionally associated with *all* sects of Protestant origin which comprised colonial society, and therefore is an altogether separate ethical concept than that ethic which is linked to Puritanism. The

Protestant ethic refers to the perception that one must work hard and to the best of his/her ability, and be continually mindful of the good being performed not only for the temporal community, but as a member of God's community as well. Today, it is commonly associated with the tenets of capitalism, which declares that success is the direct result of hard work.

In, *The Protestant Ethic and the Spirit of Capitalism* (1920), the sociologist Max Weber studied this link between Protestantism and capitalism and noted that the latter did indeed emerge in Europe through the tenets of the former, especially Calvinism. This sect's belief in God's predetermination of those souls who would enjoy eternal salvation in heaven and those damned to hell, led the Calvinists to seek, as explained by the sociologist and political scientist Dr. Ian Robertson, " 'signs' that they were among the chosen—and they took worldly success as just such a sign." (406).

The link Weber made was between the Calvinist abstinence from pleasure, which was associated with a sinful life; and diligent work, which was considered virtuous and salvational. Robertson further notes that, "(t)he more successful they were, the more likely it seemed that they were destined for heaven—and since profits could not be spent on pleasure, they had to be reinvested." (406). Hence, and as explained by Robertson, from Weber's hypothesis we find existent within early Calvinism the foundations of modern capitalism, and that through this resulting religiously derived "work ethic" emerged our recent theories of, "(t)he methodical accumulation of wealth through rational, calculated procedures, such as accounting and long-range planning. Hard work and making money are highly valued for their own sake. To spend money on idle luxury is considered disreputable; instead, the capital must be reinvested to earn yet more capital." (406).

It was from capitalism's progression that the modern industrial age was born, which in turn encouraged the increase of a more secularized and scientific view for producing wealth and guaranteeing profit. This has served to completely eliminate capitalism's religious foundation however, it still retains the Protestant ethic component of, "diligent work, thrift, and deferred gratification." (406).

Regardless of the distinction made between either the Puritan or Protestant ethic, the underlying common denominator of each lies in the religiously based attention to the community, its development, and the strengthening of communal bonds—all in the pursuit of a shared common good.

Here we find two fundamental planks upon which the whole structure of American society was set since its inception; what constituted and motivated colonial culture and thought, and what the Founders incorporated into their personal and political undertakings— namely religion and community. The former was introduced via the foundational documents drafted and inaugurated by the masses fleeing religious persecution in England and seeking religious freedom in America; the latter originating with those same groups via their socially oriented religious convictions.

This is what the United States was initially all about! This is the "home base" of American society! We were an association of people united in the commonly implied, but officially undeclared goal of the furtherance and betterment of our combined condition, through a mutually understood notion of community oriented effort based on commonly held religious beliefs.

This merging of religion and community was not odd, outdated, or an abstraction to our early American ancestors—it was familiar to their everyday lives. By comparison, in our modern more segmented society—with its tendency toward what the eminent sociologist and founder of the Communitarian movement Amitai Etzioni referred to quite frequently in his books (see bibliography) as the current "loss of community" and our overall "moral confusion"—one would need to actively seek out and pursue a collective experience similar to that known to early Americans. For example: one might have to attend a religious service; be present at a political or civil rights meeting, or volunteer for community work involving local, national, or global needs. All would encompass various levels of community involvement and include certain elements of moral effort. However, most modern day individuals would ultimately return to their lives lived separate from those collective goals.

To further clarify the issue of religious belief as not only highly contributive to the archetypal laws drafted in the New World, but also that factor which is of crucial importance to our comprehension of the community oriented structure of America's earlier populations, it would be helpful to refer to Tocqueville's observations published in the 1830s in his, *Democracy in America*. Here he concluded, "Puritanism was not just a religious doctrine; in many respects it shared the most absolute democratic and republican theories." (36). Furthermore, and again as Tocqueville so significantly stated, "(Puritanism) was almost as much a political theory as a religious doctrine." (38).

Tocqueville elaborates further by noting that the foundation of American society began in the colonies collectively known as New England. Here were sowed the seeds of, "the two or three main principles now forming the basic social theory of the United States." (35). In Tocqueville's day, those principles were perceived to be: "advanced education"; "talents and knowledge," and "elements of order and morality." (36).

Tocqueville continues to explain his observation with commentary such as, "in America it is religion which leads to enlightenment and the observance of divine laws which leads men to liberty." (45). He further noted that, "in America it was somehow possible to incorporate (the) marvelous combination (of) the spirit of religion and the spirit of freedom" (46-7), and that, "(these) two distinct but not contradictory tendencies (of religion and politics) plainly show their traces everywhere, in mores and in laws...(and) work in harmony and seem to lend mutual support." (47). Other scholars have also noted that this, "increasing interpenetration of religion and politics" (Bonomi 9), was considered, "a civilizing agent among a people far removed from traditional social restraints." (16).

What we find existent throughout the entire history of America's colonial period was essentially a newly found wilderness society seeking political and social organization and finding this, according to Bonomi, through the stabilizing influence of the church. In addition, and as explained by the respected sociologist, political scientist and scholar Seymour Martin Lipset, this social stability via the church, "predisposed them to moralism." (60). This moral element was, according to the research team headed by the sociologist Robert N. Bellah, elemental to the formation of the, "face-to-face communities that characterized early American society (and which) participated mutually in enterprises that furthered the common good" (*Habits of the Heart* 116), and in efforts undertaken toward, "the creation of a certain kind of ethical community." (29).

Lipset adds further credence to the melding of American religion and politics by quoting from the historical work done by Everett Carll Ladd in his book, *The American Ideology: An Exploration of the Origins, Meaning, and Role of American Political Ideas.* Ladd observed, "(s)ince most of the Protestant sects are congregational, not hierarchical, they have fostered egalitarian, individualistic, and populist values which are anti-elitist. Hence, the political ethos and the religious ethos have reinforced each other." (Lipset 61).

There are several influential factors involved here which in essence, created the foundation of American society. That is: the duality of religion and politics; the congregational nature of the arriving Christian sects which fostered the concept of a community oriented society, and the notion of working toward a common good.

When we speak of early America's relatively homogeneous population, we not only refer to the dominance of a particular religious tradition (Christian), or nationality (English), but those societal foundations as stated above, which essentially unified the population via the mutuality of their shared intents and purposes. According to Barton, in the case of the American experience, all these factors combined to establish an underlying unifying principle of achieving the common good via, "proposed laws and policies (to) be judged with the full cognizance of their spiritual implications." (334).

In essence, what Tocqueville noted in the 1830s to be in existence throughout his study of American history, is what many scholars today often refer to as America's unofficial civic piety, or its civil religion—to which Barton indicates is composed of, "transcendent, Biblical, natural-law standards." (241). This was highly influential upon both public and private mores and behavior. For example, the former Dean of Harvard's Divinity School, Robert F. Thiemann in, *Religion in Public Life: A Dilemma for Democracy*, commented that, "a modified version of Protestant Christianity came to provide both symbolic and institutional support for a new American civic piety." (28). His further contention is especially relevant, in that, Thiemann noted the reality of a, "peculiar version of 'civil religion' that grew up in American soil...that relates the history and destiny of the nation to divine providence." (31). This was of particular importance, in that, the existence of this "civil religion" was in evidence, "during the first two centuries of the republic's life." (27).

In fact, Barton further explains that this "civil religion" constituted a, "value system...established in the Declaration of Independence" (247), which the Founders believed was, "inseparable from good government and...essential for national success...(via) the principles of religion and morality...(and) accepted as sound public policy." (319). Moreover, Barton believed that the Founders understood that civic piety, "must be publicly encouraged and supported to ensure national longevity" (330), or, "civil government would not long survive." (327).

It is within this discussion that we now arrive at the efforts of the Founders themselves to incorporate and institute their intrinsic religiously based, community oriented concepts into a social structure predicated on a secularly oriented political system.

The central issues here are several. Were religion and religious beliefs indeed part of the decision-making process of the Founders with regard to the drafting of those sacred documents associated with the foundation of the American republic namely: the Declaration of Independence; the Constitution, and the Bill of Rights? Did the Founders consider there to be a religious nature to American's government and society and simply build upon that notion? In effect, did religion play any structural role whatsoever in the Founders' efforts to organize a framework for the new nation and were religious principles to be considered an inherent part of America's governing process?

Once again we must refer to the historical evidence. As outlined earlier, since its inception, the foundations of American government and society were based primarily on Christian concepts of natural law/moral law, which also considered the notion of natural rights. This is made evident by the early legal documents drafted by the mostly English immigrants seeking religious freedom in the New World. In addition, I have referred to the religious nature and atmosphere of colonial America and the presence of an underlying unofficial civic piety in existence throughout America's early history.

With observations made barely sixty years after the birth of this nation, Alexis de Tocqueville commented repeatedly on, "(t)he religious atmosphere of the country (as) the first thing that struck me on arrival in the United States" (295), and how religion, "powerfully contributes to the maintenance of a democratic republic among the Americans" (287), and the, "(i)ndirect influence of religious beliefs upon the political society in the United States." (290).

Therefore, in light of all the evidence noted within this book and other sources too numerous to be included in these pages, I maintain that it is inconceivable that the Founders would not have sought to incorporate religion and religious principles into their considerations, decisions and expectations regarding America's government and society. From their point of view, it was simply the practice of "good" government to include religion. In addition, many modern scholars and authors in the field of history, political science, and sociology support the notion of the Founders' realization of the benefits of religion on the governing process. For example, Barton's extensive investigation of this issue reveals that, "(t)he Founders believed that religion and morality were inseparable from good government and that they were essential for national success. Consequently, the promotion of the principles of religion and morality was accepted as sound public policy." (319). "(This) was a truth recognized not just by the Founders but even by early courts and Congresses." (324).

Bonomi also supports this contention with the following observation which I find to be the base upon which the structure of American society was originally set, "(r)eligion permeated early American life in part because religious institutions had to be built anew in the colonies, a task that incorporated the laity into the very fabric of the churches at the same time it built the churches into the structure of civil society." (217).

Simply put, as new settlements required a parallel rebuilding of each segment of society, in effect, there was a multi-symbiotic relationship among all segments for survival and stability. In this sense, the mutual benefits generated created strong links, even interdependencies, among America's early social institutions much like that experienced by multiple birth siblings as they develop.

Added to this evidence are similar sentiments expressed by some of the Founders themselves. For example: "Religion and virtue are the only foundations...of republicanism and of all free governments"—John Adams, August 28, 1811 (Barton 156); "Sensible of the importance of Christian piety and virtue to the order and happiness of a state, I cannot but earnestly commend to you every measure for their support and encouragement"—John Hancock, Inaugural Address as Governor of Massachusetts, 1780 (321); "Religion and morality are the essential pillars of civil society"—George Washington, March 3, 1797 (324).

It is here that we encounter an interesting dilemma. Why then, in light of all the evidence presented regarding the Founders' religious roots and sentiments, are America's three most sacred documents (the Declaration of Independence, the Constitution, and the Bill of Rights) virtually devoid of any specific references to religion, save some introductory and explanatory statements? Why, despite the obvious importance the Founders placed upon religion and morality as "the essential pillars of civil society" are these same individuals so conspicuously silent within this country's most profound documents regarding the function of religion and religious principles in American government and society?

Are we to believe, as the contemporary historians Isaac Kramnick and R. Laurence Moore proposed, that the Founders, "wanted religion out of politics because...the state's job was merely to be an umpire ensuring a peaceful and secure arena of economic life" (87), or that the Founders were atheists, or agnostics and had no desire to include religion as part of public life? Are we to conclude that the Founders intended there to be a strictly enforced delineation, commonly referred to as the "separation of church and state" that would forever relegate religion to the realm of, as Stephen L. Carter, Professor of Law at Yale University and one of America's leading experts on Constitutional law, feared would be, "the arbitrary and unimportant" (6); "something without political significance, less an independent moral force than a quietly irrelevant moralizer" (9); or "a hobby" (29)—in essence a locally conceived system of personal opinions, beliefs and superstitions?

I think not! Therefore, and in opposition to the above, the contention of this book is outlined as thus: considering the long litany of abuses associated with state involvement in, or sponsorship of religion throughout history; and those transgressions specifically witnessed and endured by the Founders and their ancestors under English rule; and the threat of the same to overtake America as evidenced by several early colonial attempts to legislate a state sponsored religion, I propose that the Founders' intentions were completely otherwise. Their legislative omission of religion and religious principles was a purposeful attempt to protect religious beliefs against state involvement and, as so often was the case, the oppressive and tyrannical intervention by the state into religion. However, this omission of religious doctrine in America's public documents by the Founders has been increasingly problematic throughout this country's history and has left the issue open to extensive speculation and debate. In the twentieth century, specifically since the 1950s, it has fueled a heated controversy involving the role of religion in America's public life, which remains unresolved to this very day.

The result is that contemporary America is effectively sharply divided along interpretive lines involving either the inclusion or exclusion of religion in public life. The resulting confusion has seriously undermined the moral fiber of this country and created a sociopolitical stagnation that only further exacerbates the issue.

In subsequent chapters within this book, I will examine more closely this complex issue and the resulting consequences within modern American society. Each chapter will deal with the specific factors contributing to the current changes in American's moral structure and religious foundations.

The primary focal point of the opening chapter will be the First Amendment itself and the events surrounding the drafting of the same. It will deal specifically with this amendment's controversial "Separation Clause" (which incidentally has been further divided into "The Establishment Clause" and "The Free Exercise Clause").

The remaining chapters will examine: the decline of religion in America; individualism; the advent of modern liberalism; the current muddy moral order; the problems associated with maretialism, and conclude with a chapter exploring some possible solutions to the moral dilemmas affecting America today. In closing, I will offer my final reflections.

However, I have one caveat to make: To include a detailed discussion of the Declaration of Independence; the Constitution itself, and the other amendments in the Bill of Rights would be well beyond the scope of this book. Still, these documents will not be neglected and will be referred to throughout the chapters, together with their relationship to the central argument.

As a prelude to the first chapter I urge the reader to once again consider the following: The Founders' legislative omission of religion and religious principles within the sacred documents of the United States was not intended or expected to exclude or diminish religion and religious principles from the mechanics of America's public life. Rather, the Founders in their wisdom, sought to secure religion from state abuse and control, and leave it safely protected within the hands, hearts, and minds of the American people.

Chapter 1

The First Amendment: The Theory And Theology

The Founders aspired to develop a fair, just, and equitable sociopolitical system with which they would govern the nascent United States and give direction to its society. These learned individuals sought to experiment with the extraordinary concept of a self-governing, democratic society. However, considering the complexities of their goals, their written intentions and pronouncements have often been at odds with the existing social conditions within which their efforts must function at any particular time.

Many of the Founders held classically liberal political views which included the notion that less government involvement in citizens' lives is thought to produce better government. Reflective of this is the following quote from Thomas Jefferson's "First Annual Message to Congress" given on December 8, 1801, "(w)hen we consider that this government is charged with the external and mutual relations only of these states...we may well doubt whether our organization is not too complicated; too expensive; whether offices and officers have not been multiplied unnecessarily, and sometimes injuriously to the service they

1

were meant to promote." (Website: Thomas Jefferson: Good Government).

Considering this, the Founders left their pronouncements sufficiently succinct so as not to create the possibility of an imposing and overbearing governing system. What they could not possibly have foreseen was the complete opposite occurring, for example, as burgeoning socioeconomic conditions requiring increased government assistance programs result in today's modern welfare state. Additionally, given the issues raised and the facts presented in this book's introduction regarding the Founders' religious backgrounds; their strong conviction to natural law/moral law principles as construed through their religious beliefs, and their reliance on the same in decisions arrived at in their political and governing efforts—it is logical to deduce that they believed that the duality of natural law/moral law would be at work and ever present within the mechanics of an American democratic system based upon their foundational achievements.

It is equally logical to infer that within this democracy, the Founders did not conceive of a time or system whereby natural law/moral law principles would not have an underlying, contributory, and constructive influence upon our population and its government. This was supported by the pervasiveness of religious practice and belief woven throughout early American society.

However theoretical my contentions may appear, in light of the evidence produced in this book so far, one can begin to gain a sense that this religious component was firmly entrenched and inexorably linked within the mechanics of early American society, and of the utter incomprehensibility among Americans for it to be otherwise, both then and in the future. For modern Americans to understand the dynamic and essential influence of this religious component, and the deleterious effect it would have had if removed from the mechanics of colonial society—in comparison we need only envision a future America less sports, or television.

Still, over the centuries, the Founders' penned succinctness has created a multitude of controversial interpretations of those same written decisions with regard to religion's function and relevance within the mundane concerns of the state. Current interpretations seek to clarify and/or explain the fuzziness of the original concepts and make provisions to shore-up that which, for the time being, is deemed loosely understood. Inevitably, the constant reinterpretations have succeeded in stretching the original meanings well beyond their original intent. This has created an ever loosening of the underlying natural law/moral law principles, which were fundamental to the Founders' pronouncements, in favor of the excesses of the sociopolitical environment next in existence.

I have discovered that what was so often considered to be the prime example of an ideology based on the natural law/moral law and God given rights, equality, and liberty—in essence the foundation of American democracy—is, as we begin the twenty-first century, seemingly hamstrung by the multitudinous interpretations assigned to those components and the apparent resulting excesses thereof. This is not to imply that continued effort and debate here is unnecessary—on the contrary, it is vitally important to continue grappling with these difficult interpretations involving, for example, church and state issues. Still, the goal here should be a further orientation toward eliminating the superfluous and excessive within these discussions that so often mire down the process in minutiae and detract from achieving possible permanent solutions. Therefore, as we further extend our present interpretations to suit our immediate needs, much of the Founders' meanings and intentions behind their legislative efforts seems lost, or at best—uncertain.

For example, early Americans resented the use of their tax money to be dispensed for the support of any religious institution. This was based on the possibility that the religious institution thus funded would then be able to utilize the resources of the state to promote or assist in its cause. The worst case scenario for this could eventually lead to abuses of religious rights similar to those of seventeenth century England, hence clear violations of natural law/moral law principles involving the inherent freedoms afforded to all human beings by the Creator of the universe. The issue here is not about the private practice of one's religion per se, but the potential adverse effects upon one's private practice of religion through state involvement with religion.

Yet, in 1983 the United States Supreme Court upheld a program instituted by the state of Minnesota to provide parents with income tax deductions for expenses in sending their children to private schools. However, ten years earlier it voted against a similar program in New York. Referring to Ira Glasser's analysis of this case in, *Visions of Liberty: The Bill of Rights for All Americans*, in summary the Court reasoned that the New York case was specifically geared to assisting only parents of children attending private schools, where in the Minnesota case both private and public schools would benefit.

By agreeing with the Minnesota system, the Court clearly acted contrary to the intent of the Founders with regard to the First Amendment. I believe that the majority of the founding generation of Americans would have found that this decision violated the original principle of this Amendment, which was to keep government out of religion. In effect, the decision allowed public money raised through taxes to be utilized by religious institutions.

The danger of this particular precedent is obvious: future interpretations could eventually involve government assistance of specific, or majority religious institutions and conceivably lead to violations against individual or minority religions' rights.

Here, I will pause and delve into a bit of historical analysis regarding the events involving the development of the Constitution and the Bill of Rights. This will serve as a foundation for a later discussion of the intellectual and political climate under which the issues of individual rights were debated and refined.

Faced with the responsibility of leading the new nation, these learned and religious men assembled to reformulate and draft that which would epitomize their political philosophies; better organize American government; foster their hopes for this country's social development, and nurture their dreams for continued freedom and democracy within the United States. Lofty goals indeed!

To achieve this, a call was made for each state to send delegates to a national gathering in Philadelphia in 1787. The original intention was to revise the Articles of Confederation produced during the Revolution due to what some argued were fundamental weaknesses within that document. These shortcomings left the states strong, free, and independent while the national government remained weak and subordinate. In the past, this made good sense given the colonists' history with England's powerful, centralized, monarchical government however, at this juncture of American history this strategy was found to be insufficient. Many delegates felt that the majority of the conditions within the Articles did not meet the needs of the new nation and it was determined that a completely new agreement was necessary.

Commencing on May 25 through to September 17, 1787, the fifty-five delegates (Rhode Island did not send a representative) labored to produce a document which would in effect, create a new federal government. In the end, this convention drafted: the Constitution of the United States, which was transmitted to Congress, then sent to the states themselves for consideration and ratification. On June 21, 1788 the Constitution came into legal effect.

The Constitution is a document which legitimizes American government, outlines our sociopolitical plans, and gives cause for the manner in which we will conduct our affairs. Rakove's analysis of the influence of this document throughout American history indicates that, "the Constitution has always played a central role in American politics, law, and political culture, as both a continuing source of dispute and a legitimating symbol of national values." (5).

Along with the Declaration of Independence, the Constitution further justifies our existence as a nation. Barton concludes that it is a, "well-devised (plan) for government based on specific political philosophies selected only after extensive research, study, and debate. This fact was acknowledged by Benjamin Franklin at the Constitutional Convention." (213).

Later, motivated by an original proposal by George Mason of Virginia and increasingly introduced by others who felt the Constitution needed to, as in the words of author and Professor of American History at MIT, Pauline Maier, emphatically, "assert the natural equality of men (and) mention their inalienable rights" (194), on December 15, 1791, the states ratified ten of an original twelve amendments—the remaining two were dropped. Collectively, they were proposed on September 25, 1789 by the first federal Congress and were to be listed at the end of the Constitution.

Labeled the Bill of Rights, these amendments were essentially modeled after some of the provisions outlined in Virginia's Declaration of Rights, which itself (and those similar documents adopted by several other states) was based on the English, Declaration of Rights, of 1689.

With respect to those "inalienable rights" the Founders sought to secure, it is through a brief investigation of the deliberations and decisions which produced the Constitution and a more specific study of those resulting in the First Amendment, which will serve to further support my contention of an underlying and implied religious nature to the Founders' pronouncements; of their intentions for religion to remain an essential part of the national dialogue and to be included in the national decision making process, and of their fundamental, foundational understanding and reliance on natural law/moral law principles to be at work and remain so within the American democratic system. Additionally, although libertarian in their beliefs of less government means better government, and therefore so profoundly committed to keeping government out of religion—I believe that the Founders did not intend the reverse, that is, to keep religion itself out of government whatsoever; they did not intend to negate the influence of religion on America's sociopolitical affairs; they did not intend for the strict "separation of church and state" as is practiced in our modern era, and above all they did not intend to exclude the authority of the Supreme Being in the affairs of this nation.

To reemphasize, it is my strong contention that we must understand the distinction between the Founders' desire to protect religion from government influence and control by separating the latter from the former, and the erroneous perception that this "separation" was meant to eliminate religion from any participation in government.

When the Constitutional Convention convened, the protection of "individual rights" became a primary issue. Where previously under the Articles of Confederation the national government was powerless over individuals and therefore the states were viewed as the protectors of liberty, there was little threat or influence seen emanating from the central governing body. However, once the Articles of Confederation were scrapped in favor of a more powerful national government, the issue of the protection of a citizens' rights surfaced as delegates became increasingly concerned regarding the superiority of the national legislature over that of the states, and therefore over the individual citizen as well.

To counteract the possible abuses of the centralization of political power, the delegates agreed that fragmenting the government into three branches (legislative, executive, and judicial) offered the best protection of liberty. Although their further efforts were aimed at limiting the amount of power within these branches, Glasser observed that, "no *substantive* (author's emphasis) limits on power were included. Nothing was said about what the *content* (author's emphasis) of rights should be." (37).

It was only toward the final days of the Constitutional Convention that some delegates questioned the prevailing view: that individual rights were properly protected under state constitutions. Still, doubts arose over whether these state constitutions did indeed offer sufficient protection of those rights in light of the newly created federal power. Now that Congress held supremacy over the states and had direct authority over each citizen, it became apparent that a national bill of rights was needed. Further evidence of the need for a national rights bill lay in the fact that throughout early America, many states had already established systems favoring certain majority religious establishments—for example, Georgia taxed its citizens for the Anglican Church. However, at this juncture efforts made to establish a committee to draft this bill failed.

Still, once the Convention closed on September 17, 1787, the approved Constitution needed ratification by three-quarters of the states before it became law and the issue of the much-needed individual rights bill continued amongst politicians and the public alike. The ensuing political turmoil lasted for years and centered on the unpopular Federalists, who supported the Constitution, but felt a bill of rights was unnecessary and dangerous—and the Anti-Federalists, who argued against the Constitution because it both lacked a bill of rights and reduced the power of the states.

Public opinion was with the Anti-Federalists and centered mainly on the need for a rights bill since the average citizen became alarmed over the prospect of one's liberties left under the control of a centralized government. Religious groups, especially the Baptists, also saw the need for constitutional safeguards of religious liberty lest the national or state governments pass laws establishing sponsorship of a particular church and then provide tax support of the same.

The opposing Federalists' pro-Constitution/anti-bill of rights argument was explained in a series of now famous pamphlets and articles published as what we now collectively refer to as the Federalist

Papers. Though the authors of these papers were Alexander Hamilton, James Madison, and John Jay, the essence of the Federalist position was outlined by James Wilson, himself a delegate to the Constitutional Convention, in his famous "State House Yard Speech on the Constitution" on October 6, 1787 when he stated:

> (I)n delegating federal powers...everything which is not reserved is given...and everything which is not given is reserved...to those who think the omission of a bill of rights a defect in the proposed constitution; for it would have been superfluous and absurd to have stipulated with a federal body of our own creation, that we should enjoy those privileges of which we are not divested either by the intention or the act that has brought the body into existence. (Website: Douglass: James Wilson).

Ira Glasser summarizes Wilson's sentiments in this manner, "it was not necessary to secure rights by limiting powers that Congress didn't have anyway (and that) Congress would have *no* (author's emphasis) powers other than those explicitly granted to it by the Constitution." (39).

This argument was countered by the fact that the Constitution did indeed grant Congress unlimited power by stating Congress was allowed, "to make all laws that shall be necessary and proper." This further fueled the need for a national bill of rights lest the persecutions which many recalled, or previously experienced in England, resurface under the newly proposed Constitution.

In his argument for the Federalist cause, Alexander Hamilton stated that no list of rights could ever be complete and the drafting of any list essentially left those excluded rights legally unprotected. This logic had the reverse effect on Hamilton's argument in that within the Constitution some rights were mentioned. Thus, the question that followed was: were those not mentioned, in effect, now left unprotected? It became evident to many that a national bill of rights was becoming increasingly necessary.

As a result, along with each state's ratification of the Constitution was included a non-binding recommendation for Congress to add a bill of rights to the document. Although Congress was not compelled to do so, it was unable to ignore such an emphatic message from the states.

In his ongoing analysis of these events, Glasser indicates that what was truly at issue here and one of crucial importance to the premise of this chapter is that, "none of these mechanisms (within the Constitution) protected *substantive rights* (author's emphasis) such as liberty of conscience" (Glasser 40), or the right to simply be free. Furthermore, Rakove makes an interesting point by stating:

> (R)eligious liberty differed markedly from other civil rights that Americans valued. These other rights were *procedural* (author's emphasis); they assumed that government had the authority to act, but that it had to do so in conformity to the due process of law that legislatures and courts both followed. In the realm of religion, however, what (was) contested was the capacity of the state to act at all...(t)he free exercise of religion was the most 'liberal' of all the rights Americans could claim, the one that placed the greatest trust in the capacity of private choice, and the one least dependent on positive law. (312).

True, the Constitution protected the mechanisms by which government itself would work, that is, the mechanical process by which the law would secure and ensure personal liberty and freedom, yet that process seemed severely open-ended less the identification of that which liberty and freedom would actually provide—in essence the raison d'être for both these blessings.

In a letter to James Madison dated December 20, 1787, Thomas Jefferson stated, "a bill of rights is what the people are entitled to against every government on earth, general or particular, and what no just government should refuse, or *rest on inference* (emphasis added)." (Peterson 430).

With Congress now virtually compelled to draft a formal bill of rights, work commenced in earnest on that task. Many prominent politicians of the day were in support of this issue. On March 15, 1789 and again writing to the ambivalent James Madison (himself a Federalist and against a bill of rights) Thomas Jefferson penned a crucial argument for the adoption of a rights bill by stating, "(i)n the arguments in favor of a declaration of rights, you omit one which has great weight with me, the legal check which it puts into the hands of the judiciary." (Peterson 438).

Here, Glasser explains the crux of Jefferson's argument as:

> Once established, a bill of rights would provide the legal basis for an independent judiciary to strike down majoritarian excesses by ruling unconstitutional any legislative or executive act that violated individual rights as defined in the Constitution. Such legislative acts, even if committed in response to majority opinion, could be declared null and void by the courts. A bill of rights...would put a powerful 'legal check' into the hands of the judiciary, provided it remained safely independent of the other branches of government. (43).

Madison's original position expressed concern over the effectiveness of mere "parchment barriers" versus the majority power of government. However, Jefferson's argument convinced Madison that the addition of a bill of rights to the Constitution would greatly strengthen the new American government. Madison then set about to convince other Federalists and deflate the Anti-Federalist strategy. The latter group's true intention was to shelve the Constitution, not because of the lack of a bill of rights, but rather to seek a second Constitutional Convention to redraft a document which would return power back to the states.

In addition to Jefferson's contention, here is where we find the primary arguments unfolding with regard to the inclusion of the fundamental need to protect the essential and basic rights of human beings living under the authority of a powerful centralized government, lest the potential for abuse of those rights becomes eventually realized.

Samuel Adams' position on the need for a bill of rights was stated in a letter dated August 22, 1789. In this letter, Adams indicated the reason for the creation of a rights bill was the wish of the people, "to see a line drawn as clearly as may be between the federal powers vested in Congress and...the private and personal rights of the citizens." (Barton 199). Patrick Henry warned that it was necessary to draft a bill of rights, and according to Rakove, Henry maintained that without this bill, "Congress would violate one right after another." (323).

Eventually, Madison saw how easily a powerful centralized government could possibly ignore, even abuse, individual rights without the limiting effect of a stipulated criteria of rights set forth in the primary foundational documents of that government. To his credit, he saw beyond his political belief as a Federalist into the true effect unlimited power can have on governing institutions, no matter how noble their cause, or magnanimous their intentions. Once Madison became convinced of this fact, he reversed his previous stance and devoted his future energies to designing, proposing, and gaining passage of the Bill of Rights.

Madison was also acutely aware of the fact that many states' constitutions had no bill of rights and those that did were insufficient.

What he argued for, and considered to be the most valuable addition to the Constitution, was an amendment that clearly protected citizens against any violations by the states of an individual's rights. Yet, although this proposal passed in the House of Representatives, it failed in the Senate. This failure allowed the, "(s)tates (to remain) free to violate rights, unless restrained by their own state constitutions" (Glasser 45), as there were no constitutional limitations on the states' power to infringe upon an individual's rights. Therefore, with the defeat of Madison's "most valuable" amendment, the Anti-Federalists received both a Constitution with a stated bill of rights and one that left the power of the states intact. A clear victory for the Anti-Federalists!

This power of the states to affect the rights of individuals despite the Bill of Rights' design to eliminate the national government's power to do so, sadly left many Americans' fundamental freedoms effectively denied, as state and local governments often ignored or abused individual rights to further their own interests or agenda.

Here, the question of intent is crucial. By not curbing the power of the states within the Bill of Rights, and thus leaving the rights of individuals still subject to state jurisdictions, did the Founders ignore the possibility of the abuse of those rights by the states despite the efforts of the national mandate to eliminate that possibility? On the surface it would seem that there exists a contradiction of intent however, Rakove clarifies this apparent problem. He indicates that the Founders and their generation held:

> (T)he conviction that fundamental rights were not created by some positive act but instead existed as an amalgam of natural rights and customary tradition. In the wake of the Revolutionary dispute with Britain, which repeatedly forced the colonists to explain why they were entitled to the rights they claimed, it was only natural that the constitution writers...should attach

> statements of rights to the new charters of government. Some of them doubtless hoped that such formal declarations would reduce the ambiguities about the sources of rights they had just encountered. But, that did not mean that rights left undeclared would lose their authority or be relegated to a lower status. (308).

In this case of unchecked states' power vs. individual rights, I contend that it was not the condition whereby the states were free to abuse individual rights less the curbing power of the national rights bill, but rather that of the Founders' understanding of an underlying curbing power in existence within the fundamental natural law/moral law to which all individuals and governments were subject to *before* the legislative acts of any positive law. Furthermore, that the issue of slavery was not addressed here appears to be a distinct contradiction of the Founders' intentions. However, I find it quite conceivable that within their efforts to establish a written bill of rights there was generated a commitment to a course of events which set in motion, not only a reexamination of individual rights as protected under positive law, but those inherent rights existing within the duality of natural law/moral law. In this, I also find merit in the probability that the Founders were well aware of the evil of slavery and considered that their measures taken to establish the Bill of Rights would ultimately prove foundational for the eventual elimination of the practice. That this did not come to pass till 1865 via the Thirteenth Amendment, is not so much a crime of omission by the Founders than one of the perpetuation of slavery by those whose vested interest in the practice acted contrary to the foundations laid for its eventual elimination via the national rights bill.

With the Bill of Rights now added to the Constitution, and the underlying argument for its inclusion firmly established in the fact that the obvious majority of citizens feared government abuse of individual rights, let us narrow this investigation to the issues surrounding the First Amendment, specifically those dealing with religious freedom in America. It is here that a clearer understanding of the true religious nature and intent behind the Founders' efforts will become obvious and that their design for an American sociopolitical foundation based on the principles of natural law/moral law will become further apparent.

The fear of abuses against religious freedom at the hands of government was particularly troubling to the Founders and their generation of Americans. Not only were painful reminders still fresh within the memories of many who fled England to escape religious persecution, but there were also examples of the possibility of the same existent within America's early history.

It has been noted previously that some of the earliest American colonies sought some form of mergence and cooperation between government and religion in order to further their own religious beliefs and to establish civil order to guarantee survival within the often harsh frontier and wilderness life they encountered. As a result, "(b)y the time of the American Revolution, every colonial government imposed religious tests for public officials, and eight of the thirteen colonies had established an official religion." (Alderman 62).

What motivated many to seek a formal declaration of religious freedom and forever eliminate the possibility of government intervention and sponsorship of religion was primarily the fact that so many religious groups were indeed settling within America. This created a growing tension and resentment among the new immigrants who fled to the United States seeking to gain the freedom to worship according to their beliefs, yet were met with restrictions on that freedom. It seemed apparent that their religious beliefs were simply being tolerated—in fact, some experienced outright suppression of their chosen faith.

As a result, the thinking that began to circulate among the population, and in particular throughout the nation's Baptist communities was, according to Glasser, "that religious freedom was (not) a favor, to be granted by the government (nor was) tolerance...the same as having the right." (73). In addition, many became increasingly suspicious of any state involvement in religion as an attempt to return to the old establishment.

Thomas J. Curry, author and contemporary historian regarding First Amendment issues, explains that, "(t)hroughout the states, Americans found themselves asserting that religion was a matter between God and the individual: that government possessed no intrinsic powers over matters of religion; and that when secular powers interfered in religious affairs, they exceeded their authority, violated religious liberty, and corrupted both Church and State." (190).

The concept of a formal separation of church and state then began to dominate, with arguments centering on the fact, "that unless the civil authorities were stripped altogether of the power to act for or against religion, religious liberty could not flourish." (Glasser 74). There was also concern over the fact that any government sponsorship of religion would inevitably create a majority religion, leaving those in the minority to suffer.

It was not that Americans of this era were seeking to exclude religious belief from the fabric of American's political forum and the public dialogue, on the contrary, Lipset's investigation reveals that, "they opposed church establishment, but welcomed religion." (155). In fact, religion was so integral to early American life, that some expressed concern that any amendment limiting or removing government support of religion would have the reverse effect of eliminating it entirely from American society.

This sentiment was expressed by Representative Peter Sylvester of New York during the deliberations regarding the drafting of the religious freedom amendment. Curry acknowledges that the same fear was especially prevalent among the majority of the residents of the states of New England who believed that, "since religion was necessary to a civil society, the states should patronize and promote it, that their doing so constituted no violation of conscience provided they forced no one to pay for the support of a religion other than his own. Abolishing such a system could only patronize and favor atheists...and the irresponsible elements of society, who would take advantage of freedom to support no religion." (203).

Despite this concern, Lipset indicates that here the most crucial and important point is that although, "(t)he United States (was) the first country in which religious groups became voluntary associations" (61), despite the variety of its religious denominations, America's foundation was built upon the precepts of Protestantism. Curry also reached the same conclusion and stated, "(t)he vast majority of Americans assumed that theirs was a Christian, i.e. Protestant, country, and they automatically expected that government would uphold the commonly agreed on Protestant ethos and morality." (219).

Once again, the danger of a particular religious organization gaining political influence, or advantage became a very distinct possibility. This was a fact that was all too familiar to the Founding Generation.

It is quite obvious that the majority of early Americans were deeply involved, concerned, and attentive to any restrictions on their free and unencumbered religious practice and beliefs. Most believed that religion was as fundamental a concept toward a full and productive life as was politics, law, and other social abstractions. These early Americans took for granted that religion was highly contributory to the moral character of the society, provided education and public aid, fostered community relations, and above all, religion continued to remind the individual of the belief in a Supreme Being, who it was determined, was not only aware of human affairs, but someone was intimately involved in their development and outcome.

Still, despite the concerns of some over the complete elimination of government involvement in religion—the dominant political argument favored the addition of some legal protection to ensure the free flow of religious belief and expression within America, and the elimination of any majoritarian religious dominance. Therefore, the foundation for an amendment to the Constitution guaranteeing this right was in place.

It must be understood that the Founders were mostly of Christian backgrounds, so their sentiments reflect Christian attitudes, beliefs, descriptions, and interpretations of natural law/moral law principles. However, this did not have influence over their impartial desire to allow *complete* religious freedom to fully function within the United States less government intervention and for it to remain an integral part of America's sociopolitical system. An examination of many of the Founders' personal and public writings reflects their disposition with regard to religion being a vital constituent of human life and affairs. The following few examples help to illustrate this point.

In his later reflections involving the religious aspect behind the founding generation's legislative efforts, John Quincy Adams stated, "the Declaration of Independence first organized the social compact on the foundation of the Redeemer's mission upon earth (which) laid the cornerstone of human government upon the first precepts of Christianity. (From a speech delivered on the sixty-first anniversary of the Declaration of Independence, July 4, 1837)." (Barton 164-65).

Patrick Henry declared on January 8, 1799, "(t)he great pillars of government and of social life...(are) virtue, morality, and religion." (164). In a letter dated November 18, 1801 Thomas Jefferson wrote, "(the) liberty to worship our Creator in the way we think most agreeable to His will (is) a liberty deemed in other countries incompatible with good government and yet proved by our experience to be its best support." (157).

What this sampling of observations by the Founders indicates is that their efforts during the Constitutional era with regard to national religious issues, were not products of the moment. Rather, I find that these efforts were more the synthesis of the Founders' long held personal beliefs with regard to religion and government, and their desire to offer a fair and equitable solution to the problems associated with the unavoidable interaction of each. Not only were the Founders undoubtedly aware of the underlying fundamental religious nature of their efforts, but all were acutely conscious of the ramifications their decisions would have for future generations of Americans. In fact, during the debates surrounding the adoption of the Bill of Rights, Congressman Richard Henry Lee of Virginia acknowledged that the opening statements of the First Amendment were, "for ages and nations yet unborn." (Curry 193).

It is here that this discussion uncovers an inevitable enigma. Given this historical evidence in support of the importance and influence of religion upon American history and society, its laws, its sacred documents, its Founders and their efforts, intentions, and expectations for America and its future: Why, in our modern era, has the original concept of the separation of church and state, which sought only to secure religious freedom in America by removing the possibility of government abuse of that privilege, resulted in the complete elimination of religion from the public and political forum? In effect, why has America turned its back on religion?

In the following chapter: "Religion in America: From God to Godless" I will further explore the separation of church and state in America. This will include a comparison of past and present interpretations of that concept. It will further explain why the current "wall of separation" is contradictory to the underlying concepts of the First Amendment with regard to religion and public life.

In conjunction with these themes, the next chapter will primarily and specifically cover the rise and decline of religion and religious influence on American society. It will deal with issues such as: America's growing discontent with religion; our modern tendency to trivialize religion, and the effects all this has had on morality in America.

In closing I will quote the final version of the First Amendment added to the Constitution, "Congress shall make no law respecting an establishment of religion, or prohibiting the free exercise thereof; or abridging the freedom of speech, or of the press; or the right of the people peaceably to assemble, and to petition the Government for a redress of grievances."

Chapter 2

Religion In America:
From God To Godless

During the high water mark of much of the turbulence that engulfed the 1960s, the catch phrase that was bandied about throughout much of American society was: "God is dead!"

It was not so much a statement of fact, or a resurgence of Nietzscheanism, than one which expressed this country's utter frustration with itself. Frustration with the ongoing Vietnamese conflict; the "generation gap"; the sexual revolution; escalating drug use; increasing divorce rates; domestic political and social upheaval; racial problems; assassinations of public officials, and the loss of faith in the so called "American Dream"—especially among America's hippie, yippie, soon to be yuppie, youth.

It was mainly the consequences of the latter which best explained and epitomized that increasing frustration infecting America. Yet at the time, most of its citizens were either unaware of, or unwilling to accept that rationale. Much like being unable to see the forest for the trees, I suspect.

Where once the American Dream was born as a beacon of hope in the broad smiles and expectations of the returning World War II GIs— it was ultimately found dying in the dearth of its deliverance for so many of those 'baby boomers" who were the intended inheritors of its effervescent blessings. Instead, they became the recipients of its brackish backwash.

In effect, the problems that exploded onto the American scene during the 1960s were bubbling under the surface for decades, much like a simmering volcano threatening to blow. What kept these problems in relative abeyance for so long, was the rose-tinted lens through which they were invariably viewed—that being the then thought soon to be realized American Dream wonderland to finally spread across this country.

Then, as Americans became increasingly aware of their government's limitations in causing this "Dream" to become a reality, the inevitable result was a growing disappointment with this country's leadership, especially among its post-World War II youth. During this time, the proclamation that: "God is dead!" became more reflective of both a lack of faith in the "system" and frustration with those institutions believed to be responsible for the nation's ills. Many experienced a sense of abandonment as the once implied benefits of the American Dream dissolved away into the stark realities of the turbulent 1960s.

What the American Dream bred in this country's citizens was a feeling of entitlement. According to Robert J. Samuelson (a national columnist for Newsweek and the Washington Post) in his book, *The Good Life and Its Discontents: The American Dream in the Age of Entitlement*, this concept involves the expectation of "security," "independence," and "self-fulfillment" which, "would somehow be provided or guaranteed by someone or some institution, but which was also 'fully deserved'...Americans began to expect things from their government, their businesses, and other social institutions that they had never previously expected—though they may have wanted them." (47).

However, our early American ancestors harbored little of these illusions. Theirs was a society steeped in the precepts of the Protestant ethic, whereby hard work produced its own rewards through the good being generated within both the temporal and spiritual communities of one's life. Here, the citizenry objected to government involvement in their lives, as our mostly agrarian predecessors were exceedingly self-sufficient. Still, they lived within an association composed of individuals who were bound by laws of the land set in place to benefit essentially and primarily that association.

In commenting on America's tendency toward self-sufficiency, Tocqueville's early nineteenth century observations stated, "(m)en in democratic times always need to be free in order to *provide themselves* (emphasis added) with the physical pleasures for which they ever hanker." (539).

To our American ancestors, the concept of entitlements was a non sequitur—in fact, it was simply nonexistent.

In addition, and as discussed previously, both the colonial and Founding Generation viewed God as the Creator of all things—the Biblical God who formulated a natural and moral law upon which the affairs of humankind were based. Also, and as is stated in the Declaration of Independence, humanity was, "endowed by their Creator with certain inalienable rights," and Americans in particular were seeking, "the protection of Divine Providence" in securing these rights and in developing a society based of the realization of those "rights" for its citizens. Among those rights were, "life, liberty and the pursuit of happiness."

Which leads to the following: Why did modern Americans come to view the fruits of society as merely those entitlements to be plucked from the trees of society's garden, yet early Americans' perception of those same fruits was one whereby the rewards generated for both the temporal and spiritual communities were gained via the Protestant ethic precept of hard work?

I believe the basis for this dichotomy revolves around the differing levels of importance and involvement religion (as previously defined) has had within the lives of each of these contrasting generations of

Americans. This varying degree of the religious element having influence on colonial and modern Americans has not only had a direct influence upon their perceptions regarding the reality of God's involvement within their active, daily existence, but also upon the relevance of God as the basis with which to effect and influence their immediate needs and desires within the natural law/moral law setting.

It is within this difference between the colonial and modern perceptions of the relationship between God and humanity, where we uncover the underlying shift in America's attitudes with regard to the importance of religion in our public life.

Where previously God was considered to be known through religious practice, and thus from the establishment of this intimate relationship humankind could conceivably achieve the fulfillment of those endowments granted to us by the Creator, today the reverse has become prevalent. In fact, modern Americans have turned to other means of achieving the cornucopia of entitlements that they still believe are due them.

Therefore, despite the government's past inability to secure the American Dream, the primary source for our current expectations is still perceived to be from government sources. In effect, this has created an ever-increasing involvement of government in American's lives, which is completely antithetical to the Founders' intentions. However, for today's Americans, the differences they experience from their 1950s and early 1960s counterparts is that if this government involvement fails, then the individual is left to employ whatever means are deemed appropriate to achieve what he/she believes he/she is entitled to.

In either of these two cases, God is rarely relied upon to produce the "goods." Therefore, religion has become proportionately less important within the sphere of modern public life and that which one can accomplish with it. God, formerly in cooperation with humanity and its efforts to achieve that which life affords, has instead become the God of little more than ritual and holiday festivals. God now occupies a second class status behind that which society and/or the individual have constructed to achieve the material benefits of human existence.

Hence, I have found that the underlying influence of the natural law/moral law has suffered greatly as the dominant theme projected throughout American society today, and one employed mostly by the media, is the promotion of the mischievous rascal who approaches life with a rather "thumbs up" attitude while skirting around the law (both civil and moral) to get what he/she wants. God and religion are rarely considered in the mix, except to express disdain for the restrictions either may place on this individual's realization of his/her goals.

Consequently, the once public God of America's foundational generations, whose Supreme authority and influence were felt and included in all aspects of daily life, is now, for the majority of Americans, the private God of one's personal interpretation, whose influence neither occupies a place within the public arena, nor is perceived to be involved with human affairs. God's activity in our lives, if at all, is relegated to the beauty of a sunrise, a brief Sunday morning encounter, or called upon when we lose our keys.

Currently, there have been numerous studies attempting to confirm the reality of religiousness still existent within the United States, similar to that which was instilled at its founding. However, what has been uncovered, and is increasingly disturbing, is a distinctly modern variety of religiousness. According to Guenter Lewy, a professor emeritus of political science at the University of Massachusetts, Amherst, Americans today are prone to moral relativism which stands in stark contrast to the relatively constant degree in church attendance uncovered in those studies. Especially relevant here is his conclusion that, "(w)hile religion is highly popular in America, it is to a large extent superficial; it does not change people's lives to the degree one would expect from their level of professed faith." (88).

In fact, this behavior belies an underlying disbelief in the relevance of religion and daily life due to the destructive effects upon American religiousness from increased secularization. Although Americans find religion useful and reassuring it, "is not integral to their personal lives." (125).

What this book has uncovered so far, is the basic premise for the remainder of this chapter: Implied within the religion clause of the First Amendment is an unspoken respect and reverence for God and religion. So much so, that the Founders, in their understanding of the importance of both in public life (as previously discussed) preferred to completely separate governmental influence from religion in order to negate the very distinct probability of any state involvement whatsoever. This would thereby completely eliminate the risk of governmental abuse or control of religious activity in America. Nor did they wish to institute the practice of multiple establishment, whereby all religious denominations received government support. The Founders concluded that religion was simply better off less any government involvement.

Today however, religion has been relegated to the rank of, "the arbitrary and unimportant" (Carter 6)—a superstitious, private practice. As a result, the sentiments of America's founding generation, with regard to religion and public life, are considered irrelevant to our modern society and its problems and expectations. In the remainder of this chapter I will explore what I consider to be the reasons why.

By stating in the First Amendment that, "Congress shall make no law respecting an establishment of religion, or prohibiting the free exercise thereof..." the Founders were expressing and instituting their inherent interest in not only establishing religious freedom within America, but the protection of it from government involvement and influence. However, this particular addition to the Constitution was preceded by several versions which were considered, but ultimately rejected. Each discarded version did not achieve the exact nuance of meaning the Founders intended.

Since James Madison was the chief architect for the construction of the Bill or Rights, his efforts are most noteworthy here. His first draft for a religious freedom amendment read, "(t)he civil rights of none shall be abridged on account of religious belief or worship, nor shall any national religion be established, nor shall the full and equal rights of conscience be in any manner, or on any pretext, infringed." (Curry 199).

Here we uncover Madison's original concerns. In the first part, the emphasis is on protecting one's civil rights against religious domination either from powerful religious groups or the government sponsorship of religion. The latter part sought to protect the free exercise of religious practice, or "the full and equal rights of conscience."

Many modern day interpreters of the First Amendment's religious clause (among them Robert Boston—assistant director for Americans United for Separation of Church and State, and assistant editor of *Church & State* magazine—in his effort, *Why The Religious Right Is Wrong: About the Separation of Church & State*, and to some extent Kramnick and Moore in their book, *The Godless Constitution: The Case Against Religious Correctness*) agree with the above stated contention. In fact, a close examination of Madison's surviving subsequent drafts reveals similar themes involving the protection of the free exercise of religious beliefs and practice from government influence and the avoidance of government involvement in an individual's "rights of conscience." Nowhere was it stated or implied that religion itself was to be eliminated from participation in the public forum, or that religion was to be excluded, or diminished from partaking in issues of public concern.

In addition, it is quite obvious that if those individuals involved in drafting the First Amendment intended to eliminate religion from the public arena, they had several attempts to do so. Here, I find it inconceivable that this issue did not arise over the course of their discussions and therefore, the number of First Amendment versions without any mention whatsoever of an intention to limit religious involvement in the public dialogue, further supports the fact that religion was still to be considered intimately vital to the workings of American society—both then and in the future.

By settling on this Amendment's final version, the intention was clearly made to eliminate government from the legal support of any religion. Within this legal context government could never affect, influence, or negate the practice of religious freedom in America. Madison's final draft contained the exact nuance the Founders required.

I believe that the Founders' intent was to allow religious freedom to prosper and be fully engaged within the public dialogue less government influence and involvement. They did so with the full knowledge of the valuable role religion played in the shaping of public opinion and behavior. In addition, the Founders had no intention to dictate a strictly secular agenda for America. They were determined to protect religion from any temporal control and worked toward allowing it to function unhindered within the matrix of American society—thus, remaining a vital constituent of the democratic process. Decades later, Tocqueville obviously observed this still in action when he stated that, "the main reason for the quiet sway of religion over (this) country" (295), was religion operating less government influence.

The Founders walked a fine line between the possible abuses that either institution (i.e. government and religion) was capable of imposing on the other. However, their sense was more in line with what President Thomas Jefferson wrote a few years later in 1802 within a letter responding to the Danbury Baptist Association's concerns over First Amendment religious abuses within the state of Connecticut. He stated, "the legislative powers of government reach actions only, and not opinions." (Peterson 303).

In this sense Jefferson understood that the true function of American government was to act on the decisions made by the people. In essence, those decisions were formed by one's opinions based upon, among other sources, religion. Therefore, Jefferson saw the great value in allowing the free flow of those institutions which citizens employed to reach their decisions. This created the cumulative will of the people upon which government would then act.

I believe Jefferson fully understood that since religion was only one of the sources employed by citizens to arrive at civil and social decisions, there would be an inherent check within that decision making process and thereby protection against any one source dominating the rest. Furthermore, I contend that Jefferson and the other Founders had such faith in the potential of America's democratic process; its tertiary structure; its system of checks and balances; its commitment to protect human freedom and rights, and the voting process—that the early leadership understood that combined, these mechanisms would effectively nullify the possibility of any single deciding dominant source. I believe the Founders considered that within this process, religion, or any institution for that matter, would indubitably contribute to the cumulatively derived final will of the people which would be acted upon by their government. Here, any institution involved within this system would proceed independent from the rest and continue unimpeded to arrive at its own unique conclusions, which would then ultimately contribute to a collectively derived result.

Still, within that letter of January 1, 1802 where President Jefferson addressed the First Amendment concerns express by the Baptist community in Danbury, Connecticut with regard to that state's allowance of tax money to be utilized for the support of the majority church in each town resulting in a distinct disadvantage to the minority Baptist congregation, there is a segment of that letter which has since been the subject of continuous controversy for generations.

In this response, President Jefferson penned a phrase that has since taken on such strength of meaning, that even today it is used to justify the complete elimination of religion from governmental affairs. In describing the intentions of the religious clause of the First Amendment Jefferson wrote that it was, "thus building a wall of separation between Church and State." (Peterson 303). With regard to the enormous effect this particular phrase has had upon modern American society, perhaps Barton states it best, "(t)here is probably no other instance in America's history where words spoken by a single individual in a private letter...have become the sole authorization for a national judicial policy." (48).

Yet, despite the last five decades of current controversy this statement has evoked, Jefferson's "separation" statement, which appears nowhere else in his works, was never referred to until 1879 when Chief Justice Morrison R. Waite used the concept to decide on *Reynolds v. United States*. This case determined that the Mormon practice of polygamy was not justified under the claim of freedom of religious practice in the First Amendment.

Still, it wasn't until 1947 that the "wall of separation" concept became a truly significant issue within America's judicial landscape. In *Everson v. Board of Education of Ewing Township* (a.k.a. the New Jersey Bus Case), Chief Justice Hugo L. Black stated that this "wall" had not been breached when state money was awarded to the parents of twenty-one Catholic School children for bus fare reimbursement. Several other contemporaneous Supreme Court Justices were not in complete agreement with Black, yet the ruling remained. However, Chief Justice Black's decision was momentous in that he, "reaffirmed the 'wall' principle" (Abraham 265), which many at the time, including his colleague Justice Stanley F. Reed, considered simply a figure of speech. Justice Black's belief in the "separation" concept defined the future direction for all subsequent church/state cases in the United States when in presiding over the Everson Case he stated: "The First Amendment has erected a wall (of separation) between church and state. That wall must be kept high and impregnable. We could not approve the slightest breach." (266).

With this ruling by the Supreme Court the issue of this "wall of separation" was firmly installed within America's legal process. Since then, there have been many cases involving this separation concept, and each has effectively increased that wall to the point that today any implication of involvement of religion and government evokes a storm of controversy and streams of litigation. All this done in the name of keeping each completely separate from the other.

However, despite what I have previously outlined as the Founders' focus in this matter, these efforts have also had an adverse effect in quite another way: Religion has been virtually eliminated from participation in the public arena. The reasoning here is that any involvement of religion in the affairs of government is determined to violate this modern concept of the separation of church and state.

In addition, the "separation" controversy has further complicated the issue by dividing the First Amendment's pronouncement on religion, now referred to as the Separation Clause, into two distinct entities: the Establishment Clause and the Free Exercise Clause. The former is used separately by the courts to decide cases involving government aid to religion, and the latter, again used separately, deals with issues regarding government and religious interference with each other. However, as Thiemann effectively indicates, "the two clauses can easily work at cross purposes (when) the (Supreme) Court is primarily called upon to adjudicate cases that fall into the ambiguous gray area between the two clauses…the Court has responded to this situation by dealing with the two kinds of cases in isolation from one another…(and has) created two parallel and independent standards for the adjudication of cases dealing with religion." (57-58).

This splitting of the First Amendment's Separation Clause has been so problematic within the courts, that many legal experts and institutions have objected to this disjointed interpretation. For example, "(r)eligion clause doctrine since the 1940's has exaggerated the difference between the two clauses, creating a bifurcated jurisprudence of the clauses whose operation obscures the principal values underlying them." (*Developments in the Law: Religion and the State*, Harvard Law Review, 100 (1987): 1639.)

Therefore, this tendency of the Supreme Court to adopt two independent standards for interpreting the religious aspect of the First Amendment has resulted in two separate sets of criteria for judgment. Thiemann further concluded that, "it has also created a heightened and artificial sense of the conflict between the clauses, thereby obscuring the unifying elements that hold them together." (60). This has all been based on that single phrase penned by a single man in a single private letter and which appeared nowhere else in any of his writings.

Of interest here, and in the same letter, is the sentence immediately following Jefferson's "wall" phrase. It reads, "(a)dhering to this expression of the supreme will of the nation in behalf of the rights of conscience, I shall see with sincere satisfaction the progress of those sentiments which tend to restore to man all his natural rights, convinced he has no natural right in opposition to his social duties." (Peterson 303-04).

Obviously taken in conjunction with the previous "wall" sentiment to which it refers, we see that Jefferson considered the national will (those previously referred to individual judgments and opinions which collectively shape America's ultimate decisions) and upon which he stated, "government reach(es) actions only," to be intimately involved with the "rights of conscience" (a term previously noted to be indicative of religion). This would completely contradict the implication of a, "wall of separation between Church and State" as it has come to be interpreted today.

What then are we to make of this dichotomy? I believe the weight of Jefferson's "wall" phrase simply referred to the Founders' desire to protect the duality of government and religion from the possible abuses that their respective powers could generate upon each other. Here Jefferson wished only to emphasize to the Danbury Baptists that

Connecticut's dalliance with government sponsorship of majority religion was contrary to First Amendment principles. Once again, it in no way implied that religion was to be kept separate from the public dialogue, as is often currently the case resulting from many of today's Supreme Court rulings which cite Jefferson's "wall" phrase as the basis for their decisions. However, as outlined above, the Court's logic is based on a false assumption, which renders their conclusions based on that false assumption, moot.

Still, an entire group of theories have emerged which refer to the Court's reasoning regarding these church/state decisions. A review of each is beyond the scope of this book however, suffice it to say that their variety serves to demonstrate not only how complicated the process has become, but how Court decisions are neither universal in their basic logic nor in the manner in which they are dispensed. In reality, final decisions regarding religion and government depend on whichever position the current Court considers valid and renders by its majority decision.

In addition, not only do the variety of the Court's positions further confuse the church/state controversy, but each raises the following concern: Any position taken by the Supreme Court in church/state matters, in effect, does involve government in religious matters, which essentially is completely contradictory to the supposed "wall of separation" theory. In any case, the result this has had on modern American society is the removal all things of a religious nature from the fabric of America's civic forum. Once again, I am absolutely convinced that this was not the intent of the Founders.

Consequently, this rendering of religion to the fringes of public dialogue has diminished its significance as an institution contributing to the derivation of the "national will" and has relegated religion to a rank of relative unimportance. Hence, lacking religion as that generally and historically acknowledged medium with which humanity becomes intimately aware of natural law/moral law principles as composed and bequeathed by God—Americans have become increasingly irreligious, morally ambiguous, and spiritually ambivalent. Our former unofficial civic piety has become further supplanted by a civic agnosticism. This removal of religion from the conjunction of institutions employed to decide the national will has adversely affected the entire process, much like the diminishing effect the loss an appendage has upon the life of a corporeal being.

Since the signing of the Declaration of Independence on July 4, 1776, and mainly over the past fifty-two years (from 1947 when Chief Justice Black's statement forever changed the meaning of the religious intent of the First Amendment) there have been swift and far-reaching changes in religious practice and sentiment within the United States.

Where once religion played so intimate a part in America's public life that in Tocqueville's observations of the United States of the early nineteenth century it prompted him to proclaim, "America is still the place where the Christian religion has kept the greatest real power over men's souls; and nothing better demonstrates how useful and natural it is to man, since the country where it now has the widest sway is both the most enlightened and the freest (and where) religion...helps to regulate the state." (291).

However, despite this observation, within America today religion is viewed exceedingly otherwise. In fact, practically the complete reversal of these sentiments has become prevalent.

Religion is virtually ignored within the public arena and the national agenda is determined from primarily secular sources. In addition, Americans themselves have adopted a predominantly secular attitude, while maintaining a highly individualistic attitude to life within the United States. They tend to ignore religion's general moral teachings and instead live according to a personally conceived moral code derived from the various sources they employ to best secure their personal agenda. Any sense of the civic community is becoming increasingly inactive, and whole segments of the population see themselves as completely isolated from the main pulse of society—whether from cultural, philosophical, theological, racial, or economic differences.

In addition to what I consider the resulting deleterious influence of the altered perceptions regarding First Amendment religious rights emerging over the last fifty years, just why do Americans watch as religion itself withers and public and personal morality declines? Where once the authority of the Supreme Being was an accepted premise throughout American life, why today are we often referred to by many outside sources as a godless society? Where in the 1830s Tocqueville stated, "(r)eligion...should...be considered as the first of (America's) political institutions" (292)—why has the reverse surfaced in America today?

My conclusion relies on two primary factors: the influence of America's archetypal religions upon the social philosophies of this nation, and this country's ever increasing heterogeneous population.

In the first case, religion in early America was composed mainly of Christian sects emanating from the established Protestant denominations of English and European origin. Each sect held firm to a particular interpretation of biblical understanding which formed the basis for their beliefs and community. This, in fact, was the main impetus which prompted their departure from England and Europe. Mostly, as novel interpretations of scripture resulted in the formation of these schismatic groups, each became a presence that was increasingly intolerable to the established, often state sponsored Protestant groups. These majority religions quite regularly proceeded to hinder or blatantly suppress these newly forming sects, which in turn forced many to flee to America and the promise of the free practice of their religious beliefs.

What is pertinent here, is that each of these sects were splitting off from what is generically described as the Protestant faith, which itself originated with Martin Luther's original schism from the Roman Catholic Church in 1517. Within Europe and England, the success of

Lutheranism fostered an atmosphere of dissension which promoted further sect development within Protestantism as disagreements grew over biblical and scriptural interpretations. Roman Catholicism continued on intact less the Lutherans and the multitude of sects originating thereafter from that original schismatic group. Hence, this period of history saw a great rise in the number of newly formed Christian denominations.

What Lutheranism and many of the very Protestant religious denominations, such as Anglicanism, share in common with Roman Catholicism is a chiefly hierarchical structure whereby, as Lipset noted, "(p)arishioners are expected to follow the lead of their priests and bishops." (19). However, the schismatic Protestant sects that settled in America differed, in that their structure was predominantly congregational. Despite their religious differences, each shared an elemental set of foundational philosophical principles which, as Lipset further points out, developed distinctly more egalitarian, individualistic, populist (i.e. advocating the rights of the common people), and anti-elitist values. These tendencies originated in the deep desire to escape the oppressive monarchical cultures of the past which often spawned much of the religious persecution these sects endured. Within America, this elemental set of foundational philosophical principles became the basis for colonial society, and again according to Lipset, allowed both the political and religious ethos to reinforce each other.

Furthermore, and as previously outlined earlier in this book, upon settlement in America these sects formed communities based mostly upon the religious principles they followed, which in turn were inexorably woven into much of the civil structure of their communities as well. As these settlements grew, their development formed the basis for much of what would ultimately become early American society. In essence, early America's social and legal foundation was of a distinctly congregational religious nature originating with those sects splitting off from an established hierarchical Protestant origin.

In returning to that elemental set of foundational principles America's archetypal faiths shared—of note here is not only the strong impact of the same upon all aspects of American society but, of the underlying philosophical influence with regard to that of society and the individuals of which it is so composed.

Hence, and with reference to Lipset's important observations, fostered by their congregational nature—within America's foundational religious denominations existed a powerful tendency for, "a personal relationship with God, and in many cases an interpretation of biblical truth, one not mediated by bishops or determined by the state." (19-20).

In essence, this American brand of Protestantism developed into highly individualistic oriented version, which as Lipset further indicates, placed emphasis on the development of a moral code, "determined by (the sectarian's) own sense of rectitude." (19). In fact, two of Protestantism's major leaders, Martin Luther and John Calvin, concluded that no one could help a person spiritually, and that each human being was solely responsible for his/her salvation. Here, Protestant independence and personalization of devotion further fostered the emancipation of the individual from the congregation itself.

Essentially, the Protestant religions are composed of assemblages of persons united by the common creed of the independent attainment of salvation. Hence, each individual becomes the master of his/her own destiny. In effect, the congregational nature of church attendance and unification through a commonly held belief system is diametrically opposed to the independent nature of the attainment of the congregation's member's ultimate goal, i.e. personal salvation.

This American brand of devotion is unique, in that, it was essentially derived from the duality of the personalization of religious belief and the further reinforcement of the same by this country's foundational political ethos—which itself had distinctly religious overtones, as examined in an earlier section.

I believe the repercussions of our American ancestor's individualistic tendency created the foundation for an underlying social tenet which implied a rather secondary status to the importance of church. Although attendance was often mandatory, the spiritual benefits to be gained in church were merely adjuncts to that which one could achieve through one's own private efforts. This in turn focused less reliance on church teachings as those determinants of human behavior, and more on individual assessments of the same. However, where early Americans were rather new to this concept and were still steeped in the mostly God-fearing components of their Christian roots, today's Americans have fully embraced the reverse.

In a sense, our American predecessors sought freedom from the excesses of human authority via political mandates, yet were still ever mindful of the veracity of a Supreme authority. On the other hand, modern Americans living lives accustomed to the liberating effects of those political mandates seek increases of freedom, which even include a liberation from that of a Supreme authority.

America's current social tradition fully assigns a subordinate capacity to the concept of church; is decidedly anticlerical, and has further reduced the importance of religious devotion and all things religious to a significantly minor ranking—or as Stephen L. Carter points out is one that is increasingly "trivialized," and Ronald F. Thiemann notes is one of "relative unimportance." Additionally, what the further evolution of America's underlying embracement of religious individualism has wrought for out modern society is secularization. According to Peter L. Berger, University Professor and Director of the Institute for the Study of Economic Culture at Boston University:

By secularization we mean the process by which sectors of society and culture are removed from the dominance of religious institutions and symbols...(of) the evacuation by the Christian churches of...their influence. (This) affects the totality of cultural life and ideation...(and) most important of all, in the rise of science as an autonomous, thoroughly secular perspective on the world. As there is secularization of society and culture, so is there a secularization of consciousness. Put simply, this means that the modern West has produced an increasing number of individuals who look upon the world and their own lives without the benefit of religious interpretations. (107-08).

Here, the link between America's Protestant sectarian religious individualism and the rise of secularization within this country is rather clear-cut. Lewy's analysis rings especially relevant here, "(t)he assumption that nature constitutes an intelligible order was a prerequisite of modern science, but it was Protestantism that supplied another key ingredient— the obligation of intense concentration on secular activity, 'good works' that were seen providing evidence of grace. The Puritan ethos identified industriousness with the expenditure of physical energy and the handling of material objects." (17).

Furthermore, "the Puritans also believed that God helps those who help themselves...(which) also issued in a constructive self-discipline that in America helped produce the proverbial Yankee individualism." (20). This further contributed to the rise of secularization, in that the individual was not only viewed as the locus for the realization of personal salvation, but the agent through which personal salvation was, in part, achieved via that which the material world produced and offered. This opened the door to the free association of one's work with elements of religious significance and the identification of the fruits of one's labor with levels of spiritual achievement. Hence, the Protestant ethic so often cited as the basis for America's industriousness.

In addition, this notion of a certain spirituality achieved through materiality, according to Berger's studies, "became amenable to the systematic, rational penetration, both in thought and in activity, which we associate with modern science and technology. It may be maintained, then, that Protestantism served as a historically decisive prelude to secularization." (112-13).

In this sense, Protestantism was naturally attentive to the eventual developments within the world of science and technology, in that, within the resulting material advancements, there existed for the Protestant, inherent levels of spiritual association and significance. Therefore, as so many sociologists have observed, including Max Weber in his classic 1920 effort on the subject, *The Protestant Ethic and the Spirit of Capitalism*, the Puritans brought with them the values conducive to capitalism. This was eventually made manifest through the conjunction of the work ethic and business, industry, science, technology and the expansion of each—resulting in the West's development of the capitalist-industrial economy. This has been closely associated with the increased secularization of not only the United States, but with the rest of the world as well.

The literature on the secularization of America is enormous however, for the purposes of this discussion, suffice it to state the following observation. The rise of secularization has had the deleterious effect of steadily eroding away at the underlying religious fabric of American culture, in that:

A)   it supplanted a previously underlying reliance on religious principles as the basis for explaining human existence and destiny with that of a purely scientific order of logical constructs;

B)   it replaced the natural law of God with the sole reliance on an objective natural law and an apathetic evolution of the universe;

C) it rendered religion an outdated system of irrelevancies and more the realm of the intellectually backward.

In effect, it kicked God out of the earthly paradise humanity was now attempting to create for itself. Here, science and technology sought to establish a predictable order of logically deduced results to guarantee humanity's material acquisitions. This further fueled the concept of entitlements discussed at the opening of this chapter. The parallel effect of this science/technology duality was to foster further secularization, which increasingly forced religion into an inferior role. Since the inherent nature of religion, "in its purest forms, lies beyond the reach of science" (Stark 14), as, "a system of very general compensators based on supernatural assumptions" (432), and is intrinsically unable to be immediately verified or proven—science and technology supplied the seemingly absolute answers to a waiting world.

Yet, while Stark and Baimbridge in their important study of religion in the United States (see bibliography) absolved secularization from being detrimental to religion and, in fact, considered the former a natural process, I take an alternate stance.

I consider this "process" to be severely detrimental to religion, in that, it further serves to undermine religious beliefs and evaluations regarding the material world, thereby placing religion at the mercy of secularization. Therefore, religion is forced to take the defensive position and seek to prove concepts of a supernatural nature, which require faith rather than scientific procedures to ascertain. Thus, religion is inevitably the underdog and invariably subtracted from issues involving the national will due to its faith-based nature. Religion is perceived as inhabiting the world of fantasy and speculation, which is the complete antithesis of the scientific. Religion then becomes irrelevant to the scientifically induced secularized world of which only science can influence or explain. According to Steve Bruce, a leading sociologist of religion, "(s)ecularization may be sought in the following three related changes: the decline of popular involvement with the churches; the decline in scope and influence of religious institutions; and the decline in the popularity and impact of religious beliefs." (26).

This then is where I find the godlessness that has infected America—a godlessness of elimination and disregard; of rejection, dismissal, and outright repudiation of religious beliefs and principles. Yet, as mentioned previously, American's have attended church in relatively constant numbers, but with a basic indifference to whatever is being preached once they exit through the church doors. Within the material world the dominance of another set of rules seems to apply. The basis for these rules is the individual and his/her pursuit of the material according to his/her own perceptions of how best to achieve the same. This involves a personally derived criteria subjectively achieved from internally considered rationalizations quite often less the influence of religious value systems. Berger explains this point quite clearly by stating, "(p)robably for the first time in history, the religious legitimations of the world...lost their plausibility not only for intellectuals and other marginal individuals but for broad masses of entire societies." (124).

The repercussions of this upon the underlying moral law, which served as the basis for much of America's sociopolitical structure since its inception, was most devastating. This fact was particularly evident to Lewy when he wrote, "(t)he moral capital that (had) accumulated over many centuries from a unique stock of religious and ethical teachings deplet(ed) at an alarming rate." (xii). America became a vast reservoir of newly perceived moral irrelevancies—nothing was absolute save the precepts of science and technology. Furthermore, as Thiemann sadly noted and repeatedly stated, this had become increasingly prevalent among America's new crop of liberal theorists and politicians in that, "any issue which precipitat(ed) a disagreement concerning moral truth should be removed from the democratic political agenda." (125).

As mentioned earlier in this chapter, my contention with regard to the withering of religion in America and the decline in public and private morality involved two primary factors. The second, yet one admittedly having somewhat of a lesser effect than the influence upon this country's social philosophies by the tenets of our archetypal religions, is that of America's shift from a homogeneous to a heterogeneous society.

According to Boston, "(t)he United States, lacking an established religion, quickly became a haven for those seeking the right to religious free exercise." (138). In addition, many arrived at America's shores simply seeking adventure, fortune, or a better life. Therefore, the previous and relatively uniform ancestral population consisting of mainly English Christians gave way to new waves of immigrants stemming from widely diverse nationalities, cultures, and religious backgrounds, well into the twentieth century.

For the majority, their new life in America began by settling into areas populated by those of similar ilk. This brought a sense of familiarity, community, common culture, and heritage to the arriving immigrants. America itself required nothing of these people other than obedience to her laws and sharing in her dreams for the future. Of course, other than obedience to laws—antebellum slaves, American Indians, and later many of this country's black citizens were still exempt from participating in the rest. Yet, for the balance of the population, there was unlimited potential.

However, the preponderance and evolution of this melting pot of peoples had an altering effect upon the previously unifying, implied civic piety which resulted from the original English Christian migrations, in that, many of the new immigrants did not share those same religious beliefs and principles. In addition, much of America's foundational social and cultural concepts were equally less important to the arriving immigrants as well.

It must be noted here, that the Founders never opposed pluralism, and a multiplicity of faiths was considered a basic condition of America's concept of religious liberty. According to Barton this was maintained, "as long as the beliefs of other religions did not manifest in violent or deviant behavior which might threaten the stability of civil government." (33).

Still, that underlying civic Protestantism woven throughout early American society was slowly becoming less representative of the diversity of this country's inhabitants. America's conglomeration of social and religious traditions, rather than melding into a common national identity, remained individual entities within the greater whole.

Since, as Lipset noted, the American experience, "lacked the emphasis on social hierarchy and status differences characteristic of postfeudal and monarchical cultures" (19)—it did not possess the typically European conception of identity based on nationality or common history. America was a nation, "born out of revolution...organized around an ideology...about the nature of a good society (and) founded on a creed" (31), as was outlined in the Declaration of Independence. Therefore, the country was left with little more than its physical boundaries and the promises of freedom to unify its diverse population.

Eventually, the net result was a complex myriad of social, cultural, and religious systems, with each seeking to foster and maintain their particular and independent traditions within a politically derived national concept of the common good—which itself was based upon an alternate set of principles than those of the arriving immigrants.

The relationship that this multicultural plurality had upon religion and morality in this country is very similar to what Tocqueville, in the 1830s, stated was problematic to religion and democracy in general:

> Men who are alike and on the same level in this world easily conceive the idea of a single God who imposes the same laws on each man and grants him future happiness at the same price. The conception of the unity of mankind ever brings them back to the idea of the unity

of the Creator, whereas when men are isolated from one another by great differences, they easily discover as many divinities as there are nations, castes, classes, and families, and they find a thousand private roads to go to heaven. (446).

Within America, true national "unity" remained ever elusive as the plurality of its population left so many "isolated" by their "differences," causing each group to seek its own "private" road. Steve Bruce also noted pluralism's tendency to create segments of isolated individuals within a population when he wrote, "I see pluralism as the cause of a social and political structure which allows particular groups to recreate culturally homogenous 'ghettos.'" (143).

Berger's comments regarding pluralism's specific effect on religion are especially illuminating when he observed that:

> The pluralistic situation...makes it ever more difficult to maintain or to construct viable plausibility structures for religion. The plausibility structures lose massively because they can no longer enlist society as a whole to serve for the purpose of social confirmation...The pluralistic situation multiplies the number of plausibility structures competing with each other...it relativizes their religious contents. More specifically, the religious contents are 'deobjectivated,' that is...they become 'subjectivized' in a double sense: Their 'reality' becomes a 'private' affair of individuals, that is, loses the quality of self-evident intersubjective plausibility...(a)nd their 'reality'...is rooted within the consciousness of the individual rather than in any facilities of the external world. (151-52).

In addition, as moral law principles have invariably been traditionally rooted within the foundations of religious systems, so too have these principles been seriously undermined by America's plurality of moral interpretations resulting from the steadily increasing heterogeneity of its population.

In, *The One and the Many: America's Struggle for the Common Good*, Martin E. Marty, a world-renowned authority on religion and ethics in America, puts forth the premise that this country is now experiencing a, "shock that I am calling the American trauma." (6). He further indicates that the cause of this lies within the "heightened diversity" of America's population and the loss of its national identity as each group protects and maintains the exclusivity of its history and experiences (which Marty terms its "stories") set separately and apart from the whole. Marty contends that not only do these, "contrasting motions produce a shock to the civil body, a trauma in the cultural system, and a paralysis in the neural web of social interactions" (3), but that our, "moral, spiritual, and intellectual capital are in need of restoring" (17), if the United States is to overcome this "trauma" and repair its "fragile social order."

In their contemporary study of ethics in American culture (*Morality USA*), Ellen G. Friedmann and Corinne Squire discovered that, "(t)he irresolvability of contemporary moral argument is not so much a symptom of morality's absence or loss as an indication of pluralism...This pluralism is not the tolerant exchange of viewpoints that agree to differ. It is, rather, a troubled coexistence of incompatible opinions, a babble of unmatched voices...the uneasy moral pluralism in the United States." (6).

Therefore, I have found that the effect this has had upon America's social philosophy is that there is no clear-cut version of the same. Differing opinions on moral issues take center stage in daily media reports, but rarely are there any resolutions. The resulting ambiguity flounders in a limbo-like haze of continual bickering, while the controversial issue or practice continues, e.g. abortion.

As will be dealt with in more detail within the final chapter entitled: "Conclusions, Solutions, & Final Reflections" and throughout the remainder of this book—the point I raise and associate with America's current heterogeneity with regard to the variety of very often competing religious traditions and this country's resulting moral ambiguity, is not solved by a return to the Tocquevillian assigned allusion to America's former homogeneity. Rather, solutions lie in seeking to establish a commonality among these traditions with regard to the individual vices and virtues they acknowledge and adhere to within the greater society they must then ultimately function.

The various ways to accomplish this, range from Etzioni's suggestion of the forging of a national moral identity of "core values"; to Thiemann and Bellah's considerations involving an American "civil religion"; to Marty's concept of the identification of our "common stories." Perhaps the religious scholar and director of the Pluralism Project, Diana L. Eck stated it best, "(m)utual understanding may well lead to mutual transformation, as each of us begins to catch a glimpse of the glory as seen by the other. And above all, it provides the context in which the commitments of our faith can enable us to join with one another to solve the problems of our interdependent world." (229).

Here the reference to "our interdependent world" equally applies to the interdependent "world" of America's microcosmic plurality.

This chapter's attempt to trace America's apparent shift from God to godlessness began with the failure of the American Dream; explored aspects of the debates surrounding the creation and interpretations regarding the First Amendment's religious clause; examined increases in secularization, and included my contention of two primary, contributing historical factors. That is, America's disposition toward individualism as the direct result of Protestant's personalized brand of religiousness, and the increasing diversity of public opinion and behavior resulting from America's expanding heterogeneity.

In summary, within the United States, I find the above to be the primary factors which contributed to the general decline of religion in relationship to public life in that:

A)   the failed American Dream left many Americans ambivalent about the future;

B)   needing more predictable and pragmatic means to achieve a secure future, Americans turned away from the supernatural channels offered by religion, and began to reexamine religion's basic function within the society via reinterpretations of the First Amendment's religious clause;

C)   as science and technology appeared to offer definitive and absolute provisions for a secure future, a more secularized agenda became the foundation for America's future;

D)   the element of Protestant individualism inherent within American society moved many away from the precepts of the traditional congregational churches toward a less public, more personalized interpretation and direction in order to achieve supernatural compensators (à la Stark and Baimbridge);

E)   America's heterogeneity included a myriad of existing religions which further segmented the population and eliminated the possibility of any single tradition or agenda to be representative of this diverse populace within the public forum.

Combined, these five factors have acted antithetical to the importance of religion as a vital component of civic life, rendering it more a subjective, personalized, and private function. Thus, the removal of religion from America's public forum has created a rather ambiguous spiritual and moral climate, one which I agree with Thiemann, has proved most contradictory to the common good, in that:

Given the pervasiveness and importance of religious convictions within the American populace, it would indeed be odd to deny such profound sentiments any role in public life. Given the historic significance of religion in shaping our national political culture, the removal of religion from the 'public square' would seem to violate our most ancient traditions. Given the deep connection between religion and morality, the elimination of religious symbols from public discourse at a time of perceived moral crisis would appear to be self-defeating. (3-4).

In the next chapter entitled, "Understanding Individualism" I will attempt to further explore the dominance of this social philosophy within America; the resulting rise of the autonomous individual, and the satisfaction of the untrammeled self. In addition, the relationship between individualism, secularization, and our current notions of the separation of church and state will be discussed. This chapter will also cover individualism's effect on the American community, both national and local.

Martin E. Marty wondered whether the Latin motto on the Great Seal of the United States: *E pluribus unum* (translated: One from many) still applies today as it did when first stated in 1776. So do I! Therefore, the essence of the next chapter of this book will seek to answer the following question: Are we truly a "United" States?

Chapter 3

Understanding Individualism

In exploring the influence and effects of the philosophy of individualism on modern America society, one must also include the particular dominance of modernity upon the foundation of individualism within this country. In general, the term modernity refers to the freedom to construct one's life according to personally derived ethical standards regarding right and wrong. Modernity is very often the opposite of tradition and is primarily associated with the dissolution of fixed standards of personal and social behavior.

It is here that we find the eventual withering of a previously dominant biblical tradition which stressed communal and spiritual development, and its supplantation by a social tenet emphasizing increased personal satisfaction and unbridled materialism. In addition, and as was particular to this country's development, individualism in America was heavily influenced by the peculiarly secular shifts within the religious ethos prevalent since its foundation. As explained in the previous chapter, this was based in the threads of Protestantism woven inexorably throughout America and this religion's eventual strong link with the development of an underlying secularity via the influence of a religiously vestigial, materially oriented standard which evolved directly from philosophical shifts in the Protestant ethic. This was fully explored by Max Weber earlier in this century. Also discussed previously, and of equal importance here, is Protestantism's elemental emphasis on a particularly personal approach regarding the spiritual and mundane aspects of one's existence.

Still, individualism itself has occupied a long-standing special place within the hearts of the American people in that America's revolutionary origins were based on the struggle against the arbitrary and oppressive authority of Europe's monarchical and aristocratic regimes, and the triumph of individual rights and personal autonomy. This struggle also sought to establish the inherent dignity of the human person, which was so often ignored under these regimes. Paralleling this undertaking, yet to a somewhat lesser extent, were efforts involving that which Bellah describes as ontological individualism, which sets the individual apart as the primary reality, and society as an "artificial construct" of a "second-order."

However, to avoid confusion, the philosophy of individualism construed in the modern sense, and the main subject of this chapter, will be referred to simply as individualism or modern individualism— other varieties will be specifically identified. Therefore, this modern form of individualism essentially embraces the notion of the transcendence of the subjective self above the objectivity of the social collective, in that, the needs of the individual and his/her ultimate satisfaction becomes the true locus for the social mechanics of that collective. As such, individualism finds its greatest expression within the evolution of American culture. Hence, and in conjunction with one of the ongoing themes of this book, America's embrace of this dominating individualism has resulted in an almost thorough elimination of religion from the fabric of American society, and the nearly complete secularization of all aspects of American life. Here, religion has become less effective in satisfying the needs and desires of the emancipated individual within the matrix of materialism. Hence, religion's exclusion from participation in the public forum via, what I feel, are the various convoluted interpretations regarding the separation of church and state, have resulted in a further distancing of religious influence from the mainstream of American public life.

Overall, this secularized individualism has expanded over the life of the American republic in direct proportion to the advances of modernity, and the parallel development of these two factors has greatly impacted on the roots of our republicanism. Bellah testified to this fact when he examined modern individualism's increasing dominance in American life and the withering of our republican traditions. Furthermore, Bellah expressed concern over our modern view of the self as the main form of reality and questioned whether this type of individualism can actually be sustained. Here, the issue for Bellah is not the individual's withdrawal from public life to pursue a private agenda, "but whether such individuals are capable of sustaining either a public or a private life. If this is the danger, perhaps only the civic and biblical forms of individualism—forms that see the individual in relation to a larger whole, a community and a tradition—are capable of sustaining genuine individuality and nurturing both public and private life." (*Habits of the Heart* 143).

However, the seeds of the more modern strands of individualism sown within the American tradition and fully embraced within today's America, have taken Lockeian concepts involving individual autonomy and personal liberty to the extreme. Where earlier forms of individualism were able to function along with classical republicanism and the various biblical religions, which indeed did involve a certain "moral and religious obligation" acting in conjunction with personal freedoms, modern individualism has completely invalidated the communal traditions associated with the biblical and republican traditions, and replaced the same with a sole focus on the absolute needs of the self. Once again, I find Protestantism's involvement with the duality of materialism and personally derived standards of behavior to be in direct correlation with the rise of individualism within America.

What I believe to be imperative here and extremely relevant is part of the overall conclusion reached by Lipset. He explains that the American Creed's distinctly classical liberalism which fully emphasizes individualism, "is something of a double-edged sword (in that individualism) threatens traditional forms of community morality, and thus has historically promoted a particularly virulent strain of greedy behavior (yet) (a)t the same time, it represents a tremendous asset, encouraging the self-reflection necessary for responsible judgment." (268).

Although Lipset found some merit in individualism's tendency to encourage that "self-reflection"—my investigation has uncovered more of the reverse, in that, modern individuals tend to exhibit increasing levels of "greedy behavior" in order to assure the realization of their personal wants. This negative behavior becomes even more apparent when we refer to Lewy's description of the more recent branches of individualism spreading throughout America. Here, the expressive variant is characterized by the intense, "desire for self-gratification and the display of moral recklessness" (41); and the radical version involves, "disdain for traditional values and institutions, and the espousal of recreational promiscuity without personal commitment." (41).

Thus, for modern Americans, it is my opinion that individualism has evolved to encompass more of the negative excesses of human behavior similar to those groups or individuals engaged in the pursuit of unbridled personal choice. In addition, I believe that our current tendency to further extend the limits of that behavior seems more indicative of a need to validate the ability to do so, rather than the pursuit of any positive redeeming social value.

Another consequence of individualism found in much of the literature refers to the isolation generated amongst individuals as each pursues his/her personal path of self-gratification. In, *John Dewey and*

American Democracy, Robert B. Westbrook, Associate Professor of History at the University of Rochester, states that Dewey's highly influential philosophies regarding American freedom expressed concern over this isolating effect of individualism. Here Westbrook states:

> Dewey argued (that) associated life and participatory democracy were stunted and underdeveloped, and as a consequence this society produced stunted, underdeveloped, 'lost' individuals (in that) (t)he pursuit of private gain isolated individuals from one another, and the exploitative possessive individualism fostered by capitalism inhibited the formation of the participatory communities of democratic action essential to self-development and social welfare. (434).

As I further trace the rise and influence of individualism within America, what has become increasingly apparent is that despite the liberating effects this philosophy has had upon each citizen's personal choice and self-gratification, in reality, individualism has had a rather deleterious effect on the cohesiveness of American society. Additionally, even if Lipset is correct in concluding that individualism promotes "self-reflection" and "responsible judgment" I can't help but wonder: Yes, but at what cost?

In probing the current trends within America, the late cultural and political analyst Professor Christopher Lasch expressed a distinct disenchantment with American life, and described individualism as, "a way of life that is dying...which in its decadence has carried (its) logic to the extreme of a war against all, the pursuit of happiness to the dead end of a narcissistic preoccupation with the self." (xv).

Lasch further explains that American's self-absorptive tendencies have not created more socially cooperative individuals, but rather allowed Americans, "(to) become more adept at exploiting the conventions of interpersonal relations for their own benefit." (66).

I agree with Lasch, and find the precepts of individualism completely antithetical to the concept of a unified social collective, in that, the primary pursuit of the personal has produced an increasing segmentation of individual consciousness less inclined toward both national and local communal concerns. The self-determination expressly stated by the Founding generation was of course conceived as a collective concept involving notions of the common good and mutually derived benefits.

Within this context, one should not imply that a society focused on the achievement of a common good would be composed of anonymous automatons mechanically working toward achieving a communistically oriented social compact, or simply a mass of subjects merely existing under an all-knowing sovereignty. Rather, I believe there was a definite interest in preserving each citizen's individuality—that special quality that distinguishes each person from another—and the effort to establish the dignity of the individual within society as opposed to individualism's assigned dominance of the individual over society. Here, individuality would nourish the growth of the American republic through the vitality in the variety of each citizen's contribution to the entire social experience. This contribution would be made manifest through various sources including: voting; volunteerism; community involvement, and work. In this preservation of individuality, the expectation would be to extract social cooperation toward achieving a good common for all citizens. Although many will argue that this is what we indeed have achieved, I conclude along with William J. Bennett, former presidential appointee, statesman, and currently a respected author, that with regard to the deterioration of America's public values, "(a) lot of people forgot, and many others willfully rejected, the most basic and sensible answers to first questions, to questions about what contributes to our social well-being and prosperity, what makes for individual character and responsibility, and what constitutes a 'good society.' " (255-56).

In addition, I believe that although the Founders were also considering concepts of individualism that favored a personally derived self-satisfaction above that of the society, their intention was not to achieve the same at the expense of society. Once again, and as noted by Bellah, our republicanism formerly involved certain, "moral and religious obligations that in some contexts justified obedience as well as freedom." (*Habits of the Heart* 143).

Instead, I find that excesses in individualism have resulted in a marked increase in the levels of antisocial behavior in America today. One reason for this is quite apparently the shift in influence between the two branches of modern individualism and the resulting altered perceptions regarding the self, which have evolved into the radical individualism of the modern era.

To explain further, what Bellah refers to as utilitarian individualism dominated the American scene since this country's inception. People were expected to be self-supporting and able to stand on their own two feet, with, "work, the realm, par excellence, of utilitarian individualism." (*Habits of the Heart* 83). (Once again I find the influence of the Protestant ethic fully involved here.) Bellah then goes on to describe that the primary goal of this particular brand of individualism was, "the chance for the individual to get ahead on his own initiative...the focus...exclusively on individual self-improvement." (33). This thinking is based on the conception that citizens enter into a contract with society in order to advance their self-interests.

Next, Bellah explains that by the mid-1800s many Americans began to find this approach extremely restrictive and lacking in human feelings and the deeper expressions of the self. In opposition to the "utilitarian" approach, and out of the spirit of romanticism, arose what he describes as "expressive individualism" whereby, as Bellah puts it, "each person('s)...unique core of feeling and intuition...should unfold or be expressed if individuality is to be realized." (334). Here, the individual finds the freedom to, "'merge' with other persons, with nature, or with the cosmos as a whole." (334). This concept, along with the rest of expressive individualism's precepts are what have dominated the American scene ever since.

Still, for today's Americans, there have been several far-reaching changes within society resulting from the dominance of this expressive form of modern individualism coupled with the vestiges of the utilitarian version. These changes have not only been carried to excess (hence, the term "radical individualism") but have greatly contributed to the current increases in antisocial, irreligious, selfish, and increasingly immoral behavior headlined daily throughout this nation's cities. It is from this duality of the utilitarian and expressive concept of attaining self-fulfillment that we can gain better insight into understanding what motivates the lives of today's Americans. Here, traces of the former variant still moves American's to achieve greater levels of a personally derived notion of self-improvement. However, the underlying religiously based work ethic of the utilitarian branch has been completely supplanted by the more romantic notions inherent within the expressive form. This then inspires the individual to attend to the unbridled satisfaction of his/her innermost feelings and desires. The following illustrates this contention.

In studying the incidents of the modern practice of "wilding" among Americans, Charles Derber, professor of sociology at Boston College and a leading commentator on economic and cultural individualism, came to some very revealing conclusions. Most importantly, Derber offers descriptions of wilding well beyond the recent stories of marauding gangs of youths preying on innocent citizens simply for the thrill generated. Here, Derber describes wilding as, "self-centered and self-aggrandizing behavior that harms others...(an) epidemic (that) tears at the social fabric and threatens to unravel society itself, ultimately reflecting the erosion of the moral order and the withdrawal

of feelings and commitments from others to oneself, to 'number one.'"
(6).

Derber finds wilding exhibited in *all* realms of American life.
Whether political, economic, or social—for Derber, wilding is either
"expressive" in that it reflects, as in the case of youth gangs, indulging in
one's own destructive impulses for the sheer satisfaction of the act itself;
or "instrumental" whereby fun or "pure emotive gratification" rarely
factors in, yet the absolute calculated personal gain becomes the
dominant goal. In either case, Derber's investigations uncover the
underlying cause as, "manifestations of degraded American
individualism...individualism run amok...the face of America's
individualistic culture in an advanced state of disrepair." (8-9).

In essence, modern individualism, far from promoting the sacred,
dignified, individuality of the human person as described in early
American philosophy, is today more reflective of a constant
preoccupation with unbridled self-indulgence. This self-indulgence has
become so obscenely widespread, obsessive and unrestricted, that
elements of personal and social responsibility are virtually nonexistent,
and seemingly ignored. Here, the pursuit of achieving increased
pleasure and self-gratification has become such an extreme mix of both
utilitarian and expressive individualism, that the current term for this
form of human behavior, radical individualism, is indeed a most
accurate description. In addition, the maximization of one's self-
interests and improvement is made manifest by whatever means one
conceives to achieve the same in response to the satisfaction of one's
unrestricted feelings, needs, and desires. Perhaps Lasch describes this
modern variant of individualism best by identifying it as, "(s)atisfaction
(that) depends on taking what you want instead of waiting for what is
rightfully yours." (67).

The consequences of a society composed of citizens immersed in the
precepts of radical individualism, as explained by the contemporary
legal analyst Mary Ann Glendon, is that this is not a society at all and,

"cannot be successfully democratized." (74). Additionally, and in summary of Glendon's position on this issue, this attention to radical autonomy and self-sufficiency supported by both our legal and political discourse is, "not...the language of...the Founders." (75).

Within this context, many leading sociologists (e.g. Bellah, Etzioni, Lasch, and Lipset) have found that the negative social ramifications of radical individualism's "me first" attitude are disturbingly commonplace and indicative of many of American society's present ills. For example, with regard to radical individualism's expressive roots, Lipset noted, "(t)he lead of the United States in divorce rates...presumably reflects in part the strength of individualism." (50). With reference to current sexual mores, Lipset similarly finds that, "(t)he expressive individualism of young Americans leads them to have intercourse at an early age" (51), which has led to ever increasing out of wedlock teenage pregnancy rates across America. Even more alarming is the effect this radical individualism has had upon the family unit, in that, "as a value (it) leads not only to self-reliance and a reluctance to be dependent on others, but also to independence in family relationships, including a greater propensity to leave a mate if the marital relationship becomes troubled." (26-7).

Derber expresses equal concern over the negative effects individualism has had on the various social systems that make up American society, in that, this exorbitant focus on the individual can tilt so far toward the self that it not only increasingly reduces social commitments but, "the family and other building blocks of society decompose." (111).

Here we find a distinctly moral imperative very much missing from the behavioral ethics of many modern Americans. In much of Bellah's work, he spoke of the possibility of this missing moral imperative, and the need for Americans to reestablish a "moral ecology" (the web of moral understandings and commitments that tie people together in a community)—[*Habits of the Heart* 335]—as a means toward regaining healthy institutions. Bellah believes that the way to achieve this moral ecology is by retrieving much of the moral concepts contained within the older biblical and civil republican traditions that were foundational to America. However, Bellah continues by stating that, "Americans have difficulty understanding those traditions today or seeing how they apply to their lives (because) individualism makes the very idea of (these) institutions inaccessible to many of us." (*The Good Society* 5-6).

In much the same vein, Etzioni speaks of our "hollowed or weakened" moral order stemming from the individualism that evolved from the 1960s through the 1980s whereby, "self-interest (became) the best base for social order and virtue...(there arose) a growing tendency to shirk social responsibilities...(t)he role and influence of religion declined...(and) many Americans paid only lip service to some core values and showed significantly lower commitment to others— marriage, for instance." (*The New Golden Rule* 65).

Etzioni continues by calling for a regeneration of the moral order for "societies that have lost it" via a return to a common system of "core values" as that prescription for reversing the destructive trends of our antisocial autonomy. Of course whose system remains the ultimate question. Still, Etzioni's fear of a further breakdown of moral order leading to the possibility of outright social anarchy if the excesses of unbounded autonomy continues, attests to the urgent need for an answer—an issue that I will deal with in the concluding chapter of this book.

Indeed, much of his work sadly indicates that we have begun to cross over the line toward social anarchy as increased sexual "liberation," deregulation, and "slack" enforcement of laws rises. For Etzioni, all these factors are indicative of the significant erosion of our society's foundations. In response, Etzioni's call for, "a blend of voluntary order with well-protected yet bounded autonomy" (73), reflects much of the Communitarian position, which he founded. Here, the limits of our autonomy is inexorably related to the issue of whose system will define those parameters, yet Etzioni's desire to reestablish society, "as a community of communities...(with a) social order rel(ying) on social bonds and moral voices" (141-42), is not only a viable beginning, it is distinctly antithetical to the precepts of all modern forms of individualism and their socially destructive focus on the self. I find that the Communitarian approach still thoroughly cultivates and maintains one's individuality via the unique, contributory, communal interaction generated by each member's involvement with the community. This, despite criticisms to the contrary, for example, from Samuel Scheffler, author and Professor of Philosophy at the University of California at Berkeley, whose work on human morality proposes that a community oriented paradigm might not be the panacea for our modern social ills, in that, the community could never, "take the place of more abstract moral notions like fairness, social justice, and the equal worth of persons." (16).

Still, I tend to find Etzioni's approach a more socially viable solution toward countering the destructive efforts of individualism, in that, the promotion of interaction among people already engaged in the excesses of self-gratification could only serve to reawaken, or at the very least reintroduce, these separated and isolated individuals to the possibility of establishing anew those social ties which promote a common good, and fosters those values which Scheffler fears might be missing in the often "suffocating and oppressive" atmosphere of the community. However, while I agree with Scheffler that we should not be blinded to the unfairness, injustice, and atomization often associated with many extreme forms of community (e.g. cults, oppressive political regimes, etc.) one cannot negate the fact that it is both within and through the community that "fairness, social justice, and the worth of persons" is achieved in the first place.

Continuing on, Etzioni and Lipset have produced findings that are representative of many who have sounded the alarm for a reevaluation of what truly constitutes a "good society" for Americans. It has been my experience that much of the available literature of those grappling with issues associated with America's social predicaments is replete with references to the fact that modern notions of individualism act mostly contrary to concepts involving the common good. While these sources, as do I, champion the sacredness of the human person and the pursuit of his/her individuality, many find serious fault in modern individualism's primary ethos of unbridled self-satisfaction. For example, Lewy labels radical individualism as, "the bane of modern societies (in its undermining of) civic virtue, family solidarity, and concern for others" (62), and one of many insightful conclusions reached by the Daloz team of social researchers calls attention to the limiting effect of "unharnessed individualism" in, "the growing evidence that civic participation is diminishing and that the current forms of individualism have a limited utility for society as a whole...which diminishes and hardens our sense of what it means to be human." (10-11).

Here, the general consensus finds the philosophies of modern individualism to be most contradictory to the communal foundation and cooperative nature of American society. Furthermore, in discussions involving the negative effects of modern individualism upon our society, the topic inevitably leads to the loss of a certain moral compass within America and the decline in the influence of this country's religious institutions.

This raises a very interesting, yet quite obvious, set of pertinent observations. Is it mere coincidence that the decline of religion and morality within America is directly proportional to the increasing impact of modern individualism? Is it merely coincidental that modern individualism's dominating doctrine of the unbridled satisfaction of the self runs parallel to the reduction in the general influence of religious tenets involving individual restraint and moral guidance? Is it mere coincidence that modern individualism's orientation toward the unrestrained pursuit of personal gain and self-gratification is correlational to the decline of the overall influence of religion within America's public institutions? And finally, is it merely coincidental that as modern individualism's orientation toward the self overtakes America we find increasing instances of further social degeneration amongst Americans and their interactive communities?

I believe that to maintain these observations as credible "coincidences" stretches the meaning of credibility to its furthest extent!

In addressing these issues, here is where I find further evidence for my ongoing argument regarding those factors contributing to the rise of a distinctly anti-religious atmosphere overtaking America, and further support for my previously cited contention relating to the wave of godlessness spreading throughout American society. Closely aligned to this is the deleterious effect the deterioration of this nation's religious communities has had upon the communal nature of American society. Here, the inevitable question that arises is: Excluding the highly improbable claim of mere coincidence, are the philosophies and ethos of individualism contrary, even incompatible, with religious and moral tenets, and if so, how has individualism contributed to the decline of religion and morality in American society? I believe the evidence I have outlined within this chapter points to the obvious inherent incompatibility between the unbridled, self-centered tenets of individualism, and that of the morally based, communal principles of religion. Here, the dominance of the former within all aspects of American life has caused the influence of the latter to suffer enormously.

In his highly informative study of religion in the modern world, Steve Bruce observed that, "individualism...change(d) the nature of religion and its place in the world. Individualism threatened the communal basis of religious belief and behavior." (230).

In describing the process by which this occurred, Bruce explains that in general, the slow evolution of the "sovereign individual" as an outgrowth of the Protestant Reformation resulted in previous assumptions regarding the "unitary and indivisible" nature of divine truth to be abandoned. Here, "(t)he Protestants' rejection of the priesthood meant every individual had to discern God's will and respond." (231). This resulted because previous to Martin Luther's schism with Roman Catholicism, almost all the Bibles were written in Latin and were therefore translated, interpreted, and explained to the congregation by the Catholic hierarchy of priests. Luther's translation of the Bible into German put it into the hands of the people who were now able to read it for themselves and interpret its meaning. This reduced the importance of the priesthood since the faithful were now able to find their own way to God. However, as each person was free to derive a personal interpretation of what he/she read, there were as many interpretations of the Bible as there were people reading it. In addition, the congregational nature of religion was effectively reduced since everyone followed his or her own independently derived and individually oriented path in life.

In light of this, I am compelled to raise the following point: that a switch from a central body of divine truth to a myriad of individual interpretations of the same is completely antithetical to the communal nature of not only the vast majority of our religious institutions, but virtually all other human associations as well. In this approach, the individual is actively encouraged to develop a selfhood radically separate from the pulse of society and embark on a personal road of spiritual discovery and awareness. However, in the end, this separate self can become so far removed from the balance of society and spiritual life, that he/she is completely distanced from any interactive participation in either. This then is totally contrary to the wealth of human knowledge amassed regarding God's relationship with humanity. Although the individual perceives a developing oneness with a god of his/her choosing and a related burgeoning sense of spiritual growth, I believe it is more the expansion of one's ego that is affected rather than any particularly personal brand of revelation regarding the will of God.

Surely, through private contemplation one can achieve certain levels of spiritual understanding and/or awareness. Still, as stated earlier, the wealth of accumulated knowledge and experience regarding God's interactive relationship with humanity, while often internally considered, is primarily manifested and expressed in conjunction with other humans who collectively interpret and share in God's intentions for humankind.

Returning to Bruce's earlier observations, eventually people were able to select from an emerging plurality of churches, sects, and cults—each claiming to reflect God's wishes. This created a social atmosphere steadily inclined toward eclecticism and idiosyncrasy, and thoroughly dominated by individualism. Consequently, the latter eighteenth and nineteenth centuries increasingly blurred bridges between the natural and supernatural world, as formerly dominant religious institutions and beliefs began to wither. This coupled with the resulting wave of rationality infusing throughout Western thought, greatly contributed to the overall decline in the popularity and importance of religion. Added to this was the influence of various private and fraternal organizations, e.g. Freemasonry, which celebrated the pursuit of self-interest via the curious mixing of quasi-religious doctrines and rituals. Furthermore, as religious beliefs became further diluted by the continuous evolution into other subcultures of belief, the ability of religion to perform as a unifying social institution was greatly reduced.

It must be stated at this juncture that from my observations regarding the rise of individualism as outgrowth of the Protestant Reformation, the reader should not conclude that I am advocating the superiority or preference of any one religion or set of religious beliefs over another. Instead, my efforts have only sought to explain that certain philosophical shifts in a society's dominant religious system, not only has profound direct effects upon the lives of all members involved in the philosophical dispute, but upon the balance of the surrounding social structure as well. This effect is both natural and unavoidable where a set of dominant religious beliefs are elemental to the everyday lives of a vast majority of any given population.

Therefore, as a result of the Protestant Reformation, not only was the importance of religion within society effectively undermined by the advent of a slowly dominating tendency toward individualism and its diffusive effect on the belief in the supernatural, but another ingredient of social cohesion was seriously affected by the slow demise of religion. This additional threat to social cohesion was the steady undercutting of those communities united by religious belief and the rippling effect this then had upon the communal nature of society itself.

As applied to the American experience, this erosion of the American community has lead to serious questions regarding the reality of an American solidarity. In effect, I am compelled to ask: Are we truly a "United" States?

In addition to individualism, within America the decline of religious influence in the public arena was advanced by a series of factors seemingly unique to American life. Industrialization, secularization, modernity, materialism, capitalism—all greatly contributed to a further focus primarily on unlimited self-satisfaction and personal gain within the material world, and less reliance on the possibility of a set of principles of personal behavior and social interaction as revealed to humanity by a Supreme Being.

The historical perspective of this issue offered by Etzioni's Communitarian position outlines that:

> Over the last few centuries, several major ideological movements have played down the role of values (or piety) in social life. The rise of secularism, the belief in science and in social engineering (including economic theories), the preoccupation with economic growth, and

the rising influence of individualistic philosophies all have minimized the role of values in general and of sharing them in particular. Religion—a major source of core values (was similarly affected). (T)he combination of long- and short-term neglect of shared values led to a thinning of the moral order and to the expected dysfunctional consequences. (*The New Golden Rule* 89).

Here, I must advise the reader that this chapter is not an attempt to imply, or prove that the sole means to achieve national unity is via religious channels. A social system solely dependent on religious affiliations in order to achieve a national unity is fraught with potential problems including the threat of an emerging theocratic totalitarianism. Indeed, this once was the case in colonial America within the Massachusetts Bay Colony established by the Puritans in 1630. Yet, and as expressed in the philosophical writings of Karol Wojtyla (who went on to become Pope John Paul II) and specifically those contained in his multi-volume work, *The Acting Person*, a social system based strictly on individualistic criteria fosters an atmosphere of oblivion to community ties amongst citizens and an increasing risk of the disintegration of social cooperation.

Still, as explained in a previous chapter within this book, America's political and social foundations are intimately based on strong, historical, religious principles. It quite obviously follows that if the basis of these foundations is dismantled or weakened, there will be serious effects upon the remaining structure. Therefore, what possible solutions are there to this dilemma?

The answer does not lie with simply establishing new social structures less religious foundations. In doing so, we run the risk of eliminating a vital component of our humanity and one which has been so vitally elemental in all forms of human life since we first began contemplating the nature of our existence. This component is the distinct possibility of a supernatural realm inhabited by a Supreme Being who interacts with humanity and its condition via the revelation of certain pertinent and important truths. As evidenced by the current tendency to ignore this possibility, humanity slowly enters into a state of moral decay and social disintegration—a fact testified to repeatedly by a variety of scholars occupying several disciplines and cited throughout this book.

It has been my contention throughout this chapter to indicate that as religion has been adversely undermined by individualism, so too has the nature of American society been similarly seriously affected by this self-centered social philosophy. However, although the alarm has been sounded amongst scholars, theologians, and politicians regarding the developing dangers of unchecked radical versions of individualism, there have been relatively few concrete solutions presented. One is the Communitarian position developed by Amitai Etzioni and outlined earlier in this chapter. Other emerging voices offering further possibilities are those of Ronald F. Thiemann and Stephen L. Carter, whose works have been cited previously in this book. Both have called for a cooperative merging of the religious and secular philosophies in order to achieve a unified citizenry. Thiemann even goes so far as to support the re-establishment of, "(a) civil religion (which) could provide an understanding of religious belief that would allow it to become the common possession of all members of society. (I)t would forge a bond between religions and the 'polis' in support of the common good of the society." (29).

I am in complete agreement with this. The reverse effect this civil religion would have on the detrimental effects modern individualism has had upon American society is quite far-reaching in scope. Similar to Marty's call for the development of "common stories" as unifying narratives shared by all of American's diverse citizenry—this shared civil religion would also serve to unite this country's varied population.

To explain further, as our national identity is based on strong ideological commitments involving freedom and equality rather than historical traditions stemming from birthright and hierarchy, some mergence of the religious and the secular would help to identify moral standards to be held in common by all Americans. This would thereby shape the foundation for improved social and communal interaction quite simply through the fact that citizens would share a similar moral value system with which to perform their public and private dealings.

In essence, while we must continually seek to protect and foster individual freedom, this freedom must be tempered with an underlying sense of common moral responsibility. As Lipset points out, "individual morality is an elemental component of the American polity." (275).

In addition, and extremely relevant here is the quote Lipset next offers from, *The Moral Foundations of United States Constitutional Democracy,* by the political theorist James Rutherford: "The free and equal individual with moral responsibility is the basis of communal solidarity." (Lipset 275). Here, we can maintain the strong foundation of America's social structure which is true to its primary plank based in traditions involving strong religious principles, and equally nurture the individual freedom we all so deeply covet.

In conclusion, while individualism originally sought to liberate the human person from an often inhuman life of anonymous survival at the hands of an all too common impassive state, and to celebrate the uniqueness of each human entity not only through their individual contributions to the common good, but as participants in God's divinely mysterious plan—today's variants of individualism offer the complete reversal of these intentions. The evolution into today's radical individualism has created the era of the apathetic, selfish narcissist. For Lasch, this narcissism is the isolated individual seeking survival and self-gratification within an intrinsically hostile world. For Lewy, it is the self-love of personal autonomy, self-expression, and sexual freedom. Whatever the description, the underlying theme is the primary satisfaction of the untrammeled self as the locus for the mechanisms of the social collective. In my opinion, this variant of individualism is slowly destroying American society and our formerly collectively conceived notions of the common good. I believe a critical reevaluation of America's communal priorities is extremely necessary for the future common good of American society. Here, voices such as Carter, Etzioni, and Thiemann have offered several possible solutions—both America and Americans would benefit greatly by listening very carefully to what they have to say.

In the next chapter I will compare classical and modern liberalism. I will explore the influence of certain concepts of modern liberalism that have had a direct correlation and effect upon the prevalence of the ethos of individualism throughout American society. Here, I will also discuss notions of personal and civic freedom, the ramifications of humanism, equal rights, pluralism, and the further effects all have had upon religious belief, morality, and concepts of the self within America.

Finally, as a preface to the next chapter, consider what Michael J. Sandel, Professor of Government at Harvard University, stated in, *Democracy's Discontent: America in Search of a Public Philosophy*:

> For the liberal self, what matters above all, what is most essential to our personhood, is not the ends we choose but our capacity to choose them...Nor does it matter, from the standpoint of liberal justice, what virtues we display or what values we espouse...(Yet) (d)espite its powerful appeal, the image of the unencumbered self is *flawed* (emphasis added). (12-13).

Chapter 4

Modern Liberalism: Legacy Or Otherwise?

In dealing with modern liberalism, one will undoubtedly find close, parallel, even identical connections with regard to the subject of the previous chapter: individualism. Indeed, much of the descriptions and effects of modern liberalism to be covered within this present chapter may have a familiar ring to them, however be assured the intention is not to repackage individualism as modern liberalism. Still, the affinity between these two social philosophies requires that some distinction be made here to avoid later confusion for the reader.

For each, the common underlying focus is on personal freedom and autonomy, yet I have found that both branch off from this main trunk in a rather fundamental approach toward achieving those goals. As discussed previously, individualism is extremely antisocial, in that, it extracts one from the social collective in order to embark on his/her own private quest to achieve unrestricted self-satisfaction. The individual "meanders" within the current social and political climate, be it either conservatively or liberally oriented, as a rather detached entity selecting from his/her own conceptions of what constitutes the good, thus to achieve a realization of his/her needs—so long as one does not impede another's pursuit of the same goal. Therefore, individualism promotes the self above and/or separate from the social collective and one's greater social obligations.

I find modern liberalism to essentially do the complete opposite. While it promotes the same pursuit of personal freedom and autonomy, it does so within the matrix of pluralistic social consciousness and obligations regarding the achievement of equality, justice, and rights for the mutual interests of all within the social collective. Here, the ultimate goal is the achievement of the good for everyone by allowing each citizen to pursue his/her own conception of what constitutes a good life. Where modern liberalism seeks to protect individuals from government influence or intervention which might infringe upon one's quest for a good life by maintaining governmental neutrality toward the moral and religious views of the citizenry; individualism leaves one afloat and independent from those governing influences, whatever the surrounding moral and religious climate of government may be. Where modern liberalism concentrates more on politics and the values that ought to govern the political institutions of a state so that citizens are capable of living their good life; individualism is apolitical in that it is purely and primarily seeking the liberation of the self via a rather mutual disinterest with the balance of society, its structure, and its governing mandates.

With this as a backdrop, I now begin this exploration of the development, influence, and effects of modern liberalism on American society.

The liberal philosophy which has so often been associated with the social ethos of the modern United States and this country's current distinctly bipartisan political offerings has its roots in America's eighteenth century revolutionary ideology à la conclusions involving Lockeian paradigms. However, there is a major distinction to be made between today's liberalism, which has influenced our cultural, social, economic, and personal agendas—and the liberal concepts which are identified with this country's foundational period. What existed during the revolutionary and founding eras is known as "classical liberalism." It included elements of Whiggism and was essentially a rebellion against the monarchical oppression and aristocratic restrictions endured under English rule. Here, our American forerunners sought to establish an egalitarian society which was highly anti-statist, anti-elitist, and conducive to individual advancement and meritocracy—in essence, something comparable to Lipset's American Creed of: liberty; egalitarianism; individualism; laissez-faire, and populism—that is, the advocacy of the rights of the common people. Hence, as Lipset further noted, those dominant bourgeois, middle-class values most associated with America.

It is noteworthy to mention that by today's standards, the founding generation's efforts to establish egalitarianism appear most contradictory given the continuance of slavery and the pillaging of the indigenous American population. However, relative to the social conditions of the eighteenth century, America was indeed more egalitarian, and placed less emphasis on social hierarchy and status than its European contemporaries.

Still, the distinction to be made between today's liberal tendencies and yesterday's classical liberalism becomes more apparent, in that, within the modern era this classical form of liberalism has evolved into what most Americans today would consider to be conservatism. Once again Lipset's analysis of the issue is most pertinent here, "(t)he semantic confusion about liberalism in America arises because both early and latter-day Americans never adopted the term to describe the unique American polity. The reason is simple. The American system of government existed long before the word 'liberal' emerged." (35-36).

Furthermore, Lipset goes on to explain that "liberal" referred to an English mid-nineteenth century political party which emphasized much of the social ethos already established in America a century before. What Europe had considered to be liberal thinking, in effect, was old-fashioned liberal thought to Americans, which by American standards of the same period was a rather conservative approach. Hence, in America today, regardless of the current incarnation, its "conservative" roots are considered "liberal" in origin. Moreover, today's notions of "liberal" or "conservative" are not purely political philosophies at all. Rather, each is a term framing a system of beliefs involving either broad or narrow interpretations encompassing personal freedom and public tolerance within the social collective. That either is associated with politics is, according to Samuelson, "political and polemical conveniences (that) frame political debates and create conflict as much as they reflect it...they depict a general postwar consciousness that affected a large majority of Americans, regardless of party or political outlook." (xiv).

Therefore, for today's American, conservatives prefer self-government on economic issues; want official standards in personal matters, and want the government to defend the community from threats to its moral fiber—liberals prefer self-government in personal matters and central decision-making on economics; they want government to fairly serve the disadvantaged, and are tolerant of social diversity, yet strive for economic equality.

Still, as concerns this chapter, the evolution of Lockeian based prescriptions for a liberal society into its distinctly modern counterpart involved several changes in the revolutionary era view that government should primarily be an instrument to secure and extend the liberties of individual freedom and rights. With this country's steady shift from a predominant agrarianism toward further industrialization came a new set of burgeoning economic conditions which directly contributed to the rise of the Bentham/Mill philosophy of utilitarianism. Here, the utilitarian approach essentially explained that what was useful is good and that any restrictions on one's liberty limited the pleasure that one might otherwise extract and enjoy from the useful. In addition, utilitarianism proposed that the purpose of government is to ensure the greatest possible happiness for the greatest possible number. What followed from this contention was a shift from the ethical value of conduct determined by an inner faculty of conscience, that is, moral principles of right and wrong involving the will of God—to conduct based on individual determinations of good and bad involving the resultant pleasure generated from the usefulness of one's actions. This shift, coupled with modern philosophical thought as reflected in much of the thinking of Immanuel Kant which linked individual autonomy and personal choice to the proposition that all human knowledge of reality is gained solely from experience, laid the foundation for the advent of modern liberalism.

Further factoring into this equation is the waning of America's laissez-faire idealism resulting from government's growing interest in business and the steady production of that which is useful to society. Moreover, according to John Dewey, the decline of laissez-faire became prevalent, as government was increasingly associated with, "aid to those at economic disadvantage and for alleviation of their conditions." (21). Dewey further explains that this notion of government assistance had come to represent the quintessential ideal that one normally uses to define modern liberalism. Hence, the so-called welfare liberalism that evolved from Roosevelt's first and second New Deal of the 1930s. Furthermore, modern liberalism is closely associated with reliance on science, reason, increased secularization, and as Thiemann and others have noted, the elimination of religion from the public arena. According to Page Smith, an American historian and professor emeritus at the University of California, "(modern liberalism) is hostile to religion in any form, except the religion of man." (194).

Overall, what we have here is a major shift in American economic theory and its social applications. In essence, our earlier classically liberal society identified economic development with individual and independent land ownership and an income structure based directly upon the satisfaction of one's material needs through the hard work associated with farming. The common good was advanced as the entire population either operated or participated in this system which required little government involvement in citizen's lives. However, the later shift toward industrialization created an increasing dependency on the satisfaction of one's material needs from the various sources outside the immediacy of one's life. Economic development became associated with organized production and government involvement. Here, modern liberalism became further immersed within the economic structure of the society by commitments to achieve the common good through a just distribution of the products of society.

With regard to this element of economic change attached to the foundation of modern liberalism, again I refer to Dewey, perhaps the most influential proponent of liberalism within America. In, *Liberalism and Social Action*, Dewey proposed that we, "socialize the forces of production...so that the liberty of individuals will be supported by the very structure of economic organization." (88). Moreover, he calls for a, "(r)egimentation of material and mechanical forces" (90), as the only way which will free individuals from, "the suppression of their cultural possibilities." (90).

I find all of this very reminiscent of the philosophies of Karl Marx and the resulting communistic system. Marx's observations on economic production paralleled Dewey's agenda, in that, in Marxism production was geared to primarily benefit the civil federation, which in theory would result in the equal distribution of goods to all individuals. The correlation with Dewey is that modern liberalism acts similarly, but in the reverse by seeking to first secure the satisfaction of individual needs as that priority emanating from the larder of state held goods produced. This is supported by Dewey's notion of the "state" as that secondary form of association created by an antecedent "public" which mediates and organizes those transactions deemed necessary for the protection of the interests shared by members of that "public." In Westbrook's chronicle of Dewey's theories regarding American democracy, Dewey defines the "public" as, "all those who are affected by the indirect consequences of transactions to such an extent that it is deemed necessary to have those consequences systematically cared for." (302).

Here, economic concepts of production are of equal importance to Dewey and Marx, differing only in the emphasis on the subject of their primary distribution.

As liberalism has evolved within this country, for today's Americans, there is quite an obvious link between current economic trends and the assurance of unabated materialism for the self-seeking, untrammeled individual. It is not my contention that Americans should not enjoy the fruits of their production, yet when this becomes the sole focus of existence, and acquisition of the same reflects an outright selfishness and disregard for others to the point of a breakdown in the moral order, then this apparatus of materialism completely contradicts modern liberalism's conception of the good life as that prescription for a healthy society.

Associated with this acquisition of goods is the controversy engendered over the just distribution of those goods. According to the respected political scientist and John L. Senior Professor of American Institutions at Cornell University, Theodore J. Lowi, liberal governments are essentially composed of sets of various interest groups (hence, Lowi's term "interest-group liberalism") resulting from the plurality of our society. These interest groups break down the ethics of government into various agenda and have, "led us into a crisis of public authority." (36). Here, as each group primarily pursues its particular priorities, governmental authority is effectively clogged by the variety of foci it must devote to these competing groups. Incidentally, this is just what the Founders feared when they expressed concern over "factionalism." Lowi goes on the explain that, "(l)iberal governments cannot plan. Planning requires the authoritative use of authority.

Planning requires law, choice, priorities, moralities. Liberalism replaces planning with bargaining." (67).

In this respect, Lowi raises further issues involving the inability of liberal governments to achieve justice, in that, the resulting division of powers creates, "a no-man's-land among duly constituted but politically impoverished governments" (168), leaving many "hopelessly fragmented." Therefore, in essence, Lowi's point involves the efficacy of the "interest group" to speak on behalf of citizens when these groups operate in competition with each other in pursuit of their own agenda. Within this framework, the ability of a fragmented, interest group fueled government to effect the just distribution of goods amongst its citizens appears, at the least, to be questionable.

Here, I would like to raise another observation with regard to Marx's social philosophies and modern liberalism which is both striking and disquieting. Within communism and modern liberalism exists a similar hostility to religion. This negative attitude toward religion within America's public forum has been documented in a previous segment of this book and will not be outlined again in this chapter. Suffice it to state that many scholars have indicated that at root of this elimination of religion from American's civic arena lies a distinctly modern day liberal political tendency which according to Thiemann, "(is) virtually unanimous in (its) staunch advocacy of the 'wall of separation between church and State'...(and its belief) that both religious practice and pluralistic democracy are best preserved by a constitutional system that precludes religious argumentation within the public realm." (75).

Adding to this is Kekes' most relevant analysis of the limitations of modern liberalism which indicates that this focus on the individual's unrestricted pursuit of the good life is replete with several major inconsistencies which, "(creates) conditions in which good and evil people are treated with equal concern and respect; in which justice is taken to involve the redistribution of resources without regard to whether their present holders and future recipients deserve them; and in which pluralism is restricted to options that conform to liberal preconceptions." (ix).

Kekes differentiates between a natural evil that occurs via a non-human agency (e.g. crop failure that results in widespread starvation) and moral evil which is under human control (e.g. murder). Here, Kekes' argument focuses on moral evil, that is, "evil...essentially connected with human actions that cause serious, unjustified harm to human beings." (27).

Therefore, Kekes concludes that in reality, modern liberalism is incapable of coping with the prevalence of evil resulting from the blanketing effect of equal treatment. In fact, modern liberalism is actually detrimental to the achievement of the good life it presumes is available to all according to its prescriptions, in that, through its commitment to avoid evil: such as poverty; discrimination; intolerance, and so forth, it creates conditions contrary to liberal values of an uninfluenced autonomy. Though the intention is laudatory, here the commitment to this autonomy generates a social climate which fosters the evils modern liberalism wishes to avoid, since in reality the citizen is equally free to select from any act, whether vice or virtue, in his/her pursuit of the good life. In appealing to both the negative and positive side of the issue of individual autonomy, modern liberalism effectively nullifies itself as an agent capable of achieving the good life for citizens. Once again, the notion of the autonomous and independent individual who is neither influenced by, or has influence on other individuals in their pursuit of the good life becomes an obvious fallacious and unattainable condition.

The dichotomy of modern liberalism is that in theory it appears to work well within a highly pluralistic society with its promise of the good life for an often exceedingly competitive heterogeneity, yet it promotes the notions previously discussed in an earlier chapter which foster individualism and the unbridled satisfaction of the self set free from communal considerations. Here, the dynamic forces involved in modern liberalism's underlying reliance on economic growth to sustain the needs of the untrammeled citizenry allow liberalism to become the bulwark of individualism and the champion of self-interest. Again, the contradiction is obvious and modern liberalism could never succeed by creating conditions in complete opposition to each other.

It is my contention that both the social phenomena of modern liberalism and individualism are symbiotically linked by the fact that each is based on the precept of the primacy of the self over that of the social collective. Yet, modern liberalism's pronouncement that the resulting "good life" for all constitutes a better society is flawed, in that, it fosters those discrepancies outlined by Kekes which indicate, to me anyway, that a priority whereby individual satisfaction takes precedence over that of society is completely contradictory to the foundations upon which America was established and is severely detrimental to our national cohesion. Sandel offers further reinforcement of this contention by stating, "(t)he vaulted independence of the deontological subject is a liberal illusion. It misunderstands the fundamentally 'social' nature of man...(t)here is no...transcendental subject capable of standing outside society or outside experience." (*Liberalism and the Limits of Justice* 11).

Within my investigation, I have found several additional sources which reflect similar sentiments that regard modern liberalism's focus on the individual to be detrimental to the society it professes to be concerned with. For example, Etzioni refers to modern liberalism's tendency to limit the social order to legitimize, "individuals acting as free agents" (*The New Golden Rule* 12), and Michael Lind, senior editor of *The New Republic, Harper's* and executive editor of *The National Interest* expresses concern over, "individualistic liberalism, rather than deference to legitimate authority (becoming) the organizing principle in families, schools, universities, corporations, and associations." (284-85).

Of course, one may correctly question what exactly constitutes "legitimate authority," yet here it has been demonstrated that authority based on the precepts of modern liberalism is replete with inconsistencies and is therefore an invalid foundation for that authority.

Still, there are other ideals and concepts embraced by liberalism that at first glance appear laudatory, yet upon careful analysis are mired in further contradictions. Coupled with the value of a pluralistic society is the liberal notion that government should remain neutral and equally tolerant regarding conceptions of what constitutes the good life and one's free selection from those choices. Here, the problem arises over the plurality of options. If the business of government is to formulate and maintain rules that allow citizens to create their "good life," is government acting neutrally when the rules disallow certain choices, such as those involving the removal of symbols of religious expression from public places? In this sense, Sandel raises the question of whether justice can ever be achieved within a liberal state since the priority of the individual would thus have the biasing effect of favoring individualistic values in given situations. Therefore, not only is justice compromised, but Sandel further concludes that, "the ideal of a society governed by neutral principles is liberalism's false promise. It affirms individualistic values while pretending to a neutrality which can never be achieved." (*Liberalism and the Limits of Justice* 11-12).

Added to this is the moral implication of good vs. right involved within those choices (a topic to be covered in greater depth in the next chapter). Liberal theory holds that conformity to the rules is what is right and it is up to the individual to decide what constitutes the good according to one's personal criteria of evaluation. As I stated very early on in this book, according to this system, there are as many concepts of what constitutes the good, as there are members of the system. With each considered to be as equally valid as the next—from where or who do we select that which constitutes an interactive norm? Lacking a clear definition of the same—upon what do we base criteria for social order? Therefore, government must reenter the picture to legislate laws that achieve social order—this is hardly neutral action. Additionally, when government must decide between two competing notions of what citizens consider to be good—as in the case of abortion, or church/state issues—not only is government violating the liberal ideal of neutrality, but according the Thiemann, "it misleads the public concerning government's role in the adjudication of volatile moral and political issues" (78), in that, it forces the courts to serve as a model for moral reasoning. Again, hardly neutral action.

Here, the impossibility of modern liberalism's criteria for governmental neutrality becomes quite apparent, as conformity to the rules requires government involvement in order to establish social order. Modern liberalism's tenet of an autonomous criteria of evaluation runs contrary to this no matter how it is rationalized as a means toward the achievement of the good. Definitions of the good must involve concepts beyond a myriad of myopic standards of personal evaluations if they are to be truly equal and pluralistic. For me, what modern liberalism proposes here seems quite antipodal to the requirements of our social reality. A system based primarily on autonomously derived evaluations and government neutrality seems most susceptible to a rather mercurial system of justice.

Another ideal that evokes contradictions within the scope of modern liberal theory is the issue of freedom. Essentially, this concept holds that the individual is free to choose among the variety of values and options to create his/her notion of a good life—without external interference. Here, Kekes points out that the most pressing problem with this lies not only in the obvious restriction that one's exercise of this ideal should not interfere with the freedom of another, but the presumption of our ability to make reasonable choices to avoid infringing on another citizen's freedom. Of course, this then does negate the prerequisite of a freedom "without external interference" yet even more so, in that, it is a painfully obvious fact of human history that humans quite often do not make reasonable choices. Furthermore, Kekes notes, "it is common ground among liberals that the value of freedom emerges only under civilized conditions (involving the alleviation of) starvation, disease, poverty, illiteracy, superstition, ignorance, insecurity, and so forth." (7-8).

Even here individuals are restricted into making choices to remain civilized, and for obvious reasons—eliminate these civilized conditions, and freedom becomes and "unaffordable luxury." In effect, within a social collective it is impossible to live without "external interference."

Closely linked to modern liberalism's concept of freedom is the notion of rights, which are considered those things which no person or group can do without. The most important rights are those which are required by individuals simply because they are human and allow individuals to function as human beings. These are termed "human rights" which transcend legal rights and, "define areas whose violation is morally impermissible because they constitute minimum requirements of human welfare." (Kekes 9).

The differentiation to be made here is between "human rights" which are pre-political and universal, in that they recognize the dignity of the individual human person and his/her potential to be free and self-determining and which exist previous to any social doctrine; and "individual rights" which are granted through positive law (e.g. the Bill or Rights) to protect against the unwarranted interference in the exercise of individual freedom. Here, one of the major problems of achieving individual rights within the liberal context is in its penchant for the absolute freedom from restrictions in achieving those rights. According to an explanation proffered by the contemporary political scientist, Mary Ann Glendon:

> Our rights talk, in its absoluteness, promotes unrealistic expectations, heightens social conflict, and

inhibits dialogue that might lead toward consensus, accommodation, or at least the discovery of common ground. In its silence concerning responsibilities, it seems to condone acceptance of the benefits of living in a democratic social welfare state, without accepting the corresponding personal and civic obligations. In its relentless individualism, it fosters a climate that is inhospitable to society's losers, and that systematically disadvantages caretakers and dependents, young and old. In its neglect of civil society, it undermines the principal seedbeds of civic and personal virtue. In its insularity, it shuts out potentially important aids to the process of self-correcting learning. All of these traits promote mere assertion over reason-giving...The catalog of individual liberties expands, without much consideration of the ends to which they are oriented, their relationship to one another, to corresponding responsibilities, or to the general welfare. (14).

According to Kekes, for modern liberals the problem lies in their interpretations regarding human rights. Although the vast majority agree that a liberal state should protect human rights, their disagreements lie with whether these rights are merely protections from unwarranted interference in the exercise of independent freedom, or are rights which are part of the minimum requirements of human welfare. Here, the controversy and confusion engendered leaves undecided whether human rights are independent of, or contingent upon conclusions derived from positive law, that is, are these rights immutable precepts of human existence, or subject to political and legal interpretations?

Finally, there is the issue of equality. The premise is that all human beings are equal and should be treated equally. Yet, Kekes' analysis raises the issue of whether we should be, "equalizing everyone's opportunity to achieve the benefit in question or equalizing the outcome of the efforts to make use of the opportunity." (10). In addition, are we to assume that the lives of both criminals and law-abiding citizens are to be furthered by equal treatment? Would this not violate the moral merits of law and the validity of punishment for unlawful activity? Does this equality of treatment imply that all individuals—whether needy or not; deserving or not, should share equally? Lastly, do we redistribute all equally regardless of the intentions of the recipient?

The absurdity of equal treatment under these conditions is against all logic and systems of justice. Not only is there a distinct possibility of jeopardizing our finite resources to satisfy the limitless requirements of this indiscriminate system, but we run the risk of rewarding individuals truly undeserving of such treatment. Of course, who defines the "undeserving" is a matter that has evoked controversy and debate for decades. However, as we are still unable to reach an equitable solution in this regard do we continue, for example, arbitrarily and often illegitimately to offer equal treatment to the lawless and obedient citizen alike? Here, a sense of guaranteeing human rights should always take precedence in both cases, yet what remains falls into the realm of individual rights which involves certain aspects of justice, which according to Sandel, evokes a sense of community amongst members of a social collective. Therefore, as criminal and other forms of felonious antisocial activity act contrary to any sense of community (except of course, that of criminals) should the finite resources of the community be available to these individuals beyond their human right to the minimum requirements of welfare (i.e. food, shelter, medical care, etc.)? Here, criminal activity surely qualifies as "undeserving," yet as part of modern liberalism's agenda current trends in our penal system extend virtually all individual rights (save freedom beyond the bounds of the prison) to incarceratees. The deprivation of freedom simply confines the criminal's ability to be mobile within the greater society which has voiced its displeasure of the offense via the prison sentence. Still, while in prison all criminals (save those solitarily confined or punished for infractions while imprisoned) are allowed access to much if not all of the material resources available to the balance of a society's law-abiding citizens. To me, this example is evidence of the existence of an obvious and unjust flaw in modern liberalism's contention of equality of treatment and distribution of resources. Furthermore, this is additionally indicative of the failure of modern liberalism's ability to guide and direct American society.

In the final analysis of modern liberalism's philosophies regarding pluralism, freedom, rights, equality, and justice—the core value uniting all is the assurance of individual autonomy. However, autonomy involves making reasonable and informed choices with regard to the good life liberalism seeks to create for individuals. Within this process of selection exists elements of moral responsibility, control, judgment, and an understanding of the significance of the outcome of one's actions. To be truly autonomous according to the traditions of modern liberalism requires individuals to make decisions regarding what constitutes their conception of a good life—without external interference. Once again, it is quite obvious that this is an impossible condition to achieve for human beings living within a social collective.

In addition, autonomy in the liberal sense is totally contradictory to the social nature of all human beings, yet the resulting loss of this intrinsic social quality is rendered acceptable under the guise of achieving personal freedom. Here, the freedom afforded the individual is one of singularity and separation from each other—more a conglomeration of isolated units in the vein of the theory of atomism which portrays people as solitary wanderers. Acting in this manner leads one to question where the nature of authority lies if the individual decides in separation from others. How does a community then get started in the first place? Of what use then are society's laws? All of these issues led Charles Taylor to offer the following observation, "in a world of changing affiliations and relationships, the loss of substance, the increasing thinness of ties and shallowness of the things we use, increases space. And the public consequences are even more direct. A society of self-fulfillers, whose affiliations are more and more seen as revocable, cannot sustain the strong identification with the political community which public freedom needs." (508).

For modern liberalism, this public freedom exists within the variety of choices available to individuals in selecting their conceptions of what constitutes a good life. However, given modern liberalism's various shortcomings as outlined previously, the question that remains is one regarding the efficacy of modern liberalism's agenda within the context of the social collective it professes concern over to remain a viable social philosophy for America's future.

In his historical study of liberalism in America, Alan Brinkley, author and Professor of History at Columbia University, examined the various claims against the liberal tradition within this country. He reported that many people felt, "liberalism is too wedded to liberty; that its excessive, indeed nearly exclusive, emphasis on rights and freedoms makes no room for a definition of the public good; that liberalism leaves society without a moral core and hence vulnerable to the destabilizing whims of fractious minorities and transitory passions. Liberalism is, in other words, a threat to community." (x).

In addition to sharing this view, Brinkley further argues that the last thirty years have proven that modern liberalism is not the only important political tradition in America. Furthermore, its inability to exhibit uniformity and stability is the direct result of its own, "internal weaknesses and incongruities, and from the unwillingness or inability of many liberals to look skeptically or critically at their own values and assumptions." (xi).

Surely, the vast majority of Americans instinctively agree with modern liberalism's desire to achieve those ideals examined earlier. It is because of this instinct that modern liberalism has become so popular and dominant a force within today's society. However, as my analysis proves, it is one thing, for example, to vociferously advocate unrestrained individual freedom, and quite another to achieve it according to modern liberalism's contention of: "without external interference." It is with similar observations in mind that Brinkley himself aptly concluded his study by expressing concern over, "the chronic weakness of the progressive state...the enormous difficulty liberals have had in securing and retaining popular loyalties" (278), and the apparent inability for liberalism, in general, to resolve the battle over, "the nature of American politics and American culture." (278).

It is within this context of the nature of American politics and culture that I return to the main focus of this book. That focus is, the diametrical change in American society from a once communally inclined collective primarily oriented toward the achievement of a common good in relationship to both moral and religious dispositions—to that of today's America with its escalating emphasis on the untrammeled, unrestricted self and his/her pursuit of whatever he/she can extract from the good life he/she constructs.

I believe the reader will find it quite obvious that within the context of this chapter, I hold modern liberalism to be most culpable for this shift from America's foundational principles to that of our current narcissistic condition. Here, society is dominated by a liberal manifesto based solely on scientific conclusions, intellectual reason, increased secularization, and the elimination of religion from the public dialogue. What has evolved from this has created a unique system whereby, to summarize Lewy: Morality is derived solely from human experience, and ethics is based on autonomous conclusions that are purely situational—with no need of theological or ideological influences.

In essence, according to this line of thinking, American society is to be guided purely by a secular humanism which, as the offspring of contemporary American liberalism, further promotes the total, unrestricted achievement of human needs and desires through a primarily atheistically centered and materialistically oriented foundation. Moreover, the moral relativism, situation ethics, and selfish hedonism of secular humanism together seek to function under the guise of being a legitimate, though nontheistic, religion. Here, secular humanism completely negates the human spiritual self; religious teachings, and any references to God. It is a social philosophy whereby "anything goes" in achieving complete unrestricted individual fulfillment à la the once often touted 1960s motto: "If it feels good, do it!"

Lewy further notes that proponents of secular humanism completely support personal rather than social morality and are extremely tolerant of pornography, abortion, divorce, euthanasia, suicide, birth control, and sexual promiscuity. In addition, traditional religious precepts restricting these behaviors are considered by secular humanists to be "archaic Biblical codes" and society's limitations of the same are labeled "outworn social taboos."

In essence, traditional relationships are ignored in the name of diversity; the sanctity of human life is lessened; traditional religion is considered puerile, and sex is devoid of love, compassion, or meaning. Additionally, Lewy argues that secular humanism equally weakens the moral and social fabric of society, and, "can be highly destructive to both mental health and societal integrity." (35). Furthermore, in applying the work of the mental-health expert William Kilpatrick to his own argument, Lewy refers to Kilpatrick's assessment that the pursuit of this selfish and hedonistic "pleasure principle": "is not a very good rule for social order. Sooner or later, sexual irresponsibility, adulteries, diseases, neglected children and abandoned families become everyone's problem." (35-36).

Within the debates involving the adverse effects of secular humanism upon American life we find many leading sociologists raising important questions regarding the health of our society. For example, Etzioni expresses concern over the instability of our moral order which can result in social anarchy, and Marty fears the, "conspiracy among secular humanists and liberals to propagate versions of American history and human values that are designed to rule out religious faith...(or) in the interest of keeping church and state separate...the setting forth of an alternative religion." (45).

In light of all that I have outlined so far, the question that naturally follows is: What are the beneficial elements within the philosophies of modern liberalism for American society? In general, many of liberalism's secular underpinnings are derived from the thinking that arose amid the French Revolution and took hold during the professed era of "enlightenment" which followed. The foundations of this thinking were based in the desire to achieve freedom from arbitrary monarchical rule, and the once harsh and often excessive influences of traditional religion, both within the public and private domains. Though America's parallel revolution against the same still recognized the authority of a Supreme Being and the importance of religion, the French revolt sought to start anew and eliminate all forms of rule, both secular and spiritual, which were deemed guilty of abusing their power and position. Here, absolute power was given to the people who were then considered in complete control of their destiny.

It is with similar intentions in mind, that modern liberals have sought mostly to achieve a society which neither supports any one definitive system, nor allows for the dominance of any in particular. Yet, the fulfillment of this structure would tend to contradict the premise, in that, the liberal tradition would then become *the* dominant system. In addition, modern liberalism's desire for the autonomous individual's complete control of his/her destiny would seem to eliminate the likelihood that an abusive power would force an intolerable existence on anyone. Given humanity's history of the pervasive abuse of power, one does find merit in modern liberalism's penchant to avoid this possibility. However, in comparison, the aftermath of the social liberalism and advocacy of personal autonomy, so central to the cause of the French Enlightenment, left France in political and social turmoil for ten years. Here, the unfolding ability of the individual to choose his/her own destiny less the perceived authoritarian character of the "ancien règime" was frequently stymied as democracy struggled to succeed. In addition, many objectives of the revolution regarding what we now call "human rights" were obscured due to the decade long rivalry for power among the revolutionary leadership.

For example, stemming from the sharp divisions among the various committees established to restore political and social order, during 1795 bread riots and protest demonstrations spread from Paris to many sections of the country. Furthermore, constant intragovernmental squabbling left much of France's national agenda in turmoil for years, leading to a 99 percent depreciation of French currency. Here, the toll on the populace was enormous and continued until Napoleon came to power and reorganized French society within a codified system. With this in mind, one wonders if a political and social direction determined by total reliance on the autonomy of the individual would not result in similar conditions within modern day America as had resulted in post-enlightened France? This possibility of social anarchy resulting from an unchecked liberalism is expressed throughout the works of Amitai Etzioni and is worth considering previous to any absolute adoption of the ethos of modern liberalism for America.

Of course, under Napoleon the freedoms of liberty, equality, and fraternity so dear to the hearts of the French revolutionaries as declared in their Declaration of the Rights of Man, finally became possible, but mainly due to the direct result of government intervention. Here, we find added proof that modern liberalism's pursuit of government neutrality as a required prescription for the realization of a good life is completely untenable given the French example. Furthermore, the American revolution would have wrought a similar social debacle had government not been involved from the onset in ordering society, politics, and individual life according to precepts outlined in the Declaration of Independence, the Constitution, and the Bill of Rights.

In offering a defense of modern liberalism's benefits, many find that the emancipating effects of liberal philosophy has opened the floodgates of creative thought leading to a neo-renaissance within American thinking, which has greatly improved our society, culture, standard of living, and has made the United States the envy of the world. Again, considering the numerous instances of social stagnation resulting from the oppressive suffocation of the human intellect that has existed both within recent memory and throughout history, one could well admire the motivation behind modern liberalism's philosophies. Yet, when the excesses of this creative neo-renaissance stages cultural events with works of dubious merit, such as the immersion of a crucifix in a glass vat of human urine, then one wonders just what beneficial effect this has on American culture. Here, this not only gives evidence for the often extreme, even depraved permissive climate so rampant in American society today, and one introduced primarily under the guise of freedom à la the tenets of modern liberalism, but so equally evidential of the extent individuals themselves will go in the name of exercising personal liberty and autonomy. Furthermore, what advances are made for our society when federally funded art shows use the American flag as a doormat for visiting patrons? Is all of this an indication of an enlightened society, whereby members can destroy, defile, and disfigure cherished religious and secular symbols with impunity? Shall we soon become so further "enlightened" that we defecate in public to celebrate our freedom and autonomy? Taxpayer's money (that is part of the Taylor's "public freedom" discussed earlier) should not be used to fund public events which offend that which other taxpayers hold sacred and dear. A prime example of this is the controversy involving New York's Brooklyn Museum and its decision to include in an exhibit of contemporary art an elephant dung splattered image of the Virgin Mary. That this exhibition is offensive to Roman Catholics is without question, but for the publicly funded museum to use this taxpayer money to offend other taxpayers is, in my opinion, unconscionable.

The list of similar abuses is endless, and one can find several examples of the same mentioned within the work of William J. Bennett who also questions the emancipation of America's creativity à la the precepts of liberal philosophy. Again one wonders if the ethos of modern liberalism, which champions unrestricted individual freedom, has gone a bit too far.

In addition, the tenet of equality touted by modern liberalism has done little to eliminate poverty in America, or ghetto life from America's cities. In fact, in today's liberal America there are more homeless individuals living on our nation's streets than at any other time in our history. Some may argue that in proportion to our growing population, the number of homeless is still within acceptable limits. Yet, in proportion to the magnificent strides in this nation's productivity and wealth, the idea of an acceptable limit of homeless individuals should not even be considered at all.

The issue of racism still infects American society, and the newly christened offense of the "hate crime" spreads rampantly across this nation. Perhaps the liberal conception of equality has contributed to the reduction of some of the external manifestations of racism, however we must also include the efforts of the traditional religious institutions in this effort whose tenets of human equality and freedom predate modern liberalism's declaration of the same, in some cases, by thousands of years. Still, the hidden expression of racial prejudice is a continuing problem for America, along with many of racism's obvious external components. In this respect, modern liberalism should hardly be considered completely remedial, or lay claim to being the sole component upon which America should hinge its hopes for future solutions.

Rather than continue with an enumeration of the purported beneficial aspects of modern liberalism and countering each by listing the resulting deleterious excesses so generally prevalent within modern American society, instead I will become more specific and investigate the negative effects modern day liberalism has had upon one particular segment of American society—its middle-class. Here, I refer to the study done by the well-known sociologist and University Professor at Boston University, Alan Wolfe, entitled, *One Nation, After All.*

What Wolfe has discovered surfaces very early in his work, that is, within America's middle-class there exists the possibility of, "a severe state of discontent." (13). However, it is not sufficient to state this conclusion without some background details which will lend further support to my contention that the root of this discontent is the increasing pressure of modern liberal philosophy upon the traditionally conservative middle-class value system, or as it is often referred to: middle-class morality. Wolfe's characterization of this value system is one that is spread throughout his entire study. For example, middle-class values are based on: hard work; upward striving; virtues identified with the Protestant ethic; personal responsibility; importance of family; obligation to others; civic involvement; voluntary ties with neighbors and friends; ideals concerning the common good; security, prosperity, and liberty under the law; religious belief; God; moral bearings; patriotism; physical safety—in short, those values often identified with the foundations upon which this country was based.

However, this is not to imply that these values are disconnected from modern liberalism, but according to Wolfe, the middle-class suffers from an increasing ambivalence, or confusion over the completely alternate set of choices represented by the philosophy of modern liberalism. Generally, members of the middle-class strive to achieve individuality and, "a belief in something outside oneself" (Wolfe 5), which as discussed in an earlier chapter, is something quite different from modern liberalism's strong ties to the self-centeredness of individualism. In my opinion, viewed from the perspective of modern liberalism, the set of values listed above take on a completely different priority—with the singular self the main focus for accomplishing these values, rather that the overall social well-being to be generated.

With this in mind, Wolfe makes it quite clear that when modernity entered the picture, middle-class values were not only threatened, but have been declining ever since. Here, Wolfe's definition of modernity is essentially the foundational liberal precept of, "(t)he freedom...to construct one's own life as one best sees fit. Concretely, that means not accepting God's commands regarding right and wrong, but developing one's own personal ethical standards." (9-10).

Although America's middle-class is not so inflexible as to reject any change (i.e. they have come to accept religious diversity as a fact of life), "(a)bove all (they are) moderate in their outlook...they believe in the importance of leading a virtuous life...(they are) strong believers in morality." (Wolfe 278). In this respect, Wolfe goes on to describe the middle-class as "modern traditionalists" and because of this distinction, this population group possesses values that are in complete opposition to those of modern liberalism. "For liberals, by contrast, a world without fixed moral guidelines is one that offers individuals greater choice." (Wolfe 11).

Here, we have further evidence that the drive by the adherents of modern liberal philosophy to promote individualism and unbridled individual autonomy is in direct conflict with America's founding principles which are represented by middle-class morality. Furthermore, despite the liberal contention that its philosophies are those which would best represent all of this country's citizens, Wolfe goes on to explain that, in effect, the liberal experiments in social justice have been almost exclusively in alliance with the upper-class and the lower-class, leaving the middle-class the "forgotten" Americans. As a result, here we uncover the foundation for Wolfe's additional contention of a "culture war" existing within American society which further contributes to the state of "anger"; "lethargy"; "apathy," and "withdrawal" which is often associated with today's middle-class Americans.

Finally, in identifying those who are clearly at odds with all things representative of the middle-class, Wolfe points to the primary adherents of modern liberal philosophy, that is, America's "intellectuals"; "activists," and the "cultural elite" who, "have never had much sympathy for the middle-class morality praised by the right. The left tends to believe that middle-class morality is bad, and the only good thing is that it might become obsolete." (11).

These contentions and conclusions examined within Wolfe's work are truly disturbing. In effect, there exists a complete polarization of the upper and lower classes, who are unified under the umbrella of modern liberalism, and the middle-class who still adhere to a morality that many liberals simply label an outdated conservatism. However, in actuality, this conservatism is very close to those principles once dear to the hearts of this country's Founders; their generation, and upon which American society and its laws are based.

Still, Wolfe's work is essentially empirical, and the balance of his study then attempts to prove if the contentions outlined above were in fact the case, or if other factors caused or contributed to this middle-class discontent. Deemed the Middle Class Morality Project, Wolfe's efforts carried on lengthy and detailed interviews with many middle-class individuals across America. After much documented analysis, Wolfe concluded that there is indeed a "culture war" within America, and, "it is one that is being fought primarily by intellectuals, not by most Americans themselves." (276).

Here, intellectuals are representative of the cutting edge of modern liberal philosophy, and although there are differences among members of the middle-class themselves over the degree of interaction between moral and cultural questions, the intellectual/liberal agenda, which is so completely opposed to a world of "fixed moral guidelines," has created the culture war which Wolfe so often refers to throughout his study. I find that the "war" has been declared through the determined effort to install an intellectual/liberal agenda for America with the "battle" being waged over moral issues, yet the middle-class is an unwilling participant in either. Wolfe expresses similar sentiments in that:

> If middle-class Americans do not understand themselves to be that divided culturally, they are even less likely to see themselves at war. Conflict, dissent, controversy—all of which define the tone of the culture war—are not foreign to intellectuals, for argument is in their lifeblood. What I heard as I talked to Americans from all walks of the middle-class, by contrast, was a distaste for conflict, a sense that ideas should never be taken so seriously that they lead people into uncivil, let alone violent, courses of action. (284-5).

Here, Wolfe has found that although many middle-class Americans are "morally frustrated" by this assault on their value system, they are not angry, in fact, they are quite tolerant and understanding of American diversity. While members of the middle-class have definite opinions about the morality of many of the issues and behaviors that exist within America today, most are content to live their lives in private and according to traditional moral principles. Still, many interviewed by Wolfe feel that the continuous efforts by intellectuals to poll and survey, "divide(s) people up (and gives) the impression that there is more disagreement that there may actually be." (276-277).

Of course, the greater issue here involves whether people should have the "right" to their own view and not be disturbed by others—to which I offer a resounding: "Yes!" However, using Wolfe's study as evidence, and the daily blitz of modern liberalism's influence in every aspect of American life which middle-class Americans view as, "the establishment, protecting their monopoly of ideas by insisting on standards of political correctness" (283)—the issue then expands even further. The question I now raise is: Should one group's "rights" usurp the "rights" of another, and given the plurality of the American experience, should one group's agenda determine the social course for the entire balance? I think not! Rather, a synthesis of knowledge and philosophical direction should guide the course of our nation—a concept I will discuss more fully in the concluding chapter of this book.

In this sense, Wolfe finds that intellectuals are very comfortable in establishing two competing sets of values. Theirs is a style of approach whereby once an association is made with one of the two views within the set, intellectuals pursue their choice with exceptional vigor. Here, the "liberal camp" of intellectuals have become, "(c)onvinced that whatever is more modern is usually better" (282), and since the 1960s have sought social changes that have supported the liberal agenda. Yet, in essence middle-class Americans are "Jeffersonian moralists" who subscribe to a general theory of moral obligation that Wolfe calls "morality writ small" and which is also rooted in Catholic social thought. This he describes as, "not only should our circles of moral obligation never become so large that they lose their coherence, but morality should also be modest in its ambitions and quiet in its proclamations, not seeking to transform the entire world but to make a difference where it can." (290).

Still, Wolfe explains that this desire to live a "morality writ small" life is always violated when government and politics becomes involved. In fact, the most interesting conclusion Wolfe has reached is that middle-class morality has no politics at all, "(i)t is an outlook on the world that grows up from personal experience, not down from ideological commitment." (315). The significance of middle-class "morality writ small" is that in the close interaction between people, especially those closest to each other, it matters less what the formal rules are if behavior based on morally derived principles is not taught by the moral lesson set by personal example. It is not that middle-class individuals are seeking to define an absolute truth, or impose an all encompassing definition of moral behavior for all Americans to follow, but rather, "(f)or middle-class Americans, the ideal set of obligations are those in which people can monitor the reciprocal impacts of giving and getting, and only small-scale morality can achieve that objective. Americans want to see that their efforts at caring are noted: a reciprocity between giver and receiver, when more personal, is also more visible. They also want to insure that their moral concern is effective: a morality of modest proportions, they believe, is a morality under control." (292).

In reality, middle-class Americans do not like their morality corrupted by politics, yet any disagreements they express with liberal thinking are met with disdain and criticism.

In conclusion, Wolfe sought to determine if America was "one nation, after all." What he found was that middle-class Americans, "are desperate that we once again become one nation (which) would uphold middle-class values (and) reduce class inequality (through) moral equality." (321). Yet, Wolfe explains that modern liberal tradition consistently denies this moral idea of one nation. In fact, as is the case with the modern liberal approach to welfare, "the idea that there would exist a permanent class of dependent people—a nation within a nation, if you will—of individuals whose fortunes would not be under their own control (is) a conception (most) at odds with the middle-class belief in one nation." (321).

Although my conclusions and analyses have been threaded throughout this synopsis of Wolfe's important work, let me emphatically state once again that I firmly believe and have offered evidence to support my contention, that the greatest threat to national cohesion, unity, and morality is modern liberalism. In summary, it acts completely contrary to that which is in disagreement with its agenda. Since, it attracts many leading intellectuals and culturally elite, liberalism has become remarkably tolerant and all embracing of the various views of its erudite proponents, and openly hostile to those of its "grass roots" opponents.

In this respect, and as Wolfe concluded, lines have been drawn between certain classes of people within America, leaving a culture war raging as the proponents of modern liberalism seek further headway and control of American society. The liberal disdain for the foundational principles of this country as represented by their contempt for middle-class morality, is slowly changing America into a nation that is often at odds with its own founding principles.

Of course, one would expect this to be the case since modern liberal ideologies have become the dominating factor behind individual behavior and social thought. Here, the proponents of modern liberalism occupy many of the influential positions within our society and continue to shape America's direction according to liberal philosophy. In addition, modern liberalism itself has become increasingly attractive to each succeeding generation of Americans, who in the name of self-satisfaction and individual autonomy pursue further limits of the: "If it feels good, do it!" mentality.

The underlying problem with this "culture war" is that simply put, and as is the case with human nature, hostility breeds hostility—and while the majority of middle-class Americans are content to exercise "morality writ small" some have reacted by offering an organized offense. Sadly, this has invariably deteriorated into mudslinging and even violent responses mainly from some Protestant evangelical groups, fundamentalists, televangelists, and organizations such as the Moral Majority and the Christian Coalition—which Wolfe found were not very well received by those middle-class Americans with whom he spoke.

Once again, it is the "politicizing" of religion and morality that the middle-class finds most distasteful. To my way of thinking and one that Wolfe raises quite repeatedly, this tends to cloud and corrupt the entire debate process which rather gums up the possibility of arriving at some form of consensus to benefit the common good.

Furthermore, I find that mostly due to the pervasive effects of the liberal elite, America is slowly disassembling itself from a country once based on a moral and religiously oriented conception of the common good, to one that continually descends into moral chaos (as in the case of the Clinton/Lewinsky affair) and increased social disorder (as evidenced by greater levels of violence among this nation's youth as exemplified by the social phenomenon of "wilding"). Sadly, we barely resemble the nation we were once conceived to be, as the effects of modern liberal philosophy strips Americans of their social interaction and moral responsibilities and ultimately replaces the same with a selfish, individual autonomy and unbridled, moral recklessness. I do not believe this is the proper course that America should be taking towards achieving social harmony and the common good. I will discuss alternatives in the concluding chapter of this book.

In the next chapter of this book that follows, I will explore "The Muddy Moral Order" that is clouding America's conceptions of the good and creating an ambiguous moral field. In addition, I will examine the apparent resulting breakdown in our social order. Also included will be the effect this has had on our ability to govern, and on this nation's religious institutions. I will also discuss the need for the development of a new moral order within this country.

In closing, I would like to leave the reader with the following thought: Along with the greater importance modern liberalism places on individual autonomy as that central prerequisite for one's personal pursuit of the good life, is the moral standing of one's chosen actions and the responsibility for those actions which are under one's control. Here, Kekes elaborates further, "(b)ecause responsibility is an essential feature of morality, the further importance of autonomy is that morality would be impossible without (autonomy). The basic liberal values, which protect autonomy, and autonomy itself, therefore, are supposed to express not merely the essential constituents of a particular political morality but also a precondition of all morality." (22).

Chapter 5

The Muddy Moral Order

From the loosely linked bands of hunters and gatherers of eons ago, to the interconnectedness of our modern metropolises spread across the earth—humankind's social evolution has been continuously conjoined with one primary and particular goal: cooperation amongst both individuals and their collective associations.

In seeking to achieve this cooperation, most elementary systems of guidance were designed to set limits on the human inclination to do that which may be personally pleasing, yet might impact negatively upon the general well-being, or outright survival of the greater group. More modern systems employ variants of these guiding measures in the hope of achieving social harmony and personal dignity, private and public safety, and both individual and group-based interests among the ever-increasing diversity of human associations.

Since the underlying foundation of these guidance systems involves elements of self-sacrifice and the curbing of an oftentimes powerful inclination toward selfishness, human behavior is thus engaged within a framework of choices, actions, and judgments relating to principles of right and wrong. Here, the emergence of a code of moral reasoning becomes essential to human interaction and the basis for all human endeavors. That we do require this moral element within our lives is indicative of the fact that the human experience so often involves situations developing contrary to the common good, and therefore quite opposed to the general well-being. In this sense, human morality not only involves the expectation that the individual will act as an effective moral agent, but that our social associations also include a framework of moral evaluations.

According to a conclusion reached through the combined efforts of two contemporary scholars of modern ethical and moral issues, Elaine E. Englehardt and Donald D. Schmeltekopft, "moral norms (are also) applicable to business corporations, political bodies, medical organizations, colleges and universities, churches, sects, and so on, as well as individuals qua individuals. While moral theories and concepts are designed to deal primarily with individuals, moral categories can be sensibly applied to these various institutions and groups." (3).

While ethics is the study of our moral actions within the context of our social settings, this chapter will deal primarily with our conclusions and applications regarding morality itself and the inherent obligations, or absence thereof, assigned to our human capacity to act as moral agents within the framework of human undertakings. Furthermore, most of what is pertinent to this book regarding the origins and reality of humanity's distinctly moral nature, and its significance for human existence in relationship to concepts involving natural law is outlined in this book's introduction. Here, my added intention is to discuss the concept of morality as it applies to human actions and the pertinence of the same to act as a valid system with which to establish and maintain social order.

By "order" I do not mean to imply that we institute and adhere to a rigid system of absolutes within given situations with regard to human actions, and with severe consequences for any deviation from that "order." Rather, I seek a fellowship of citizens sharing a common solidarity of purpose which primarily involves the concept that the establishment and maintenance of their mutual association, interactions, and intentions be based upon determinations which move beyond the general notion of the good and bad outcome of *one's* actions and instead makes those determinations based upon moral precepts involving the right and wrong outcome of *human* actions.

Here, a brief summary of moral theory would be most helpful and aid in clarifying my position. Among the majority of moral philosophies I've encountered for this study, it is generally agreed that the ultimate goal of each human being is to achieve a state of happiness. Faced with performing an action which will result in a happiness producing (or good) outcome, the human being proceeds voluntarily and deliberately, through the motion of the will, toward the progression and completion of that action. If the action fails to produce the expected happy outcome it is a "bad" action. However, prior to, or during this process, the human mind employs an internal knowledge of the purpose of the action and to freely judge whether that action will result in a proper end. This "proper end" or that which results in a natural point of conclusion, is determined to be morally right—results contrary to this proper end are considered morally wrong. The phrase "natural point of conclusion" refers to that result towards which a being, activity, object, or event is directed by its nature. For example, the nature of the eye is to see, and human actions (save those of necessity, e.g. medical conditions) which deter or eliminate sight, are morally wrong.

Here, theories regarding the origins of these right and wrong judgments range from the early Greek and Aquinian conceptions involving an objective system of moral truths and attributes which all human beings innately sense and participate in; to the late eighteenth century doctrine known as Utilitarianism which considers all human actions to be motivated solely by the desire to obtain pleasure and avoid pain; to much of modern philosophy (e.g. Kant, Marx, Sartre) who abandoned this concept and argued that since this moral system could not be verified, our moral decisions are relatively determined and based on expressions of feelings and/or any combination of experiences based on our cultural, social, and economic realities rather than any objective criteria. Hence the term—moral relativism.

According to many modern thinkers, this abandonment of an objective moral system is fraught with problems, in that, humanity is then considered left to employ completely subjective moral determinations that, according to former UCLA and Harvard professor and public policy expert, James Q. Wilson, "do little more than utter personal preferences, bow to historical necessity, or accept social convention." (5). Here, lacking a firm moral compass with which to orient human actions leaves humanity in a state of uncertainty with regard to moral judgments. Wilson goes on to characterize this state as an "emptiness of being" which sometimes forces people to retreat, "inward to mystical or drug-induced self-contemplation or outward to various fanatical ideologies." (5). In any case, for Wilson, this "emptiness of being" leads many to believe, "that they are free to do whatever they can get away with." (9).

In understanding the motivations behind human actions, one must realize that as we mature and become further aware of our own selfhood we also gain an increasing knowledge of the uniqueness of our identity and the strength of our will to freely reason and realize the ends we seek. We also become conscious of our responsibilities towards others. Here, the notion of a strong subjective nature to our moral determinations, which modern philosophy upholds as valid instead of an objective system of moral truths, in my opinion becomes more the exercise of human free will. The subjective nature of our option to either accept or ignore a moral truth in the pursuit of a good we hope to achieve, is in fact the utilization of our free will to select either the right or wrong approach toward attaining the proper end of that pursuit. That our action is performed according to our personal determinations does not negate the existence of the moral truth to which we referred to at the onset of our action. This is quite opposed to the Utilitarian characterization of human beings as amoeba-like creatures motivated solely by the instinct to seek pleasure and avoid pain. Although basic to our human psychology is the condition that we instinctively react to an opportune moment, we similarly temper our actions according to moral determinations—we don't steal the neighbor's empty, idling car because we are tired of walking.

According to Taylor, we often reach conclusions regarding what is right to do in relationship to a combined moral and spiritual intuition which encompasses, "notions (of) justice and the respect of other people's life, well-being, and dignity." (4). Taylor goes on to point out that these moral and spiritual intuitions are quite different from evaluations involving what makes life worth living, in that, the former includes independent conclusions regarding right and wrong whose validity is not determined from the latter which relate to personal standards of taste and desire. What is most important within Taylor's explanation of humanity's moral nature is in the depth, or "gut" reaction with which we sense its evaluations; our response to these evaluations, and our belief that these evaluations apply to the whole human race. Here, Taylor finds these moral reactions to be so strongly ingrained within our human nature, that we demand they function independent of our "de facto reactions." Taylor further explains that although many modern philosophers, "scrutinize and criticize our moral institutions for their consistency or lack of it (human beings in general) feel the demand to be consistent in (their) moral reactions." (7).

In describing human behavior, one must assign an absolute human value to the outcome of our voluntary actions. This value must be something which we consider a supreme end to achieve; conforms to a standard of right actions, and is beneficial to the common interests of the entire community. We arrive at these conclusions through our experiential knowledge which assigns the confirmation of the good to those positive outcomes which have acted to produce happiness and bring a sense of completeness to our endeavors. In this sense a value becomes a guiding principle—a norm, with which human actions are ultimately judged. Here, actions that are virtuous are those which are consistently performed to produce a proper end; are done well, and remain right. Vice is a habitually contrary action performed in direct opposition to the proper end and is intrinsically inclined toward the wrong. Furthermore, closely aligned to vice are actions deemed to be evil, which are described by the author and ethicist, Rev. Thomas J. Higgins as, "the privation of good which ought to be present (and) is brought about by a cause which destroys or hinders some being." (46). Here, the ultimate manifestation of right is virtue; and of wrong is evil.

Human actions are therefore classified as either good or bad in their achievement of happiness, together with being right or wrong according to the properness of their end result. One of the most pressing problems humans face is in this classification process. Collectively, the human race has deemed many actions obviously bad and wrong. Thus, within every culture's spiritual and secular community the act of murder is considered a bad/wrong/evil action. This then becomes a norm with which human actions regarding the continuance and protection of human life is judged. Other acts, such as gambling, are not so obviously defined and require an appeal to some authority for clarification. Here, the concept of authority is crucial to our understanding of this classification process and in the establishment of those norms with which a society governs and judges the actions of its citizens, and seeks to achieve social order. At this point I forego the general informative nature of this chapter's introduction and return to specifics regarding the subject of this book, which is American society.

As discussed primarily in the introductory chapter and threaded throughout subsequent sections within this book, is my contention that in their attempt to draft a governing system for the new nation, the Founders were also addressing many issues involving natural law/moral law principles. Here, the nature of authority within civil institutions was of particular concern to them as they faced two opposing schools of thought regarding this problem. The first stated that human reason alone is sufficient to discern and understand principles involving natural law/moral law; the second stressed that human reason is insufficient for this purpose and these principles become more clearly defined via the process of revelation. The former placed authority solely within the realm of human construction, that is, the state; the latter set authority within the source of the revelation, that is, within the supernatural—which involves the existence of a Supreme Being, religious belief, and the ecclesiastical. That the Founders were well aware of their responsibilities regarding the moral nature of their decisions seems evident from the following within Section 8 of the Constitution, "The Congress shall have power to...make all laws which shall be necessary and proper." Here, I find "proper" expressed in the sense of the morally right condition of achieving a "proper" end, that is, the natural point of conclusion to an action—not simply the achievement of the good, which is based solely on actions that achieve a state of happiness and do not necessarily rely on moral considerations to attain their goal. Furthermore, one must not imply from the Founders' statement in the Declaration of Independence regarding our inalienable right to the "pursuit of happiness" any judgment or suggestion regarding a preference for the good above the morally right. Here, I find that the Founders sole intention was to emphatically state their belief in one's right to pursue happiness, and their objection to any governing authority infringing upon this right.

Furthermore, throughout this book I have argued in support of the inherent religiousness of the Founders, and their efforts to incorporate both previously mentioned opposing schools of thought regarding the nature of authority within the establishment of our governing system. In addition, this governing system developed both civil and social order through the procedures of positive law based upon our human reason to conceive of a moral law and discern principles of natural law as revealed to humanity by the Supreme Being—the ultimate authority of the universe and all things in it.

Here, the Founders intimately understood the concept of a naturally occurring order within the universe as composed by a Supreme Being and that Being's interaction in human affairs via revealed truths regarding that order. Similarly, I have offered added proof of the Founders' desire to incorporate these natural law/moral principles throughout their legislative efforts for the new nation and thus establish civil and social order based on these principles. However, to circumvent the possibility of those abuses associated with an evolving theocracy (of which the Founders had first hand knowledge) and to equally protect those various institutions associated with belief systems involving supernatural revelations (i.e. religious organizations) and after much deliberation, the Founders realized the vital need to keep "church and state" separate with regard to the nation's governing process. Still, this establishment of a primarily secular governing authority did not negate their intrinsic knowledge of the important continuance and incorporation of a supernatural authority within the affairs of humankind. Here, via the voting process, the Founders relied on the strong religious nature of the American citizenry to keep check on the possible abuses of the secular authority of government.

With regard to the maintenance of social order, the Founders were cognizant of the requirement of cooperation amongst citizens if a common good was to be achieved. Here, I wish to explain this conjunction of social order, cooperation, and the achievement of the common good more fully by offering a brief summary of the social organizing process.

Berger speaks of the socialization process as being composed of an, "ordering of experience (whereby) a meaningful order, or nomos, is imposed upon the discrete experiences and meanings of individuals." (19). He goes on to confirm the, "collective character of this ordering activity (which is) endemic to any kind of social interaction (in the desire to achieve) common meaning." (19). Although this "nomos" could never include the totality of individual meanings, those marginal experiences are still part of the "totalizing" process as the "nomos" expands throughout its existence. Here, the "nomos" includes both objective and subjective elements, yet according to Berger the objective (moral maxims, traditional wisdom, and "interpretative schema") is foundational to the organizing process, in that, to participate in the society one must share in its collective objective knowledge. Furthermore, the resulting society becomes the guardian of order and meaning via the objective knowledge contained within its "institutional structures" and the structuring of the subjective consciousness of individuals. Through this process the society becomes an, "area of meaning carved out of a vast mass of meaninglessness (and) the individual is provided...with various methods to stave off...anomy (sic) (what Berger describes as separation from the social world) and to stay within the safe boundaries of the established nomos." (24).

Therefore, the collective cooperation of all within the established society becomes of paramount importance for the future continuance of that society—lest it fall into chaos; and for the benefit of individual needs as well—lest he/she is plunged into "anomy."

Furthermore, within this evolution of social order through collective cooperation, there develops definitions of reality and existence that become fundamental to the society's understanding of both the cosmological and anthropological "nature of things." Berger considers these definitions to be derived, "from more powerful sources than the historical efforts of human beings" (25)—a notion closely aligned to much of the information uncovered by Stark and Bainbridge within their influential work, *The Future of Religion*. Here, Berger finds that religion significantly enters into the picture together with the concept of a sacred cosmos, that is, the reality of a mysterious power, "other than man and yet related to him...an immensely powerful reality other than himself (which) addresses itself to him and locates his life in an ultimately meaningful order." (25-6).

For Berger, it is through this "sacred cosmos" that human beings come to believe in the reality of "ultimate forces or principles" which rule all things in the cosmos. In addition, Berger goes on to indicate that once this "sacred cosmos" is established, humans then begin to view, "(t)he routines of everyday life (as) profane unless...they are conceived of as being infused in one way or another with sacred power...(this) dichotomization of reality into sacred and profane spheres...is intrinsic to the religious enterprise." (26).

Lastly, before I return to the Founders' efforts in the establishment of social order for the new nation, I would like to briefly explore the influence of an underlying moral order upon their decisions.

Within the Founders' religiousness was an understanding of, and inclination toward actions involving considerations of moral principles of right and wrong, coupled with a deep desire to achieve the common good. This led these learned men to establish a system of association heretofore unknown to humankind—that of a self-governing social order. That one's religiousness is closely associated with one's underlying morality is confirmed from many sources, not only within the fields of ethics, moral philosophy, and religion, but also government, law, and other related areas. Iris Murdoch's efforts in the field of moral philosophy led her to declare, "(r)eligion symbolizes high moral ideas which then travel with us and are more intimately and accessibly effective than the unadorned promptings of reason." (484).

She commented further on the "moral-religious continuum" as being most evident within our precious and positive pursuit of virtue, which I defined earlier as those actions which are consistently performed to produce a proper end, are done well, and remain right. Similar sentiments regarding the link between religion and morality were expressed by Harvey Cox, a Professor of Divinity at Harvard

Divinity School, who stated, "(it is) right to recognize that morality and religion are intertwined inextricably." (206).

Therefore, one can safely assume that the Founders' efforts in establishing social order contained elements of Murdoch's "moral-religious continuum." It would be inconceivable that within those discussions involving the establishment of social order via the drafting of the "laws of the land" that questions concerning the moral order of society would not have arisen. Although this contention was more fully discussed in the first chapter of this book which examined the theory and theology behind the First Amendment, here a sampling of comments from the Founders themselves would be most illustrative of this conclusion regarding the Founders' attentiveness to a moral order. Of course, "moral order" for the Founders was distinctly democratic in its manifestations, and Christian in its underpinnings.

In his "Farewell Address" of September 17, 1796, George Washington stated, "(o)f all the dispositions and habits which lead to political prosperity, religion and morality are indispensable supports." (Barton 117). Once again he issued almost the exact same statement in a letter dated March 3, 1797, where he wrote, "(r)eligion and morality are the essential pillars of civil society." (324). In a letter dated October 16, 1778, Samuel Adams wrote, "(r)eligion and good morals are the only solid foundation of public liberty and happiness." (320). Throughout their lives, similar sentiments were expressed by John Adams, Thomas Jefferson, and James Madison—to name a few.

Here, one must ask why these issues of religion and morality would have been considered, or were of any concern whatsoever to men involved in drafting the mostly objective legislation required for the governance of a nation? With reference to the Distinguished Professor of Criminal Justice at Pembroke State University and Chairman of its Sociology Department, Frank Schmalleger, "(the) first, and most significant, purpose of the law can be simply stated: laws support social order." (111). In addition, Schmalleger firmly includes the protection and credibility of the philosophical, moral, and value systems of the creators of the law within that purpose of producing social order. Here, the Founders were establishing laws which would include their understanding of the essential and fundamental rights of freedom and liberty which they agreed were guaranteed by the Creator to all human beings. Furthermore, according to Higgins, "(a) right is totally a moral power both as to legitimacy and inviolability" (231), and rights do not have their origins in force, they originate in the law. Higgins goes on the state quite emphatically that, "(t)he juridicial order is the total system of rights and justice: laws defining rights, duties corresponding to rights, and rights themselves." (231).

Here, I believe it becomes quite obvious that for the Founders, there was an inexorable correlation between both rights as an extension of moral principles; religion as an expression of those same principles, and the law—which was the manifestation and realization of both in the pursuit of justice through the establishment of a morally based social order.

It is at this juncture that we arrive at a most perplexing puzzle: As outlined earlier in this book, modern American society has completely separated religion from the legal process and removed religion from partaking in our public dialogue. Secondly, the moral foundation of our nation has been in a steady decline roughly since the end of World War II, so much so that not only do other nations consider the United States an immoral nation—but many of our own scholars, educators, politicians, legislators, religious leaders, and citizens have arrived at this conclusion as well. Most have become increasingly alarmed over the apparent widespread disregard among all segments of the population for considerations involving right and wrong, which are so very distinct from those concerned with good and bad, as previously examined earlier in this chapter.

In light of the founding principles of this nation; its underlying historical elements of religiousness and morality, and those sacred, revered documents and legal principles which still outline and structure our social order even after well over two centuries of existence—to what do we owe this current antithetical and destructive condition of an apparent lack of moral and religious considerations to?

First, let me offer a historical foundation to the main answer which I will outline shortly. It is my opinion that the continuance and perpetuation of slavery was that inceptive condition chiefly to blame for the first seeds of moral confusion to be spread across this nation.

The obvious flaw in the Founders' pronouncement in the Declaration of Independence, "that all men are created equal" was that despite the desire to achieve the goals outlined in that document, there were still hundreds of thousands of abused and exploited individuals shackled to a life of servitude as slaves. In, *Notes on the State of Virginia,* written in 1781 and later updated in 1782, Jefferson's own estimate of the slave population in his native Virginia alone was 270,762—this among 296,852 free inhabitants. (Figures taken from Peterson 127.) Jefferson himself, as well as Washington and several other signers of the Declaration of Independence owned slaves. The First Census taken in 1790 set the population of the United States at: White—3,172,444; Free Negro—59,557; Slaves—697,624. By 1860, the total slave population was 3,953,760 among a free citizenry of 27,489,240.

I steadfastly maintain that the continuance of this inhuman practice despite the sublime ideals and visionary intentions announced by the Founders on July 4, 1776, appeared contradictory not only to the American people, but to the rest of the educated world as well. In fact, according to Glasser, "(b)y the time of the Revolution in 1776, slavery was nearly universally believed to be 'the absolute political evil.' " (57). Glasser goes on to indicate that, given their grievances with England, revolutionary era Americans were very concerned with the abuse of power and believed it should be "sharply limited." To these Americans, "slavery represented the death of liberty, the end result of the failure to limit power." (58). In addition, while visiting the United States, Alexis de

Tocqueville, who was a French citizen, questioned the existence of slavery within a supposed free society, and among his many conclusions was the fact that he too considered it, "an obvious abuse of strength." (354). These observations are perhaps reflective of a contemporaneous and universal view held by many regarding the continuance of slavery within the United States, that is, it continued because America wanted it to. Furthermore, despite the later condemnations of slavery by Jefferson and Madison, to name but a few—Rakove raises the distinct possibility that the Founders conveniently transferred the responsibility for the elimination of slavery to a later generation even after they drafted the Constitution because, "once (their) fellow planters grasped that (the Constitution and the Bill of Rights) would extend to the law of slavery" (337), the passage of the Constitution would have been doomed.

On the other hand, although Jefferson was decidedly against slavery, as is evident from his letter to Edward Coles dated August 25, 1814, Jefferson felt it a greater injustice to simply free a large group of people without an education, or social skills beyond the farmstead—and quite probably others at the time agreed. Here, Jefferson wrote:

> For men probably of any color, but of this color we know, brought from their infancy without necessity for thought or forecast, are by their habits rendered as incapable as children of taking care of themselves...until more can be done for them, we should endeavor, with those whom fortune has thrown on our hands, to feed and clothe them well, protect them from all ill usage, require such reasonable labor only as is performed voluntarily by freemen & be led by no repugnancies to abdicate them, and our duties to them. The laws do not permit us to turn them loose, if that were for their good: and to commute them for other property is to commit

them to those whose usage of them we cannot control.
(Peterson 546).

Perhaps this is the true reason why Jefferson never formally freed his slaves—he felt it was his moral responsibility to care for these people who were so deficient in the basic skills necessary to become self-sufficient within eighteenth century American society.

It is well beyond the scope of this chapter to offer a detailed examination of the arguments for and against the failure of the Founders to eliminate slavery. Perhaps, their avoidance of this issue is not a contradiction at all, but a sad economic reality of their era and/or simply the dominant influence of those various groups with a vested interest in the continuance of the practice. Many, including Jefferson, raised the point that slavery was introduced by the English who based the entire American colonial economy on forced labor, and a sudden elimination of that labor force would have caused economic collapse. Quite possibly as I stated in the chapter dealing with the First Amendment, the Founders did not shift the responsibility of eradicating slavery to a later generation, but rather did indeed take the first steps toward its elimination by passing the Bill of Rights, which would eventually strengthen the growing arguments for the cessation of the practice. In fact, there are many references by the Founders, specifically Jefferson, to the notion that sudden freedom of the slaves was not the best answer, but rather working through government to eliminate the institution of slavery itself seemed a far better solution.

Rakove admitted to the latter possibility when he speculated on Madison's thinking during the drafting of the Constitution. Gleaned from Madison's writings, Rakove finds that Madison was guarded in his thoughts on slavery so as not to doom the ratification of the Constitution. However, as a delegate to the Constitutional Convention although Madison reluctantly accepted slavery as, "the positive law of the states (he agreed that) the Constitution should not imply that slavery might be legal in a more fundamental sense" (Rakove 91), so the word "slavery" was stricken from the Constitution. Furthermore, Rakove believes that although Madison's primary concern was, in Rakove's words, to "reconstitute the union"—the hope was that the passage of the Constitution would, again according to Rakove's analysis, "in its wake" one day allow for a veto of state laws, "and thereby provide an entering wedge to weaken the hold of slavery and its evil effects." (337).

Whatever the case, at issue here is the fact that it did continue, and the resulting impact this condition had upon the founding population and all subsequent generations of American citizens. Here, I firmly believe that the signal sent was one involving the dichotomous perception that it was acceptable to state in theory the political and social goals, intentions and aspirations for our nation—but in reality it was quite another thing to commit them to practice. The underlying ramifications of this ambiguity allowed individuals to rationalize that what was good, that is, acts that brought about the achievement of personal happiness, took precedence over what was morally right, that is, acts that reached the properness of their end result—their natural point of conclusion, or that result towards which a being, activity, object, or event is directed by its nature. In effect, while the slaves toiled quite contrary to their human nature, which included the right to be free, the white population reaped all the rewards (i.e. happiness) from those efforts.

Slavery is not the proper condition of a human life—it is the privation of our intrinsic need for freedom, and according to the definition given by Higgins cited earlier, slavery is evil, in that, it causes the destruction or hindering of the human being. For the slave, the only hope of liberation was through membership in the various Christian communities which offered eternal freedom in the afterlife; or escape which often led to severe punishment when captured—quite possibly death. Still, slave membership in a religious community, despite the appeal for the conversion of these supposed "infidels" was often resisted by the slaveowners who thought it encouraged rebelliousness. According to Bunomi, there was always conflict between the secular and religious communities, with the former, "(always) accus(ing) Christian missionaries of fomenting disorder." (119). Even well into the nineteenth and twentieth centuries Christian churches, specifically those in black communities, were associated with rebelliousness. Here, through the churches, black Americans sought the improvement of their condition by appealing for an end to racism and prejudice, and the securing of one's basic rights based on fundamental moral grounds associated with Christian religious principles. It is a well-documented fact that most of the civil rights movements originating in this country began at the pulpit.

In fact, much of the discriminating practices that are so sadly part of America's legacy (i.e. those based on gender, class, race, or religious belief) are opposed and often openly contested on moral grounds by the majority of this country's religious communities.

Still, returning to the era of slavery in America, even in rare instances when a group of slaves had owners similar to Jefferson who were most magnanimous to their human "property"—the basic need for freedom was absolutely denied these people.

Furthermore, free citizens were surrounded daily by the poverty, abuse, exploitation, and ignominy of human beings held in slavery, despite what was solemnized in America's sacred documents regarding human freedom. This point was made apparent in Jefferson's letter of August 25, 1814, where he described being, "(n)ursed and educated in the daily habit of seeing the degraded condition, both bodily and mental, of these unfortunate beings." (Peterson 544). Citizens were also constantly exposed to a double system of justice which, according to the highly regarded nineteenth century sociologist W. E. B. Du Bois, "erred on the white side by undue leniency and the practical immunity of red-handed criminals, and erred on the black side by undue severity, injustice, and lack of discrimination." (200).

These conditions (including the mistreatment and systematic destruction of America's Indian population) must surely have had an undermining effect upon the underlying moral structure of not only the general community, but the individual citizen as well. I contend that this set in place an elemental plank of what I call "rationalized reasoning" which I define as the determination that actions resulting in the accomplishment of a subjective good were preferable to those concluding in an objective right. For example, with reference to slavery: the thinking whereby although outwardly many Americans may have sympathized with the slaves' condition—given the society's dependency on forced labor, inwardly most whites could not conceive of simply setting all the slaves free. Here, the objective right (freedom) is rationalized away via the seeming reasonableness of the subjective good, which in this case is the assurance of a readily available, unpaid work force, and a stable economy. This is not to say that suddenly moral laxity became the order of the day, and every citizen engaged in debauchery. Instead, what seeped further into the foundations of American society was the slow eroding of this country's moral field, which today occupies a severely weakened position and stands as a stark contradiction to many of the ideals articulated by the Founders. According to Glasser, "the price (of slavery) included maintaining the fiction that skin color matters, that it is a legitimate distinction among people...like a cancer, the fiction...spread throughout the body politic, seeped below the surface of our professed ideals, and corroded them from within." (59).

Here, we find the fine line drawn between slavery as the prime cause of further discriminations infecting American society, even to this day, or slavery as an example of the social reality of discrimination. I contend that the latter is surely an unhappy legacy throughout human history, and the founding generation was no stranger to experiencing discrimination as it was foisted against themselves and their ancestors both in England, and in the colonies by the English still loyal to the king, and abroad by the king himself—where incidentally the latter was the primary spark which ignited the American revolution. However, as the Founders chiefly sought to end discrimination and establish freedom, liberty, and equality—I believe the continuance of slavery caused the erosion of this country's moral field rather than exemplified the same. Here, the Founders' groundbreaking principles established a legal and logical end to a discriminating society, of which slavery stood as one stark example. That slavery did not cease once the Founders' pronouncements became law allowed slavery to remain as the *cause* of any further moral erosion, in that, once the legal and logical arguments for its end were already made in the Declaration of Independence, the Constitution, and the Bill of Rights—the contradiction of these arguments, that is, the practice of slavery in America, allowed for the "rationalized reasoning" explained earlier. This thinking then found its way into America's collective consciousness ever since. For example, on a large scale this country's once touted tenet of "manifest destiny" reflects this thought process whereby our territorial expansion (the subjective good) was reasoned to be inevitable and divinely ordained, while the inherent freedom and sovereignty of a people or those nations (the objective right) that we "acquired" or "annexed" is rationalized away by our supposed "divine ordination." On a smaller scale, this type of thinking exists when we ignore the requirements of the community at large for reasons involving the satisfaction of our personal needs (e.g. double-parking).

Still, the dawning of this "rationalized reasoning" regarding the moral concerns that slavery itself wrought is not the main cause for the deteriorated moral condition within our modern day society. What is most culpable here and so fully furthered this perception was the rise and influence of individualism and liberalism within America.

As outlined in the previous two chapters: Modern individualism promotes the autonomy of the individual and his/her unbridled self-centered self-gratification according to a personally conceived system of right and wrong. Modern liberalism is concerned with the advancement of the autonomous citizen's pursuit of his/her personal conceptions of what constitutes a good life. In each case, the transcendence of the subjective self above the objectivity of the social collective becomes the true locus for the social mechanisms of that collective. Here, the underlying "rationalized reasoning" regarding moral concerns, originating in our social and political body since the days of slavery, and incidentally still present in the racism expressed towards America's black citizens despite the end of slavery in this country over 130 years ago, found fruition in the tenets of individualism and liberalism.

The conditions created by these two essentially antisocial philosophies fostered the notion that *the* primary concern is the totality of the individual's untrammeled happiness. In this sense, moral concepts of right and wrong within any given situation are blunted and substituted by rationalizations involving the achievement of that happiness based solely on good or bad actions directed toward the accomplishment of that end. Here, the value of one's actions is not in the realization of the proper end, that is, the natural point of conclusion, but in the satisfaction of the individual's needs regardless of the improperness of the end result. Of utmost concern here is gaining happiness and eliminating the tension created by the materialization of the initial need.

For example, in the case of abortion: The desire to have sex results in an unplanned pregnancy which is perceived to be a bad outcome and which causes unhappiness to those involved; to once again achieve happiness, the act of terminating the pregnancy is considered a good action, and an abortion is performed. However, the natural point of conclusion of the pregnancy, or its proper end, if at all considered, is ignored. This proper end or morally right action is the birth process and that which is the sole reason for the existence of the gestation period in the first place. The act of abortion interrupts this proper process and is therefore not only morally wrong, it is evil in that it causes the destruction of a human being engaged in the process of being gestated in preparation of that being's birth. Like slavery, abortion is destructive to the proper end of human life.

The point made here is that when steeped in the tenets of individualism and liberalism, whereby one is continuously exposed to claims that the purpose of human existence is the accumulation of happiness via unrestricted self-satisfaction, people ultimately become desensitized to the moral implications of their actions. These moral implications restrict or negate the performance of certain actions perceived to be good in their production of happiness, yet are not right in their achievement of a proper end. Here, according to the philosophy of individualism what is right and proper is the satisfaction of one's needs, notwithstanding the proper end of those individuals or objects employed to satisfy those needs. On this point, Lasch aptly observed that individualism's pursuit of pleasure is actually a disguise for the struggle for power, in that, "Americans...have merely become more adept at exploiting the conventions of interpersonal relations for their own benefit." (66). In addition, Lasch concludes: Where activities once done for the enjoyment engendered between participants, today the real object is "doing others in"; in sexual relationships "exploitation is the general rule and some form of dependence the common fate" (67); that we take what we believe is rightfully ours rather than wait to receive it, and that the only, "universal obligation (is) to enjoy and be enjoyed." (70). To which I add that we have become a culture of users, in that, we employ whatever is at our disposal (people, places, things) to satisfy our needs in spite of the proper end of that action.

Coupled with this is that which is right and proper in liberal theory, which holds that the individual should have free and unhindered choice from the larder of options regarding what one could conceive of as being a good life, notwithstanding the ultimate separation of the individual from the social collective while in pursuit of the good life, which is contradictory to the nature of all human associations and social obligations. According to Berger this, "separation (of the individual) from the social world...(causes) the individual (to) begin to lose his moral bearings." (21-2).

As a result, the adverse ramifications for modern America from this underlying framework of personal interpretations and rationalizations further augmented through the precepts of individualism and liberalism are such, that our society has lost its moral compass. Where once this moral compass seemed to be more clearly oriented, today it has been completely clouded over by a myriad of individual conceptions regarding what constitutes acceptable personal and social behavior. Not only has this trend sought to eliminate religion and religious principles from the fabric of American society, but the confusion wrought regarding issues involving right and wrong has left our authoritative, organizing, governing, social, and cultural institutions increasingly ambiguous and vacillating over moral issues. In addition, and perhaps even more alarming, is the concern expressed by many leading scholars and educators regarding the burgeoning breakdown of our social order, as citizens continue to place the pursuit of personal needs and desires over that of the social collective.

The vast majority of Americans understand the need for social order, and therefore the potential to achieve the common good through the promotion of shared values via those laws and obligations previously agreed upon. For Etzioni, and many others including myself, these shared values represent the core values which are considered foundational to the social association, and are the beliefs held in common by the members of that association. These values, derived from both secular and spiritual sources, are the moral field upon which commitments to right and wrong behavior within the social collective are based. Here, the members are not forced to comply with these values, but will freely abide by them simply because of the belief that the maintenance of the social order is contingent upon one's compliance with these core values.

Again, as stated earlier, the "order" I refer to is not an adherence to a rigid system of absolutes, but rather a cooperative venture amongst citizens to achieve a common solidarity of purpose within the matrix of moral right and wrong actions. According to Etzioni, the point of contention amongst many liberal thinkers is in the "thickness" of this social order. Previous generations believed that a large portion of commonly held core values were an integral part of the social order, while today, "libertarians and liberal individualists are troubled by social formulations of the common good that are a core part of thick social orders. They argue that each person should formulate his or her own virtue, and that public policies and mores should reflect only agreements that individuals voluntarily form." (*The New Golden Rule* 11).

The flaw in this liberal approach is that much of the social order decomposes within the individualistic paradigm, in that, with the focus primarily on individual action and outcome, attention to the social collective is stunted. Here, individualism and liberalism are inherently antithetical to the promotion of social association as they are relatively devoid of the primacy of social considerations. Within these liberal systems is less a commitment toward attaining the common good, and more of one which emphasizes personal gain through unbridled autonomous action. Although these liberal systems propose that the common good is faithfully served via the advances one makes through one's personal achievements, as Derber points out in his study of the erosion of our nation's character from increasing levels of greed and violence, "(a)s individualism intensifies, the balance of commitment can tilt so far toward the self that the family and other building blocks of society decompose...Americans converted to the reigning ideology of 'looking out for number one' are proving ready to sacrifice not only outsiders but their kin on the altar of their own needs and pleasures." (111).

I find this theme echoed throughout the majority of the sources cited within this book. Although each source has compiled independent evidence and proposes different solutions regarding the vexing problem of the breakdown of social order in America (i.e. Etzioni's communitarian approach, and Thiemann's commitment to the inclusion of religion in public life) the common denominator underlying all is the decline of moral order within our society.

Perhaps the most important reflection of this sentiment can be found in, *Judgment Day at the White House: A Critical Declaration Exploring Moral Issues and the Political Use and Abuse of Religion,* edited by Gabriel Fackre who is the Abbot Professor of Christian Theology Emeritus at Andover Newton Theological School. This book is composed of a series of essays from twenty of America's leading scholars of religion and public life, some of whom also belong to the ninety member committee who penned the "Declaration Concerning Religion, Ethics, and the Crisis in the Clinton Presidency." In fact, the book itself, compiled during Clinton's tenure, functions as an extension of that Declaration. Within its pages the contributors (among them: William J. Buckley and Stephen Carter) not only sought to provide "substantive discussion" regarding the moral issues raised during the Clinton presidency with regard to: the social effects of sinful acts; the manipulation of religion in the debate about presidential responsibility, and the exploitation of words for political advantage—they were also providing a forum to bring to the public's attention the committee's desire, "to bring clarity to the moral confusion caused by the presidential scandal." (From the back cover).

Here, the thread that united all committee members and contributing authors alike is "The Declaration" itself, which among many of its concerns states:

(W)e protest the manipulation of religion and the debasing of moral language in the discussion about presidential responsibility...The resulting moral confusion is a threat to the integrity of American religion and to the foundation of a civil society... (P)olitics and morality cannot be separated...(C)ertain moral qualities are central to the survival of our political system...(T)he moral character of a people is more important than the tenure of a particular politician or the protection of a particular political agenda. Political and religious history indicate that violations and misunderstandings of such moral issues may have grave consequences...We urge the society as a whole to take account of the ethical commitments necessary for a civil society and to seek the integrity of both public and private morality (lest) the moral basis of the constitutional system itself will be lost. (1-3).

These are very powerful statements which cannot be ignored. Although the committee's actions were prompted by former-President Clinton's indiscretionary, extracurricular, sexual shenanigans which scandalized not only himself, but the institution of the presidency and the nation itself—these statements also reflect the consistent concern by so many of America's leading citizen, in every walk of life, as to the steady decline in the moral fabric of American society. The Clinton case, by far, reflects only the tip of the iceberg regarding this widespread and nocuous problem of America's moral degeneracy, which shows no sign of abating.

Among other things, that while during his tenure as President of the United States, Clinton could publicly proclaim that he did not consider oral sex to be sex, and therefore render groundless any evidence accusing him of being an adulterer, was not only completely contrary to practical reality, but to humanity's inherent moral sense as well. However, the fact that this defense was even considered valid and reasonable, in my opinion, reflects the sadly deteriorated state of morality in this country, and the distortions of moral values one is capable of conceiving when purely personalized interpretations and rationalizations regarding one's actions (à la the individualistic tradition) are employed. That many Americans even accepted this explanation attests, far more than any other incident, to our deep confusion over what constitutes right and wrong human behavior.

Of course, this is not to imply that issues of a moral nature should not be debated or included within the public forum. Rather, what I still find to be so prevalent among many proponents of liberal and ultra-left wing philosophy is the contention that moral considerations are deemed to be irrelevant when dealing with issues of private behavior which impact directly upon the public good. In the case of former-President Clinton, the rationale offered by many adherents of modern liberal philosophy for his private immoral behavior is that it is "private." However, the effect this reasoning has on the general public is that it strongly implies not only a loosening of the social taboos regarding the "worker/boss" relationship due to the fact that Clinton's sex scandal involved a female White House employee, but of the further withering of the inviolability of the marital union.

This then is the tradition we have inherited and fully implemented within our modern society. If, when in office, Clinton could offer the American public such an obvious piece of moral relativism in defense of his blatantly immoral actions, and fully expect his actions to be considered within the realm of acceptable behavior, then what signal does this send to the balance of our population—especially our young?

As outlined earlier with reference to slavery, much of this type of distorted reasoning regarding one's right and wrong actions is already deeply implanted within American society. In the pursuit of one's personal happiness (i.e. the good) we have completely ignored the moral (i.e. the right) ramifications of our actions. Therefore, in the vein of the 1960s proclamation: "If it feel good, do it!"—now anything goes, and as a result of this attitude there have been serious effects upon the social order of this nation.

For example, in a study done by the contemporary sociologist Jay MacLeod on two groups of young males inhabiting one of America's inner city, low-income neighborhoods, the author found that one group adhered to the concept of being "bad" as a survival technique throughout their lives. As one youth explained, being "bad" is actually good. In essence, it is giving evidence of one's masculinity and prowess by exhibiting antisocial and contrary behavior in virtually every situation one encounters. It is engaging in the daily practice of breaking all the rules, for example: fighting; stealing; getting arrested; taking drugs; drinking, and foregoing school. All the subjects within this group rationalized that this behavior was necessary in order to avoid criticism and an important, normal criterion for gaining status and acceptability within the group.

What I find most revealing are the larger ramifications of MacLeod's study, in that, groups of similar ilk are very common across this country and all tend to exhibit identical antisocial behavior as a reaction to their social status and relatively impoverished lives. Here, each employs a "rationalized reasoning" which then gives validity to the good they personally achieve for themselves as the result of their negative acts and criminal exploits, yet nowhere are the moral implications regarding right and wrong considered. Of course many citizens and scholars alike will say that their actions are a direct result of poverty; their struggle to survive, and their dysfunctional family life. However, I raise the following point: Is it a given, that by living an impoverished life one must relinquish all sense of the moral? Poverty existed in the past; exists in the present, and no doubt will continue in the future, yet throughout our history most individuals who struggled with poverty still lived life according to natural law/moral law principles, especially those common to the various religious traditions. Therefore, to what do we attribute the lack of morality within those groups described above? I conclude that the recent and current signals sent by our society (as exemplified by the aforementioned Clintonian reasoning) and which promotes the unbridled pursuit of personal satisfaction as the ultimate reality of one's existence, has served to eliminate much of the moral from the consciousness of not only the lower strata of our society, but the entire balance as well.

In addition, and even more disturbing are some of Derber's findings from his study involving the growing phenomenon of "wilding" among this nation's youth, and similar forms of "legitimate sociopathic behavior" exhibited in families, business, and politics. Here, Derber explains that in the exercise of individual freedom, Americans have become ruthless in their pursuit of self-interest to the point that this behavior threatens to unravel society itself.

In its most basic sense, Derber defines "wilding" as, "individualistic behavior that advances or indulges the self by hurting others." (10). Furthermore, Derber finds that, "(w)ilding partly reflects a weakened community less able to regulate its increasingly individualistic members. In this sense, the American wilder is the undersocialized product of a declining society that is losing its authority to instill respect for social values and obligations." (16-7).

Of course, this issue of living a life based on moral principles involving right and wrong is not restricted to the poor and unfortunate members of our society, or our "wilding" youths. Granted, poor individuals surrounded daily by the expanding latitudes of our materially oriented society, and which are so often unavailable to them, may have found it difficult to live up to the conditions of a moral life, especially when abandoning those requirements very often brings an increased chance of procuring that which is so denied them by their poverty (i.e. engaging in criminal activity can give one an opportunity to illicitly acquire that which one is legitimacy unable to secure). In addition, it is the nature of the majority of our nation's young to reject much of conventional wisdom and engage in faddish, even antisocial behavior and thinking in the pursuit of their newfound mental awareness. Yet, what of both the financially fortunate and model members of our society who by virtue of their income, personal wealth, position, or status do not want for anything—what moral conditions are expected of them?

Here, the same principles involving right and wrong apply equally to them. I believe that a moral "right" is an eternal condition and cannot be modified by the financial or social status of the individual involved. The moral "right" is true in all places and for all time. Although there is nothing wrong with the successful and fortunate members of our society enjoying the material fruits of their income, or status—however, if their condition causes them to abandon, or ignore the morally "right" in any given situation, then they are as equally guilty as those in the opposite end of the social spectrum of employing "rationalized reasoning" in the achievement of the good they desire. Once again, if one's success or status breeds the promotion of an unbridled pursuit of personal satisfaction less morally right and wrong considerations, it is not the action of achieving success or status that produces this condition. Instead, the fault lies with the individual, who because of his/her success or status thus ignores moral principles, and therefore is then guilty of moral laxity. As I stated earlier: Living an impoverished life does not absolve anyone from relinquishing all sense of the moral, and the same applies to every strata of our society as well.

Here, I find that in our feverish pursuit of personal interests, à la the prescriptions of individualism and liberalism, Americans have ignored, "the moral constraints that hold stable communities together." (Derber 101). I believe that many are caught up in the confusion between what is perceived to be the necessary and ambitious pursuit of the fruits of our society, and the intense competition generated amongst individuals and groups to secure those fruits for themselves. Somewhere within this confusion an "anything goes" mentality has become prevalent.

That there exists a correlation between adherence to moral standards and the maintenance of social order, I believe, has been made obvious from this chapter. In fact, much of the goal of Etzioni's Communitarian movement has been geared toward, "the regeneration of moral values and commitments" (*The New Golden Rule* xiv), with respect to "the full significance of the deep-seated sociological and historical need for order." (xvi). This is a theme repeatedly stated by the majority of the sources utilized in the research and preparation of this book—no doubt there are many others. Indeed, continuous vacillating and often contradictory government rules and regulations, and our inordinately hamstrung religious institutions contribute greatly to this confused social order. In this sense, and as Etzioni admonishes, we have lost our equilibrium between the lessons of tradition (those shared, substantive, moral values passed from generation to generation) and the advances of modernity.

Of course, the question that naturally arises is: What form will this new morally based social order take? I will deal with this issue in more depth in the final chapter of this book entitled: "Conclusions, Solutions, and Final Reflections" but as a prelude, let me offer some initial comments.

First, I do not advocate a return to some supposed "Golden Age" of American social history—since there was none. The purpose of dealing with the majority of the historical themes in this thesis was not to imply that at some point in the latter 1700s or early 1800s America was the quintessence of humanity's moral and social capabilities! Instead, my hope was to utilize these founding and early national periods as focal points with which to view and compare just how far we have currently strayed from the original principles upon which this nation was founded. Still, those principles were not perfect, they needed some improvement and refinement—not to be virtually abandoned, as in the case of the elimination of religion from public life masking as the separation of church and state, or brought to excess, as in the case of an unbridled personal autonomy masking as freedom.

Secondly, I do not advocate the formation of some sort of religious tribunal to lead this country, or guide it out of its moral/social confusion. What I do propose is similar to the Communitarian position which seeks, "a way to blend elements of tradition (order based on virtues) with elements of modernity (well-protected autonomy)...(of) finding an equilibrium between universal individual rights and the common good...between self and community." (*The New Golden Rule* xviii).

However, Communitarianism is essentially opposed to the larger structures that organize our society in favor of a more locally based and privately organized framework of communities which would then serve as the focal point for a regeneration of moral/social order. I don't believe this will work since the complexity and vastness of our society and its problems needs those larger structures to effect solutions— reliance on local or private groups to produce the same is too diverse and decentralized a framework to truly produce widespread and lasting changes.

So, what do I propose? I believe we should reevaluate the individualistic concept which prescribes the unbridled pursuit of one's self-satisfaction, and reexamine the liberal notion of the primacy of a personal conception of what constitutes the good life—which together are heralded as the ultimate goal of human happiness and existence. Here, I am not advocating the abandonment of individuality, but simply calling for a re-focusing of our national priority from one which promotes the preeminence of the untrammeled achievement of individual good, to one which seeks the primacy of the realization of the common good. In order to achieve this common good, I believe there should be a purposeful effort to devise a revitalized system of moral and social norms with which to orient our society. This effort, which could perhaps begin with a nationwide internet/telephone/mail survey and culminate in a committee composed of both our religious and secular institutions and representative of all traditions, could accumulate the data needed to compose recommendations which would accurately reflect the guidelines for achieving a true common good. This would be a monumental task, but the time taken to accomplish it would be well worth the effort.

While related to Marty's notion of sharing "common stories" as one means toward composing a common good, and Eck's conception of an "interdependent" community advancing toward a wider sense of "we"—here, what I propose and label as the National Social Morality Project (NSMP) would encompass a wider range of problem identification, dialogue, interaction, and ultimate solutions. The NSMP would foster what no doubt Thiemann had in mind when he voiced similar concerns over America's declining morality and the effects it has on our "public sphere" by stating, "(i)f a genuine political consensus is to be built, democratic governments cannot occupy an imagined place of neutral transcendence above the fray of contending substantive points of view; rather, such governments must discover the 'common ground' present among those who hold diverse and conflicting comprehensive schemes." (82).

I strongly believe that as a nation we must assign the highest priority toward the attainment of a morally derived, collectively determined common good lest the notion of an American community further unravels into anarchy. This and other themes I previously raised will be further explored in the concluding chapter of this book. However, the next section will explore the dominance of materialism within American culture. I will trace materialism's influence, effects, and ramifications on post-World War II American society, and the problems it has engendered ever since, especially among the current younger generation of Americans—the so-called "GenXers."

Chapter 6

A Malignant Materialism

There can be little doubt that humankind would never have become *the* dominant life on Earth, if not for our technological abilities. In fact, even our survival as a species hinged on the fact that we were most adept at making things to meet our immediate needs. From the first campfires of our distant past, to the fiery ascent of the Space Shuttle's climb into space, the case for the continuance of our species rests on our ingenious use and adaptation of that which we have discovered, invented, and then applied in order to ensure or improve our daily existence. Hence, our preoccupation with the delights and dangers of the material world which surrounds us has always been the focal point of humanity's attention—and for one obvious reason: A good life is better than a dead life.

In this sense, humankind's legacy is inexorably inclined toward the material. Since we are primarily physical beings, where else would our orientations mainly lie except within the material world? The orbit of each human being's life not only intersects, but also revolves around that which has been produced for our use. Therefore, throughout the course of human events, among the many theories and concepts that have emerged seeking to explain the essence of humanity's condition are those that attempt to relate our reality solely within the sphere of the material world. Collectively known as "materialism," the two most fundamental prongs of this term are defined as: A) the theory that matter is the only reality and that everything is reducible to matter and to the energy inherent in matter; B) the doctrine that physical well-being and worldly possessions constitute the greatest good and highest value in life; the tendency to take greater interest in material possessions and comfort than in spiritual values. The first is a strictly philosophical concept dating back to pre-Socratic Greece, while the latter is considered a cultural phenomenon frequently exhibited by, but not restricted to, more affluent societies and often considered a ramification of the economics of capitalism and consumerism.

In comparison, one can correctly extrapolate the obvious relationship between these two elemental prongs of materialistic theory, in that, each is based on the, "view (that) nature itself is ultimate and sovereign. In essence, (making) a god of nature (and creating a form of) nature-worship dressed up as secularism or science." (Stanton 122). Furthermore, I find the common link between the philosophical and economic brands of materialism to be inherently atheistic, that is, a purposeful effort to replace God with the supremacy of physical nature. Hence, the many branches of philosophical materialistic theory that have arisen since the end of the Medieval period and which have had the most profound influence upon modern society, have not only been distinctly atheistically oriented, but as noted by the historians J. Bronowski and Bruce Mazlish in, *The Western Intellectual Tradition,* have ultimately, "served as a basis for a large part of future thought." (198). For example, the Elizabethan Age fully embraced the theories of the astronomer Nicolaus Copernicus and the mathematician Thomas Hariot as indicative of a materialistic, rather than theistic origin of the universe. According to Bronowski and Mazlish, both theories became the basis for modern materialism in science. In the seventeenth century, Hobbes contributed greatly to the philosophical thinking of his age, and that of subsequent generations, when he concluded that the universe is solely corporeal and materialistic. In fact, human history is replete with a wide range of interpretations regarding materialistic theory which have formed the basis for much of modern thought. Who can doubt the enormous effect of Charles Darwin's theory of evolution (Darwinism), or the magnitude of Karl Marx and Nikolai Lenin's dialectical materialism (Communism) upon the human condition since the mid-1800s? Both are fully atheistic, in that, God is completely removed from speculations and conclusions involving humankind's origins, direction, and interactions. Even the religious tenets of the Protestant ethic, which formed the basis for much of colonial America's attitudes and thinking, have today been fully discarded in favor of a purely secular, materialistic conception regarding human work and business practices à la the tenets of capitalism.

Although the focus of this chapter concerns the latter of the two definitions outlined above, most of what modern Americans consider to be materialism is, in essence, a branch of the latter which is the basis for much of the themes explained throughout this book. That is: a purely ego-oriented self-satisfaction based on the untrammeled acquisition of whatever one desires and thus fully determined by a personal moral code favoring a "good" rather than "right" outcome which very often excludes God and/or religion. This attitude is typified by the earlier notion of: "Keeping up with the Joneses" and today is epitomized by the bumper sticker which proudly announces: "Whoever has the most toys when he dies—wins!" Hence, we are dealing with an atheistic economic materialism, that is, a malignancy which further tears at the very heart of our religious foundation, and seeks to further supplant God and religion with a fully secular agenda for America. According to Charles Derber, Americans have had to struggle, "to choose between the materialist dream and the moral dream (and although the) market system was an excellent vehicle for delivering the promises of the materialist dream…it was far less effective in preserving the moral fiber of society." (155). Therefore, the balance of this chapter deals specifically with this current form and will be what is meant by "materialism" throughout this section.

Among Americans, there is an underlying competition to succeed. Evidence of accomplishing this goal is measured in mainly material acquisitions: the nice car; the fabulous house arranged with beautiful furniture; the fashionable clothes; the expensive gadgets and "toys"; the wonderful vacations; investments; artwork; collectibles—in short, anything that money can buy! No matter how subjectively we adorn our lives with our "things," when an individual believes he/she has attained this plateau of existence, that is, a successful life, a certain sense of pride, relief, and contentment is realized—life appears to be complete and all seems well. The message we exude is of having "made it," and now we can relax and enjoy life within our personally constructed world of relative comfort and luxury. Juliet B. Schor, author and senior lecturer and Director of Studies, Women's Studies at Harvard University, in her book, *The Overspent American: Why We Want What We Don't Need*, noted this tendency and offered the following observation, "(w)hat (we) acquire and own is tightly bound to (our) personal identity…and support(s) a particular image of (ourselves) to present to the world." (3). Additionally, we utilize our purchases not only to adorn ourselves and our private spaces, or as tools or implements to assist in our daily lives, but more importantly to establish and announce our social position to others.

The drive to succeed has become America's all-encompassing legacy. Yet, that so many prosperous Americans seem immersed in empty lives; are unhappy; depressed, and even suicidal—despite their achievements—testifies to the distinct probability that a successful human life is not measured solely with the yardstick of increased achievements and the continuance of unrestricted material acquisitions. Equally unfortunate is the reality that such a large part of our fact and fiction centers on this same theme. We are all familiar with the literary motif of someone graduating from "rags to riches," only to spend the rest of his/her life yearning for the "good old days" before they had "made it" in life. However, for the majority of Americans, the drive to succeed is so much more powerful for it is fueled daily by the various media as we are bombarded by commercials promoting a "better" life; entertained by shows and movies extolling the "good life," and informed by newscasts and documentaries about someone's "perfect" life. Of course, little attention is paid to the downside of a life lived steeped in the perversions of the purely material.

In commenting on the possibility of just such a negative condition arising from a culture dominated by materialism, in the early 1800s Tocqueville observed, "(d)emocracy favors the taste for physical pleasures. This taste, if it becomes excessive soon disposes men to believe that nothing but matter exists. Materialism, in its turn, spurs them on to such delights with mad impetuosity." (544). Tocqueville continues by labeling materialism, "a dangerous malady of the human spirit"; materialist doctrines as, "pernicious," and the proponents of materialism as being, "full of a pride" that seems to announce to all that they are gods. In addition, many of today's scholars have reached similar conclusions. For example, in another book by Schor entitled, *The Overworked American: The Unexpected Decline of Leisure,* the author states, "(m)aterialism has not only failed to make us happy, it has also bred its own form of discontent—even among the affluent." (116). That discontent is the ever increasing chipping away at one's family relationships and leisure time resulting from the added working hours needed to support our addiction to the accumulation of more possessions. Furthermore, later in the book Schor notes that, "(s)urveys show that many (Americans) believe materialism is ruining the country, perverting our values, and damaging our children…(a)fter drugs and crime, people see materialism as the most serious problem affecting American families." (24). It is quite apparent, that within many segments of our society, many of us feel truly uneasy with this new form of consumerism.

I believe that materialism is the natural result of a society steeped in the precepts of individualism. Here, members of that society have so divorced themselves from the matrix of community oriented life and engagement in the achievement of a common good, that they have sought to assemble a private and completely self-satisfying microcosm all to themselves. This universe of "one" is furnished with what its sole inhabitant interprets to be the material extensions of him/herself, that is, tangible reflections of their inner being meant not only to announce a separation from the other "universes" around them, but to project a sense of liberation from the rest of the world as well. That this inward journey is fueled by increasingly "greedy behavior" was noted by Lipset in, *American Exceptionalism: A Double Edged Sword,* to be a sad consequence of many American's inordinate desire to achieve the realization of their personal wants. Furthermore, according to Etzioni, a life based on the preoccupation with material success has even more serious consequences for the children of these detached individuals. Here, "(t)he community –that is, all of us, suffers the ill effects of *absentee* (author's emphasis) parenting" (*The Spirit of Community* 69), as the drive for the accumulation of the material leaves more young people "latch key kids" with far too much unsupervised time on their hands. In addition, Etzioni states that studies have shown that these lonely children were twice as likely to be abusers of marijuana, tobacco, alcohol, and other drugs; prone to delinquency, anger, stress, family conflict, gangs, and risk-taking; engaged in sexual experiments at an early age, and inclined toward increasingly antisocial behavior. All this, as many adults have their attention diverted from neighbors, friends, family, spouses, and children—to focus mainly on themselves and the satisfaction of their personal wants, needs, and desires.

Moreover, I maintain that the rise in America's materialist culture is further sustained by the philosophy of liberalism which has evolved within this country. Here, liberalism champions the personal freedom and autonomy of the individual in his/her pursuit of the "good life." In essence, while this "good life" purports to be the direct result of the realization of the common good that liberalism so vociferously strives to achieve, in reality it is simply just another vehicle for the unbridled achievement of one's own self interests which are invariably material in nature. As much of the fourth chapter of this book points out, liberalism is quite responsible for this country's shift from a, "once communally inclined collective...to that of today's America with its escalating emphasis on the untrammeled, unrestricted self and his/her pursuit of whatever he/she can extract from the good life he/she constructs." As a result, this current narcissism running so rampant throughout America furthers the rise of materialism, in that, the construction of one's "good life" is mostly assembled from the material acquisitions one accumulates.

With so many resulting consequences attached to a materialist culture, why exactly do Americans cling so tenaciously to the procurement of more and more "things" in their lives? Why are we so fascinated with piles of possessions, while our children wait in day care centers as we work ourselves to death so we can purchase more "things" for ourselves? Perhaps a brief history of this country's current consumerism would offer an answer to these questions.

In the early 1900s, almost every aspect of American society was slowly being changed by advancements in science and technology. Although in everyday life much of this came to a temporary standstill as the United States entered into World War I, science and technology was fully employed in transforming the "art" of warfare from swords and horses to machine guns and tanks. As a result, once World War I ended, the average American's former puppy love with science and technology had now become a full time affair, and breakthroughs on the battlefield consummated the relationship with the promise of unlimited potential for improving everyone's life. Furthermore, the imagination of inventors everywhere were fully ignited by the sudden need for "bigger, better, faster," and businessmen across the country fired up their factories to meet the new dreams of this post-war generation. It was here that the seeds of the "American Dream" of the later post-war generation of the 1950s were sown; only here it was referred to as "the American way of life." Thus, the famous "Roaring 20s" were, as Schor described, a decade where, "(t)hrift and sobriety were out; waste and excess were in." (*The Overworked American: The Unexpected Decline of Leisure* 117). Schor further explains that the 1920s ushered in not only the breakdown of longstanding values and the growth of America's middle class, but the birth of something that many historians view as the bane of modern human culture: consumer credit! Here, "(t)he growth of the middle class created a large group of potential buyers and the possibility that mass culture could be oriented around material goods," (117) and banks were more than willing to extend credit to consumers in order to fuel the new economy.

It was at this juncture in American history that the foundations of modern consumerism was born, as businesses everywhere employed "hard sell" advertising to convince the public to buy their product. In effect, and as Schor explains further, this technique was a psychological weapon used against consumers in the hope of forcing them to, "develop an association between the product and one's very identity (which) (e)ventually...came to promise everything and anything— from self-esteem, to status, friendship, and love." (119). The effect this had on the American public was that, "the middle class and above (to whom virtually all advertising was targeted) were no longer buying to satisfy basic needs...(these needs) had been met. Advertisers had to persuade consumers to acquire things they most certainly did not need." (119). Here, the foundation of America's current unrestrained materialism was firmly set in place.

Still, there was one other great event in American history that further solidified the newly laid foundation for our modern materialistic culture. This event was so traumatic to those that lived through it, that it forever shaped the psychology of the American consumer—it was the

Great Depression of the 1930s. Here, the survivors of this tragedy struggled to ensure that their progeny would never experience such insecurity, instability, or downright wanting again. Continuing on, Schor points out, "(o)ne of the legacies (of the Depression) was a longstanding emphasis on finding security in the form of material success." (122). In effect, the Depression served to either instruct the ignorant; introduce to the unaware; prove to the unconvinced, and reinforce in those who were already converted, that materialism was a valuable and viable approach toward assuring personal and social survival throughout one's life. Therefore, the acquisition of possessions, goods, "things" directly translated into not only the ability of the individual to sustain and secure his/her existence, but to achieve certain levels of status during that existence which could conceivably further enhance and assure his/her existence. In effect, our materialistic consumerism became a way of life for most Americans, and as Schor observed, we walk around with an ever-present "wish list" of things we must buy or get. We have become so enamored with what money can buy, that shopping has become our national obsession.

In, *Lead Us Into Temptation: The Triumph of American Materialism,* author and educator James B. Twitchell notes that Americans have about four times as many things as Middle Europeans, and even more than the less developed areas of the world. Still, we complain that we are victims of capitalism as though it is some mind-controlling, alien force that has forever subjected us to a life of "shopping till we drop." I agree with Schor, in that, this thinking is part of the psychological denial we exhibit regarding the connection between our buying habits and the social statements they make. Furthermore, as Twitchell indicates, the reality, "*is* (author's emphasis) our better judgment. Not only are we willing to consume, and not only does consuming make us happy, 'getting and spending' is what gives our lives order and purpose." (20). Despite some initial opposition, this has become the triumph of capitalism!

In addition, here we find the rise of the "new consumerism" which Schor characterizes as spending habits based on making comparisons with a social group above our own strata. Therefore, the people in this group become the "reference group" with which we identify, emulate, and then completely engage ourselves to, in a life of "upscale spending." This particular form of materialism arose in the 1970s, and as Schor found evidence for, by the mid-1990s the average person spent about 30 percent more on "upscale" buying—some studies place the figure nearer to 70 percent! Whichever is the more accurate figure, no one denies that the "new consumerism" has led to a mass "overspending," especially among middle-class Americans—a fact that businesses all around the United States have obviously been all to eager to accommodate.

The problem is, of course, that as the lifestyle of the most affluent escalated, "the need that many others felt to meet that standard (also increased) irrespective of their financial ability to maintain such a lifestyle." (*The Overspent American: Why We Want What We Don't Need* 18). Hence, we are truly "overspent Americans" engaged in a, "daily struggle to survive." (14). In addition, with television as the modern marketplace, and the Internet further expanding the boundaries of our shopping time, Twitchell found that the potency of our materialistic culture causes us to spend, "more time at the carnival, less and less in church." (27). Thus, we make purchases to satisfy our own perceived needs and project those same needs onto our children via a stream of automatic rationalizations based upon the tenets of materialism.

Therefore, in answer to the question I raised earlier: Why are we so fascinated with piles of possessions, while our children wait in day care centers as we work ourselves to death so we can purchase more "things" for ourselves? Because, we have all been psychology convinced that not only are we providing for ourselves and ensuring our own survival by increasing our material accumulations, but that this is one of the primary ways we provide for and love our children—by continuously buying them things. Sadly enough, the underlying insidiousness of the seemingly innocent modern "power ad" campaign is that the drive to convince us to keep buying has tapped into the materialistic legacy handed down to us from both the excesses and needs of previous generations. This has served to unconsciously seduce and convince us to substitute the natural, nurturing, parental love of our presence and daily interaction with our children, with the unnatural, uninvolved, absentee, superficial love of supplying things to our children instead of the giving of ourselves. What we have bought more than anything else is a lie, and for quite some time now we have all suffered the effects of this malignant materialism. We have especially begun to see the effect it has had on our adolescent children, especially teenagers. Not only have we further removed ourselves from the world around us by constructing our own private universe, but we have also succeeded in removing ourselves from our very own family unit. We have filled our children's rooms with every conceivable toy, sat them in front of innumerable videos, bought our spouses hundreds of gifts, and spent any free family time *appearing* together in the malls, yet engaged in more buying and with our attention diverted toward comparison shopping and scanning the shelves for more "things" to purchase.

The negative ramifications of our modern materialistic culture are many and most deleterious. For example, in, *Sources of the Self: The Making of the Modern Identity*, Charles Taylor commented repeatedly on materialism's effect on religion and morality in general. Taylor wrote, "materialism...can form part of a quite different moral outlook (that is) the basis of a despairing amoralism (or) a reductive morality, in which, aspiration to honour (sic) and altruism have no place." (333). He goes on to indicate that a, "(m)ore dangerous...morality of purely egoistic gratification...could find a basis in radical materialism," (334) and that, "(t)hose who were drawn to materialism...were indeed concerned to subvert traditional religion and morality." (348). Clearly Taylor saw that the overt tendency for materialism to cater to the individual's every whim would ultimately lead to the erosion of one's "parochial allegiances and attachments" as one's life was transformed into the selfish pursuit and achievement of material goals. I believe it would only be logical to assume this to be the case, for both religious and moral codes would ultimately serve to offer impediments to those whose primary quest is obtaining gratification solely within the sphere of the material. In essence, as the drive toward furthering one's possessions increases, one's prohibitions decrease.

Thus we find the modern consumer as the locus from which the ebb and flow of our contemporary temporal society originates. That is, it is the tendency of our current code of consumerism to foster an inordinate preoccupation with increasing our cache of personal property. Born of the capitalistic system which seeks to produce goods and sell them at a profit, consumerism's main intent is the promotion of goods produced solely for the consumer's interest. Though functioning more out of necessity in past eras, the consumerism of today's marketplace, serves as an all too willing vehicle with which one can achieve any level of satisfaction no matter how perverse, depraved, or taboo. Here, the modern consumer is bombarded daily with hundreds of suggestive, crude, and coercive ads and slogans meant to entice and attract the individual to make a purchase. According to Friedman and Squire in, *Morality USA*, this daily effort undertaken for the consumer's attention creates a "moral drift" whereby we develop an inner conflict between our moral traditions and those which are presented to us in the various advertisements flung our way—that is, our moral traditions are held together in an "uneasy coexistence" with what we find around us. The effect this has on consumers is that we are continuously forced into the dilemma of either tolerating the ambiguity we are experiencing or we seek to "get out." In either case, consumers are met with a constant inner moral negotiation as we try to make sense of the "new moral conditions" which surrounds us, and deal with the "moral conflicts" within us. Friedman and Squire have found that, "(c)onsumption itself can be seen as a form of production, producing a new kind of surplus value, an excess of meaning that challenges existing moralities and provides a kind of everyday resistance." (213).

Which leads me to ask the following question: If the average consumer's day is so adversely affected by the continuous assaults by our modern materialistic culture, what then is the effect it has upon our society as a whole? Here, in, *American Exceptionalism: A Double-Edged Sword*, Lipset found that our modern political system has such a large number of powerful special interest groups, lobbying organizations, and social movements intertwined within the political process, that not only are political candidates most vulnerable to the influence of these groups and/or dependent on the money they produce for running a successful campaign, but, "(t)his results in American politics appearing more materialistic...than elsewhere." (44). To many countries and cultures that do not give materialism so preeminent a position within their political or social systems, it is no wonder that America is often considered the bane of the planet, or referred to as the "Great Satan." We tend to project and promote a materialism which seemingly takes precedence above all other systems, be they religious, social, political.

The consequences of all that I have discussed so far has become most apparent in the children of the "Baby Boomers," that is, the so-called "Generation X"—the first of which who came of age in the early 1990s, and the balance who will reach that same plateau in the first decade of this new century. Many scholars consider this particular generation of Americans to be perhaps the most jaded of this country's inhabitants. What these young people have inherited from the pervious generation is a materialism that is bereft of any limitations, and what Derber characterized as, "the dominant dream (which) has equated freedom and fulfillment with the right to get as rich or famous as luck, talent, or hard work permits." (151). In themselves, neither of these ambitions is inherently nocuous, if pursued within reasonable limits. However, to paraphrase Derber, coupled with the central values of American life, namely: aggressive competitiveness; untrammeled material success; and a super-achievement of personal ambitions, this younger generation of Americans has taken their particular brand of materialism to levels that their parents would never have thought possible—and quite often with very serious results.

There have been numerous studies regarding the apparent apathy of Generation X toward many of the seemingly "idealistic" 1960s values of their parent's era, and their almost complete refusal for, even violent rebelliousness against, what they consider to be the hopelessly "old-fashioned" values of their grandparents. Perhaps the most violent statement these "GenXers" have made is examined in Derber's book which deals with the recent phenomenon of "wilding." As Derber observed, Generation X ushered in "The Age of Indifference" which he states is best characterized by a New York Times article he references which was written in the summer of 1990. The report stated, "the materialistic preoccupations of the young were turning them into the generation 'that couldn't care less,' " and possessing an indifference to the pain of others. The report labeled them, "self-centered know-nothings" who were so, "self-absorbed that they would not act to help others even in the most dire emergency." This apathetic indifference actually led to the coining of the term "Generation X." Continuing on, Derber notes that by 1995, the youth of the 1990s were deemed a:

> '(S)lacker' population that had moved from indifference to nihilism. Suffering from dysfunctional families and an economy offering them 'McJobs,' they are hooked on TV, relate to the Brady Bunch, and have no heroes...they inhabit 'Wayne's World'...(t)hey have 'boomer envy,' jealous of the wealth of the baby boomers and afraid of facing 'lessness'...(i)n fact, they are the first American generation who will live less well than their parents." (96).

How sad, and we have only ourselves to blame because, as Derber concludes, "(t)o weave grandiose materialist dreams in an era of restricted opportunities is the ultimate recipe for wilding." (13). Here, once the bubble burst after the first oil crisis of the early 1970s, even the baby boomers were scrambling to shore up their crumbling segment of the American Dream. However, propelled by our society's almost unquenchable appetite for things, most Americans still flocked to the malls and continued to pile mountains of gifts around their children for their birthdays and on special holidays. It was business as usual, and the children growing up in the 1970s and 1980s considered it all simply a normal way of life. Then, as they grew into teenagers, and later entered into their early twenties, the stark realization that it requires increasingly larger salaries; longer work hours, and additional effort to maintain the level of materialism they have come to expect, has left many of them confused, alienated, upset, and quite disillusioned. Most try their best to adjust and survive, while others become so very angry that they lash out against the society they feel has betrayed them. Hence, the violence we've witnessed over the last decade emanating from our children—this Generation X—so given to wilding, "drive-bys," school shootings, mayhem, escalating gang violence and a general penchant for obnoxious behavior. In my opinion, and as explained throughout this chapter, I find that one layer of this complex problem is that of our inordinately materialistic society—a fact which Twitchell apparently agrees with when he stated, "(w)hat is clear is that most of these things in and of themselves simply do not mean enough. So we have developed very powerful ways to add meaning to goods...and their meanings is how most Western young people cope in a world that science has pretty much bled of traditional religious meanings," (12)—and of God, I might add! Include with this the malignant materialism so rampant throughout or society; the selfishness of individualism, and the autonomy of liberalism, and no wonder our children seem so lost and seemingly beyond our reach.

It is quite apparent that the meaning we have attached to all those "things" falls so far short of sufficient, that our children are turning increasingly apathetic, indifferent, and suffering emotionally stunted lives. What then must we do to counteract this social scourge blanketing our nation and infecting our youth? Although Derber's conclusion refers specifically to the recent wilding epidemic in America, perhaps his advice applies equally well to the more general problems affecting our young people, "(we) will have to rediscover and refashion a version of the moral dream in order to temper the current fever of individualistic materialism and resurrect civil society." (150). In my opinion, this will take a great and collective effort by every segment of our society, that is, a much less selfish society, and one more inclined to create a truly "common" good among its members, rather than a society which perpetuates an egotistical catering to the needs of the "self."

In the concluding chapter which follows, I raise some additional problems associated with our current materialistic, individualistic, and liberal oriented society, and offer some possible solutions to the most deleterious effect this triad has had upon America.

Chapter 7

Conclusions, Solutions, & Final Reflections

The current complex multiplicity of modern American society is such that the once prevalent comparison of the United States to a "melting pot" of peoples is now mostly invalid. Lipset agreed with this perception when he referred to the, "depreciation of the melting pot as the image of the future of American ethnicity." (250). Though emigration to this country continues, conceptions involving the assimilation of immigrating groups into the supposed "mainstream" of American culture and society are increasingly, if not completely, untenable. The fact is, that although the United States remains the quintessential "land of opportunity"—the vast majority of immigrants place one foot squarely on our shores in the hope of bettering their previous condition, yet leave the other foot firmly implanted in their former country. Although physically here in America, their heart is given to the homeland. This in no way implies that immigrants to America should abandon their previous identities upon entering this country. However, there is quite a difference between previous generations of immigrants who, as Thiemann noted, understood themselves, for example, as both Italian and American, and today's immigrants who, I believe, feel so excluded from the pulse of American society due to vast cultural differences that they cannot, or will not identify, or understand themselves as Americans.

It has been my experience both within certain generations of my own family and that gained from over twenty-five years of discussions with a great variety of newly transplanted and recently settled immigrants from a diverse range of regions including: Russia; Haiti; Africa; Central America; South America; Canada; Europe, and some Oriental and Middle-East countries, that their ultimate dream is to return to the land of their birth and live out their lives in relative comfort via the savings accumulated from years of hard work in America. Furthermore, their added intent is to be free from what they perceive to be our inordinately materialistic, confusing, irreligious, and even immoral culture—which they add is not the case in their homeland. Whether they succeed or not, is not the issue here. What is relevant is that as long as they stay in America, the common theme among the great majority of immigrants I've encountered over the years is that they always harbor a desire to leave America and either live, retire, or be buried in their homeland.

Thus, the "melting pot" has been replaced by the "rainbow" as the symbol for America's current social state, and the conception of being an "American" is more a detail on one's passport, than a designation of ethnic origin. Instead, immigrants retain and protect an identity independent of that which is identified with Americanism, leaving American society itself a rather complex mix of sentimental references to "being an American"—coupled with all the various extra-Americanisms that exist here at any given time.

Like a round peg in a round hole, individualism fits perfectly into this scenario just as Tocqueville predicted over one hundred sixty years ago, when he not only coined the term "individualism" but also speculated and expressed concern over the distinct possibility that it could someday "attack and destroy" American society itself, as citizens and even whole communities detach and separate from the mainstream of the social collective to pursue an alternate agenda.

Sadly enough, but true to Tocqueville's predictions, and to paraphrase a familiar television commercial—while in the United States any immigrant can be all that he/she can be while remaining emotionally, philosophically, and ideologically separate from America itself. In this sense, while those born in this country are divorced from the social collective through the pursuit of self-satisfaction and personal autonomy; those transplanted to these shores remain similarly separated from the "American community" as they pursue a personal agenda in reference to an ongoing loyalty to their former homeland. By "community" I not only refer to the standard definition of a body of people living in the same place and under the same laws, but of a fellowship among those in pursuit of a common good, that is, a social collective engaged in the realization of a shared interest—not just an assemblage of people.

Within this country today, I find this notion of fellowship to be so completely lacking, and the concept of the "American community" to be nothing more than an anachronistic, even myth-like property. Still, this sense of a unified national commonality is so embedded within the collective psyche of this country, that despite their noninvolvement in the public collective, most individuals truly believe that the "American community" is waiting for them just outside their front door—if they become so inclined to participate in the same. However, upon careful inspection I believe it has long since been replaced by the community of "one" that we have all become, that is, a myriad of singular entities engaged in the lifelong pursuit of seeking out all that we can achieve to satisfy our "self." Hence, the subtitle of this book: *Of The People; By The People; For The Self.*

This then is a vastly different America than that which existed for the Founding generation and those who coined the motto: *E pluribus unum,* and one they could not have possibly envisioned given that which has been outlined and explained in the pages preceding this final chapter. As author, former associate professor of history at Harvard University, and special advisor to President Kennedy, Arthur M. Schlesinger, Jr. points out in, *The Disuniting of America: Reflections on a Multicultural Society*, what held America together for over two centuries was the:

> (C)reation of a brand-new national identity, carried forward by individuals who, in forsaking old loyalties and joining to make new lives, melted away ethnic differences. Those intrepid Europeans... *expected* (author's emphasis) to become Americans. Their goals were escape, deliverance, and assimilation. They saw America as a transforming nation, banishing dismal memories and developing a unique national character based on common political ideals and shared experiences. The point of America was not to preserve old cultures, but to forge a new *American* (author's emphasis) culture. (13).

Although echoes of Tocqueville ring clearly from these words, Schlesinger and Tocqueville part company in their experience of American society. Here, the former actually lived through what the latter could only speculate over regarding the possible problems associated with the great mix of American culture, that is, the emergence of what Schlesinger calls "the cult of ethnicity" resulting in what Tocqueville similarly referred to as the "(loss of our) common interest." Schlesinger further explains that since the end of World War II:

> (This) new ethnic gospel reject(ed) the unifying vision of individuals from all nations melted into a new

race. Its underlying philosophy is that America is not a
nation of individuals at all but a nation of groups, that
ethnicity is the defining experience for most Americans,
that ethnic ties are permanent and indelible, and that
division into ethnic communities establishes the basic
structure of American society and the basic meaning of
American history. (16).

Therefore, the diversity of this country's different cultures has more
fragmented modern America into competing sections of independent
populations engaged in conflict and separatism—which Schlesinger
concludes, "nourishes prejudices, magnifies differences and stirs
antagonisms" (17), and which Marty laments caused, "groups...to turn
their backs on one another and to oppose the idea of any national
common ground (and where) tribalism prevailed." (98). For Marty,
"tribalism" refers to the groups that people belong to as the sole
providers for the harmony and identity needed within their lives, rather
than the nation itself supplying the same.

Today, the elusiveness of America's once great internal fellowship
leaves a huge hole within the commitment toward the achievement of a
common good, and to my way of thinking, produces ever expanding
cracks in the foundation of American social cohesion.

I am reminded here of the contemporary sociologist Robert D.
Putnam and his articles dealing with America's "social capital"—a term
he uses when referring to, "features of our social organization...that
facilitates coordination and cooperation for mutual benefit" (Putnam,
1993, 1) that is, investment and reinvestment in that which promotes
the "public good." Here, Putnam finds that America's agenda regarding
its social capital is mostly "complementary," resulting in a, "social trust
(that) has declined for more than a quarter century." (6). Furthermore,
Putnam goes on to find fault with liberal social policies which tend to
enhance the opportunities of individuals and focus less on the

community—even to the point of, "destroy(ing) some forms of social capital in the name of individual opportunity." (7). In a later and more renowned article entitled "Bowling Alone: America's Declining Social Capital" Putnam develops his argument even further and finds statistical proof of America's waning social capital in the loss of civic participation in everything from church groups, to labor unions, to bowling clubs.

In identifying this trend, Putnam believes that the culprit is an erosion of all forms of social connections brought about by the advent of television which has removed intra- and inter-group connections, and, "inhibit(s) participation...(in) nearly every social activity outside the home." (Putnam, 1996, 47). Though his solutions involve the obvious fact that Americans should get out of the house more often and once again simply spend time together in networks of "associational life" and that this should engender ties of a "horizontal" rather than "vertical" nature, there are those who find Putnam's thesis to be somewhat lacking—myself included.

While I believe television has severely reduced the "quality time" anyone spends with everyone else, and I can envision myself quite possibly "shooting the breeze" with the next door neighbor a bit more if TV had not been invented in the first place, I can't conceive of how switching off the "boob tube" will suddenly foster connections between groups so isolated from each other, that even their TVs speak a different language. I find that television is simply another in a long line of "props" used to wile away the time already created as we slowly separate from each other in pursuit of our personal agendas. That we don't bowl together anymore is more indicative of the fact that we simply don't want anyone else around while we construct our lives rather than, as Putnam suggests, are empty bowling lanes part of the blueprint for the destruction of society as we know it, together with the steady invasion of "Monday Night Football" into our homes—though some sports widows may vociferously refute this last contention.

Furthermore, we have the current findings of Everett Carll Ladd, executive director and president of the Roper Center for Public Opinion Research at the University of Connecticut, who completely disputes Putnam's findings (via various demographic charts and graphs) and states that, "the country's civic life isn't declining, but rather churning, transforming itself to meet modern conditions" (4), and finds evidence of this in the "explosion" of voluntary groups and activities spreading across this nation's towns and cities. Ladd further argues that any reference to a decline in Putnam's social capital is more reflective of, "our persistent anxieties about the quality of our citizenship...blind(ing) us to the many positive trends that have been occurring." (5). However, though Ladd's "charts and graphs" may statistically prove that bodies are filling up the bowling alleys of America—once again, I am not satisfied that anyone really cares at all about anyone else, or that my next door neighbor won't shoot my head off if I lope into his yard to retrieve my bowling ball if it chances to roll there one dark, moonless night. Sorry, but I am still not convinced that all is really A-OK with our society.

Here, I believe Putnam would find Ladd's statistical evidence misleading in the sense that increased membership in, for example the Sierra Club, does not automatically denote a similar rise in human interaction and participation within the club. Being a dues-paying member of the Sierra Club is quite different from attending meetings and actively working within a Sierra cell to improve the environment. I believe many individuals, myself included, join clubs such as this in order to make donations to a worthy cause, then rarely think of their membership until it is time to renew the same. Here, Ladd has the statistics to prove membership has increased, but produces nothing, save a few comments from club representatives, with regard to increases in member participation.

In addition, Ladd does not explain the apparent disparity between the "nation of joiners" he attempts to prove exists in America versus the skyrocketing rates of divorce, crime, and other antisocial activities infecting this country—each quite opposed to the notion of a rise in America's "social capital" and collective cooperation. I'm sure Putnam would like Ladd to explain this obvious contradiction.

Then, in contrast to Ladd, we have the advent of cyberspace and the problems associated with the virtual communities sprouting up around the Internet. As originally conceived these communities were to usher in a new commons, a "virtual" place where many individuals experiencing limited or restricted access to various areas of public dialogue—whether due to gender, age, national origin, or physical appearance—could find a forum for expression and participation.

Proponents of this concept, for example Howard Rhiengold, author of, *The Virtual Community: Homesteading on the Electronic Frontier*, argued that virtual communities: allow people who don't do well in spontaneous spoken interaction time to think about what to say and then offer valuable contributions; create a "third place" or neutral ground which levels all participants to a "condition of social equality," and permit physically handicapped individuals, either confined or excluded from the mainstream community as a result of their disability, to forge new friendships, relationships, and conversations otherwise unavailable to them. Here, Rhiengold sees this new technology as forming rather than destroying our sense of community.

Still, over the years numerous studies have uncovered several underlying problems associated with these cyberspace communities that, in effect, have created quite the opposite of the original intentions. In fact, what has resulted is more the reverse, in that, many individuals have retreated from America's traditional face-to-face communities in favor of engaging in a virtual communal setting on the Internet. In a presentation given to the International Communication Association in May 1995, Jan Fernback and Brad Thompson warned, "CMC (computer-mediated communications such as chat rooms, e-mail, etc.) does not, at this point, hold the promise of enhancing democracy because it promotes communities of interest that are just as narrowly defined as current factions defined by identity (whether it be racial, sexual, or religious). (Website: The Well: Texts).

Furthermore, Fernback and Thompson continued by explaining that virtual communities: reduce the "cohesion of the larger collectivity"; foster anomie, and "reinforce the already fragmented landscape of the public sphere."

In addition, Sherry Turkle, writing in *The American Prospect* found similar problems with these cyberspace communities which she characterized as: creating "the loss of the real"; causing us to forsake our real problems by investing in unreal places, and eliminating the revitalization of community by placing us "alone in our rooms, typing at our networked computer and filling our lives with virtual friends." (Website: Prospect: Archives 24).

Finally, contributing to this confusion regarding the current status of the American community is a study done by Roger Finke, associate professor of sociology at Purdue University, and Rodney Stark, professor of sociology and comparative religion at the University of Washington, entitled, *The Churching of America 1776-1990: Winners and Losers in Our Religious Economy.* The premise here is the reverse of Putnam's, in that Finke and Stark find proof of the *growth* of America's religious "social capital" (as Putnam would put it) over the last one hundred years, from the steady increase of religious participation culled from various sources, mostly census statistics and church membership roles. From this data, the authors seemingly also refute my contention of a strong religious element threaded throughout America's colonial, founding, and national periods. In fact, Finke and Stark quite unabashedly state in the second paragraph of their work that, "America shifted from a nation in which most people took *no* (my emphasis) part in organized religion to a nation in which nearly two thirds of American adults do." (1).

If we rely on Finke and Stark's analysis, the conclusion we may reach is quite opposite to that which I stated early on in this essay and to which Schlesinger attests: namely, that the concept of an "American community"—which was so inherent a part of the founding generation's lives—in fact, no longer exists in modern day America. After all, haven't the authors of this study "proven" that more people go to church today than two hundred years ago, and from this couldn't we find proof for the existence of the American community? Maybe citizens and immigrants don't bowl together anymore, but they sure do spend time together in church and within its related components, such as church organized social functions, community meetings, community assistance programs, and the like.

Yet, the danger with the Finke and Stark study lies in the simple fact that while their data may be statistically accurate, the resulting conclusions drawn from it are erroneous because of the following fatal omission. Here, the great majority of colonial, founding, and national period churches consisted of Protestant denominations, and although church attendance was strongly suggested, there was no doctrinal requirement for any of their members to regularly attend church in order to attain salvation. For example—neither Lutherans, Baptists, Congregationalists, nor Presbyterians mandate church attendance as a means to gain heaven. In fact, as outlined in an earlier chapter of this book, "Religion in America: From God to Godless" adherents to the various forms of Protestantism were encouraged to develop a *personal* relationship with God. Here, Protestant independence and personalization of devotion further fostered the emancipation of the individual from the congregation itself. Moreover, if there was any pressure at all to attend services it probably originated from *social* rather than religious sources. Still, if early Americans were as morally lax as Finke and Stark suggest, then any social pressure would have fallen on deaf ears. Therefore, statistics on church attendance is not an accurate reflection of the degree of religious participation, or commitment within early American culture. Neither, is it indicative of the internal religious convictions of the individuals involved, again a point under contention for Finke and Stark when they audaciously announce that, "Boston's taverns were probably fuller on Saturday night than were its churches on Sunday morning" (23), and admonish us to balance our "nostalgic" images of pious and faithful colonists with, "colonial scenes of drunken revelry and barroom brawling, of women in risqué ball-gowns, of gamblers and rakes...(and of) single women in New England...more likely to be sexually active than to belong to a church." (22).

Secondly, Roman Catholicism does consider regular church attendance at the Sunday Mass to be a necessary component for salvation in accordance with the prescriptions of the third Commandment, that is, to keep holy the Sabbath day. Still, Catholics were but a minority religion within early America and it was not until much later in this nation's history that Catholicism grew to become a major religious institution within this country. Therefore, statistics of those attending church services would naturally increase due to the mandatory nature of the same upon all Catholics and in direct proportion to the rise of Catholicism within America. Of course, not all Catholics attended church despite the third Commandment however, the fact is that many did because of it.

Here, Finke and Stark would find less church attendance in the early Protestant dominated years of our history and more attendance once Catholicism spread throughout the American population. Therefore, a study involving either the lack, or proof of participation in religion within America's population during any given time based heavily upon church attendance statistics is meaningless given the above. Furthermore, for Finke and Stark to consider that the, "faith (of colonial Americans) lack(ing) public expression and organized influence" (23), was somehow then indicative of an era of less religious involvement than we customarily associate with the same era is, once again, useless given the above explanation.

Perhaps statistics involving the proportion of those individuals within a given population who regularly frequent taverns and/or engage in barroom brawling, and/or sales of risqué gowns and those women who actually wear them, and/or rising crime rates, etc. would be a more accurate reflection of the religiosity of that population than the sole reliance on church attendance. It would be of note that if figures involving all these questionable activities are proportionally high and church attendance is down, then one *may* conclude that religiosity is waning. In any case, a more multidimensional statistical model is required in order to determine a population's religiosity that that singular compass employed by Finke and Stark.

So, what is the point I wish to make here? Quite obviously that for any given study (e.g. Putnam, Ladd, Finke and Stark, and no doubt hundreds of others) the statistical data can be skewed or interpreted to reach quite different, even diametrically opposed conclusions. Therefore, evidence to uncover proof of the loss of the "American community"—that is, the dwindling fellowship among Americans once joined in the collective pursuit of a common good and the realization of a shared interest—from a once healthy component of early American life to one of relative nonexistence within modern American culture, requires avenues of evidence from other sources and topics. I believe this "evidence" must be extrapolated from those philosophical reorientations which evolved over the course of this nation's history and affected not only our society's collective thinking, but its direction as well.

In this sense, this book sought to offer a credible explanation for the major changes in the American community since its founding, through a detailed examination of what I consider to be those "philosophical reorientations" having had the most permutational impact upon that community, namely: individualism; modern liberalism, and changes in the importance and involvement of religion within the lives of Americans. In addition, this book also sought to explain the collective effect this triumvirate had upon the overall moral framework of this nation, and the resulting far-reaching consequences this has had upon both our individual and collective interactions. Hence the title of this book: *Changes in American Morality: Of The People; By The People; For The Self.*

In Etzioni's analysis of the loss of the traditional community (i.e. crisscrossing and reinforcing relationships among individuals and commitments to shared values, norms, meanings, history, and identity) within America, especially during the latter half of the twentieth century—he refers to the "liberating" effect many small town individuals felt once they left their communities and moved to the "big cities." There, "the atmosphere was said to set people free (as) anonymity would allow each person to pursue what he or she wished rather than what the community dictated." (*The Spirit of Community* 116-17). Here, a "rampant individualism" followed as towns and cities swelled with people infused with, "the mood of self-centered 'making it.'" (118).

That we again find individualism linked with the withering of social bonds within this country is, to my way of thinking, no mere coincidence. In fact, I find this same contention mentioned in almost every source cited throughout this book. Here then, must be a strong bit of evidence which points to individualism as a major contributing cause for the changing patterns in our culture with regard to the conception of the "American community."

Needless to say, the basic principle of individualism is the focus on the needs and satisfaction of the "self"—the complete antithesis of the communal or "common" good. I believe it is safe to say that more of the latter would be found within a traditional community (as defined by Etzioni) than within a population of self-oriented individuals. So, let us say that individualism is exhibit (A) in this case involving the loss of the American community.

Next, I offer into evidence the social philosophy of modern liberalism. Many sources, including William J. Bennett and Alan Wolfe to name but a few, indicate that adherents of modern liberalism exhibit scorn for what Bennett refers to as the "traditional underpinnings of American society" and which Wolfe interchangeably labels the "values of middle-class morality." That Bennett links these "traditional underpinnings" with America's sense of community and Wolfe considers "middle-class morality" to be reflective of the basic values of the American community, seems indicative of another cause for the loss of that community. That is, if each of these so scorned concepts were removed from the fabric of our society, then the existing structure of the American community itself would alter or be replaced. Furthermore, that modern liberalism has for decades been a highly influential social philosophy within all aspects of American culture clearly points to another culpable source for the demise of the American community characterized by Bennett, Wolfe, and many other credible sources. Therefore, I now enter exhibit (B): modern liberalism.

The final evidence offered here is: changes in the importance and involvement of religion within the lives of Americans. This country's Christian roots established what many sources consider to be a "civic religion" which was threaded throughout America's social and legal systems for nearly two hundred years. According to Thiemann, this allowed for a common ground between the political and religious spheres within our society, "(which) provide(d) a common rhetorical and ideological context for the development of public policies (and) (n)otions of citizenship, civic virtue, and public service...(and where) the raw material from which a sense of public virtue emerged." (32).

However, over the last fifty years the influx of so many divergent cultures and ideologies found this underlying "civic religion" to be increasingly less representative of this country's different belief systems, resulting in a steady loss of this religious element within our society. In addition, Thiemann goes on to state that less this religious orientation, "the moral context for public decision making became fluid and ambiguous" (34), and also cites this lack of religion as causing the development of what sociologists refer to as the rise of America's "three disestablishments" that is, legal, religious, and moral.

The first involves the current controversial interpretations regarding the religious clause of the first amendment and the resulting withering of the, "symbolic power of our culturally established religion, Protestant Christianity." (34). The second refers to the fragmentation of our civic piety and the waning of the dominance of what Thiemann calls our "cultural Protestantism" which formerly fostered, "remarkable cooperation among communities of faith (which) burst asunder...during the late 1960s." (35). The third was spawned by, "(t)raditional religious differences combined with political disagreement (which created) (d)ivisions within the American body politic (which) rendered America's civic faith incapable of providing the common principles for personal and public morality." (35).

That all "three disestablishments" involve elements of a religious nature, testify to the once seemingly inexorable strength of the role of religion within America's notions of the common good, public welfare, public consciousness, and public life. Here, Thiemann argues that the removal of this religious element from the public forum has so seriously affected America's associational life, national identity, and common enterprise that, "we are experiencing an atrophy of citizenship (and) a serious decline in the vitality of civil society." (152-53).

Hence, I enter the waning of religion as exhibit (C) in this case involving the loss of the American community.

The collective effect this triumvirate of individualism, modern liberalism, and changes in the importance and involvement of religion within the lives of Americans has had, has been most significant within the realm of both public and private moral integrity. In addition, the inconsistency between a self-centered, autonomously oriented, and irreligious social direction and that of a national community engaged in the pursuit of the common good is quite apparent.

Here, when the moral nature of a people becomes fixated within a foundation of the satisfaction of the independent self, and the entire social collective orients its direction toward the accomplishment of the same, and references to the moral are more oblique considerations of that which we can accomplish for ourselves in the achievement of an untrammeled personal gratification—then the result in invariably moral uncertainty. In addition, this moral uncertainty, according to Friedman and Squire, is the direct result of an uneasy pluralism within the United States which is, "not the tolerant exchange of viewpoints that agree to differ. It is, rather, a troubled coexistence of incompatible opinions, a babble of unmatched voices." (6).

Furthermore, although Friedman and Squire admit that within a liberal democracy it becomes increasingly more difficult to develop a moral consensus, they go on to link much of the twentieth century's most negative events (e.g. the First and Second World War, Nazism, Auschwitz, McCarthyism, the Vietnam War, the assassinations of John F. Kennedy and Martin Luther King, Jr., Watergate, Irangate, and the 1995 Oklahoma City bombing) with "breaks in moral certainty" (10) and our modern tendency toward moral relativism, which Friedman and Squire suggest is a, "prelude to a postmorality...(that may) give rise to an antidemocratic morality resting on individual or state power." (17).

In another sense, our moral uncertainty is the result of a suspicion generated among individuals and groups resulting from the absence of social norms which induce people to live together in peace, despite humankind's legacy of war and other atrocities which act quite contrary to peaceably living together. According to James Q. Wilson, "(t)hose (social) norms are part of a collective consciousness that produces...varying degrees of solidarity." (14). Lacking the same creates conflict, and burgeoning unresolved conflict can lead to anarchy and ultimately the breakdown of a civilized society. Many high ranking religious leaders from around the world have echoed this concern, such as Pope John Paul II who warned that freedom without values and without God is anarchy.

As our social bonds deteriorate due to the segmentation of the American community—not only from the vast cultural differences among individuals and groups, but from the myriad of subjective moral systems within our social collective—has this nation lost any hope of achieving cohesion? As we pay inordinate attention to the community of "one" that we are challenged to be, and as Charles Taylor observed, "puts the autonomous individual at the centre (sic) of our system of law" (195), have we already begun to disassemble ourselves into an atomistic society whereby all activity is reduced to local motion, or is part of the reality postulated by Bertrand Russell which is composed of independently existing objects?

All this is reminiscent of Freud's tripartite division of the personality into the id, ego, and superego. The first is our instinctual impulses seeking immediate gratification, which are tempered into socially expedient modes of achieving the same by the ego, which in turn are controlled through the moral scruples of the superego—that is, the conscience. However, I have found that the tenets of individualism and modern liberalism appeal primarily to the ego, not only in the Freudian sense, but in the bolstering of our excessive need for self-importance and the furthering of that conception of ourselves to appear to others to be masters of our personal universe. Needless to say, within this structure, moral scruples involving right and wrong, conscience, and religion are mostly out of place.

I believe the case I have presented strongly suggests that by choosing the supremacy of the "self" we are increasingly losing our social cohesion; dismantling the last vestiges of the American community, and have severely reduced the possibility of reconstructing the same. However, I would like to offer some possible solutions.

In order to regain our former sense of fellowship I propose the following, some of which I have already mentioned at the conclusion of the fifth chapter.

A) the National Social Morality Project (or NSMP)—in an effort to extract a true consensus of the moral and social norms with which to orient our society and achieve a more collectively defined "common good" for all groups within American society, let us implement a nationwide internet/telephone/mail survey which would accumulate the data needed to identify not only the needs to be addressed, but the structure and process by which this effort could be accomplished. Here, the goal is to begin that dialogue amongst and between all of America's diverse religious and secular institutions and traditions, à la the proposals advanced by Marty and Eck, which would thereby create a truly open and inclusive public forum seeking to extract solutions rather than disagreements; commonality rather than separation; concern rather than suspicion.

Although some may say that our responses to this survey may serve only to reflect the dominating effects of our self-centered individualism, I would rather we begin with at least this point established and then proceed toward extracting solutions to this problem, then do nothing at all and allow our modern society to further deteriorate through selfishness.

B) Communitarianism Plus (or C+)—Amitai Etzioni has spent a lifetime developing the Communitarian movement which, "seek(s) a way to blend elements of tradition (order based on virtues) with elements of modernity (well-protected autonomy)...an equilibrium between universal individual rights and the common good...between self and the community, and above all how such an equilibrium can be achieved and sustained." (*The New Golden Rule* xviii).

This all-encompassing proposal is, to my way of thinking, closest to the position necessary to bring stability and social order to our nation, and realign ourselves with many of the original positions upon which this country was founded. It allows the individual to retain his/her individuality within the larger scheme of public life less the isolation and self-absorption generated by individualism, through the development of strong communal ties. It is a wide enough system to embrace all facets of this diverse American society through the melding of tradition and the modern. It acknowledges the fact that there are excesses in both the conservative and liberal positions however, through the development of a set of "core values" citizens can strike a healthy balance between the two and therefore develop a "third social philosophy" with which to orient our nation.

I am hard pressed to find fault with Etzioni's position, so let it be noted that I prefer to consider the following merely improvements of his themes. I believe if these improvements were implemented, the Communitarian position would be vastly more appealing to a greater number of Americans and better representative of its highly pluralistic nature, hence the designation: Communitarianism Plus, or C+.

In seeking to align traditional and modern values, I am disturbed by Etzioni's conclusion that, "religious values are a good example of the kind of values that need not be shared by all." (*The New Golden Rule* 92). While I can surely understand his concerns over the excesses and fanaticism of the Inquisition and religious fundamentalism throughout the world, including the West (to cite those examples Etzioni mentions)—I simply find it rather impossible to extract religion from the value system Etzioni proposes, or any system that seeks to include a moral framework into its foundation—a fact I have steadfastly maintained throughout this book.

In my opinion, by minimizing the role of religious principles in the formation of moral order, Etzioni's quest for the establishment of "shared values" runs the risk of once again allowing for the removal of religion from the public forum through the preponderance of the secular agenda Etzioni proposes within the Communitarian paradigm. "Shared values" will most certainly involve enormous amounts of religion in their structure since the underlying foundation of many values, if not most, are set within the matrix of religious principles. I simply do not agree with Etzioni's conclusion regarding religion. In fact, I find that, as Thiemann noted, this could eventually leave those citizens of faith excluded from the national discourse and forced to participate in an "artificial unity" by being relegated to the fringes of the public dialogue. All this due to fears related to past actions of the Inquisition and concerns over today's fundamentalist fanaticism. Even worse, once again it leaves the authority of a Supreme Being removed from human affairs and the power of the state as the sole determinant of society's direction—this despite the Communitarian opposition to the domination of our society by its larger organizational structures. By rendering religion a value "that need not be shared by all" Etzioni has effectively sentenced religion to the realm of what Carter complained was, "the arbitrary and unimportant." (6). Hence, I believe the Communitarian platform would be greatly strengthened if religious values would be included as an integral part of its position. Of course how to arrive at a set of religious values could be achieved at through the National Social Morality Project (NSMP) mentioned earlier.

Secondly, as the Bellah team noted in, *The Good Society*, "communitarians are opposed to the state, the economy, and all larger structures that so largely dominate our life today" (6), and are in favor of face-to-face solutions involving families, congregations, and neighborhoods. Here, I agree with the team's conclusion, that is, that this position is deficient given the fact that the ever-increasing problems of our contemporary social life invariably include, and is particularly dominated by, those "larger structures." In this respect, to maintain the current Communitarian position is rather simplistic given the complexity and vastness of our society. Furthermore, by limiting itself to the local level, I believe the Communitarian approach is rendered too narrow a notion to produce widespread and lasting change within the whole of American society, despite its claim to accomplish the same less the incorporation of those "larger structures." Local change would result, but I doubt anything beyond that, and surely not on a national level, given the above.

C) Reevaluate Individualism/Reconsider Liberalism (or RIRL— [pronounced "real"])—I can make no stronger point for the adoption of this agenda than that which this entire book represents. Therefore, I ask: How can we as a nation continue to maintain a policy of the supremacy and satisfaction of the self as that basic constituent of our social collective, when the nature of that collective was founded on, is steeped in, and has been organized and oriented towards an association engaged in the achievement of a common good? To my mind, this is a complete contradiction, not only of terms, but also of direction. The philosophy of individualism can no more promote the social health of this nation, than can a scattering of leaves be considered growing a tree. As Ladd pointed out, there are growing frustrations within this country with regard to individualism, leading many to condemn its principles. He acknowledges individualism's far-reaching influence within the United States and further testifies that to avoid its "dark side" we must develop, "a more elevated sense of what individuals can accomplish when they accept the responsibilities of citizenship and work together more constructively." (155).

Secondly, the other half of my equation is to "Reconsider Liberalism" and by "liberalism" I refer to modern liberalism. As is the case with all human endeavors that become extremely one-sided and severely excessive, the inevitable result is a society engaged in a host of constant and emerging vices which John Cowles Professor of Government at Harvard University, Judith N. Shklar considered, "more a recipe for survival than a project for the perfectibility of mankind." (4). That she finds this to be the case within liberal democracies testifies further to my contention of the need to reconsider the true advantages of a society dominated by the philosophy of liberalism. She further accuses liberalism of hypocrisy in that it has fallen short of its original moral goal of eliminating oppression through progress and instead has cultivated a host of, "politicians who habitually promise more than they can deliver, who profess beliefs they do not hold, and whose moral pretensions are intolerable." (67). For Shklar, liberalism has put, "enormous burdens of choice upon all of us (which are) very demanding" (248), and in the end causes us to abandon, "certainty and agreement as goals worthy of free people." (249). In summary, Shklar concludes, "liberalism imposes extraordinary ethical difficulties on us: to live with contradictions, unresolved conflicts, and a balancing between public and private imperatives which are neither opposed to nor at one with each other." (249).

Throughout my investigation of the influence and effects of modern liberalism on American society, perhaps the most pervasive problem with its precepts is the contradictions it engenders between: social requirements and individual satisfaction; government involvement and independent human "autonomies"; civic duty and private objectives, and moral responsibility and personal pleasure. In each of these antipodes, within our society today it is modern liberalism's singular purpose to promote the latter case much to the detriment of the former.

Of course, just as Etzioni admonished, my equal concern here is primarily with the excesses of individualism and modern liberalism that have so engulfed our society and brought it to its current state of moral confusion and social instability. Again, I believe the first step towards extracting solutions is through dialogue and consensus, both of which I firmly sense can be accomplished through the NSMP. Together, we have our best chance of achieving stasis in this matter, that is, a balance among the diversity of our systems and equilibrium between their competing agendas.

D) Reintroduce Religion (or R2)—as outlined within the first two chapters of this book, I, along with so many learned individuals within this country and in all aspects of life, consider this nation's excessive preoccupation with the exclusion of religion from the public forum and the maintenance of a strict and high wall of separation between church and state—as it is now interpreted—to be an artificially contrived construction; contrary to the foundations of this country, and quite simply wrong.

Despite those who maintain that religion is a private concern and therefore not to be included in the public dialogue on the grounds that it is "invisible" and "inaccessible" to external scrutiny, I maintain, along with Thiemann, that, "religious convictions...do not differ in kind or in function from the fundamental commitments that orient the lives of nonreligious persons" (155), such as, for example, freedom, love, and justice. Therefore, just as any human expression of thinking, or system of knowledge is open to scrutiny, and is engaged in public affairs, so too must religion occupy a likewise status. Furthermore, since religion reflects much of the moral values with which humanity has oriented its social structures since we "descended from the trees," excluding it from the public arena, as is the inevitable result of many of this country's policies and legal decisions, or at best assigning it to the fringes of our public dialogue where its voice is barely audible, lessens the validity of the framework with which we direct human activity. Here, the point is not to elevate any one particular religious faith, but to arrive at a synthesis of religious thought with which to define a common moral purpose for America.

Added to this is the condemnation of violence expressed by the majority of this country's religious traditions which often stands in stark contrast to actions ordinarily considered appropriate by the secular state. For example, in the *Religion and Ethics Newsweekly* broadcast of April 17, 1999, Rev. Richard John Neuhaus, Editor of *First Things*, represented the Roman Catholic position; and Rabbi David

Saperstein of the Religious Action Center of Reform Judaism, expressed the fundamental Jewish position. Each spoke equally with regard to what constitutes a "just" war, specifically the recent conflict in Kosovo. Here, both speakers upheld their religion's conviction that some of the conditions to be met in this regard are: that there must be a reasonable chance of success; that there is a swift resolution, and that one does not promote undue human suffering. Yet, the prolonged and seemingly excessive bombing of Kosovo had in effect not only created the opposite effect of these stated conditions, but caused massive refugee problems and tremendous hardships and suffering for millions of innocent people. In this sense, both religious traditions represented here strongly objected to the perpetuation of this violent action and the furtherance of human suffering, yet little of these concerns had any effect on that violent action which continued for months with minimal reduction. Perhaps if the positions, or proposals for peace stated by these and other religious traditions were taken more seriously, or fully and equally included within the ongoing political negotiations, that conflict would have been resolved much sooner. However, there was little indication in the abundance of daily media reports that the nonviolent alternatives offered by the various religious traditions were ever seriously considered, or that their objections and opinions regarding what constitutes a "just" war were ever truly included in the political dialogue.

My contention here is that although leaders from all camps voiced their opposition to the Kosovo bombing and offered their alternatives for a peaceful solution, the public dialogue, which was delivered and/or broadcast to our homes daily, rarely treated those religiously oriented possibilities as equally viable options. This was made obvious and apparent by the paltry few references made within the media to the religious position, yet those of military advisors, politicians, and other secular pundits dominated the airwaves and this nation's plethora of print publications. In addition, that there was even a religious position at all could only be determined by chancing upon it within a few public television programs, or found as part of the opening monologue of some late-night talk show host.

Why? I believe it is the direct result of the domination of a political agenda which seeks levels of persuasion involving force, either real or implied, via this country's military might—and the inherently pacifistic religious approach is completely antithetical to this agenda. Since this reliance on force has worked almost every time for America, and the machinery of government, etc. are conditioned to react militarily to perceived or actual threats—peaceful solutions emanating from religious sources are rarely considered viable or practical. Thus, the religious position is effectively ignored, rarely seriously discussed, and even silenced.

Equally related to religion's potential to counteract these types of violent excesses are the comments of the founder of the International Peace Research Institute, Johan Galtung, who advised in a speech to UNESCO in 1994, "(l)et us now proceed more systematically by exploring the peace potential of the religions." (*Cross Currents* Winter 1997-98, 439). Within the remainder of the article in which this quote appears, Galtung calls upon humanity to engage in a, "theological dialogue (whereby) religious messages (can) be understood in a way that makes them maximally peace productive." (449).

Here, in appealing to UNESCO members to consider the "peace potential of the religions," Galtung echoes the concerns of many who feel that the removal of religion from the public forum leaves unheard religious prescriptions for anti-violent solutions, and negates religion's role as a potential mediator in difficult social situations that threaten to erupt into violence. This is not to imply that this country's secular state prefers, or promotes violence, however there are often times where the state's parallel path of extracting peaceful solutions is paved far less extensively than that path our religious traditions follow.

With this in mind, we must realize that in our search for truth and an understanding of the human condition, religion is equally engaged in the same process. However, as Thiemann noted, to pick and choose those arguments that we will allow into the public sphere in effect violates this country's notion of free speech. Therefore, the continued elimination of religion from participating in the public forum stands in direct contradiction to one of this country's most basic principles.

Allowing religion entry into the public forum does not constitute state involvement with religion, or vice versa, but rather simply permits the voices of people of faith to be heard within, "the pluralistic conversation that constitutes a liberal democracy." (Thiemann 167). In addition, religion offers alternative conceptions, interpretations, and meanings to those arrived at by our dominant secular culture, and as such, can constructively participate in both the criticisms, conclusions, and solutions reached in the continued effort to further advance our society.

We must cease ignoring the huge impact religion has on public affairs by our continual engagement in policies of exclusion. Religion must be allowed full and equal entry into the national dialogue. Although there have been some advancements made in this direction, I find most very similar to taking two steps forward and one step back. I believe that through the efforts and results of the NSMP consensus, America will undoubtedly rediscover its religious voice and once again allow it to speak.

In returning to the theme expressed throughout this chapter, that is, the need to regenerate a sense of community within America, the four "solutions" I have proposed and discussed above have the distinct underlying and unifying matter of religion threaded throughout each. To my way of thinking, this inclusion of religion is inescapable, and the reliance on religion to foster a resurgence of the American community is not only obvious, it is logical. Here, almost all of this country's religious traditions are intrinsically social and community oriented.

Although there are some that act contrary to this orientation, I find them to be more aberrations to this universal theme.

Therefore, as Americans steadily divorce themselves from their local and national community in their pursuit of the self through the ethos of individualism and modern liberalism's call for personal autonomy, it is quite apparent that religion stands completely diametric to these self-satisfying proposals. Here, I believe it is as natural as the tendency of light to eliminate darkness, for religion to redirect Americans toward a refocusing of their energies from the destructive preoccupation with themselves, in favor of one which involves constructing a new sense of the American community given the demands of the modern era, and a rebuilding of community involvement based upon the traditional values upon which this country was founded.

Of equal consideration here, and as maintained so often throughout this book, religion and moral principles involving right and wrong are inexorably intertwined. Therefore, it is inevitable that as religion enters into the public forum, questions involving human morality increase. That morality occupies a vital role in the social health of our communities, and that individualism acts contrary to this condition, is definitively expressed by Etzioni throughout his work. For example:

> The incontestable fact about human nature is that the good and virtuous character of those who have acquired it tends to degrade. If left to their own devices, going through the routine of life, individuals gradually lose much of their commitment to values—unless these are continuously reinforced. A major sociological function of the community as a building block of the moral infrastructure, is to reinforce the character of individuals...In general, the weaker the community...the thinner the social web and the slacker the moral voice. (*The New Golden Rule* 187.)

Furthermore, Etzioni goes on to state that churches, synagogues, and mosques are those associations that, "make much more room for the moral voice than many other voluntary associations do." (188).

That modern liberalism promotes a system of relatively conceived notions of good and bad as superior to that which involves moral principles of right and wrong, is apparent from the details outlined in the fifth chapter of this book. That these liberal notions have contributed to, if not caused, America's current moral degeneracy and secular hedonism is, to me, equally apparent.

It is my firm and unequivocal conclusion that a renaissance of the American community would soon follow, if the severe antisocial, self-satisfying tenets of individualism and modern liberalism are reviewed and reduced, and the important involvement of religion within America's public life is both recognized and realized. Here, not only would individual isolation be markedly diminished, and the social and cultural separatism and fragmentation experienced by so many settled and arriving groups be significantly decreased, but all will begin to experience a commonality in orientation through the fostering of a fellowship geared toward the achievement of a truly *common* good— instead of the current heterogeneity which emphasizes adherence to independent groupings of moral codes, rather than to one more collectively achieved and oriented. In addition, that *common* good would take on new and valuable dimensions spurred by the realization that not only are we a united people, but that we share a *common* moral heritage of core values and beliefs emanating from the reality of the existence of a Supreme Being, who is acutely aware of, and intimately involved in human affairs. That we are, as was once repeated daily throughout America's communities in our Pledge of Allegiance, "one nation under God."

This project emerged from two sources. The first developed from an increasingly uncomfortable feeling that most of us are truly unconcerned with the lives of those outside that closed and select group of people we surround ourselves with, namely family and very close friends. Added to this is the fact that from years of personal experiences and observations, I have been left both saddened and puzzled over the growing apathy, insensitivity, and downright selfish behavior we humans have exhibited towards not only those unconnected to our daily lives, but to many of our most intimate relationships as well. Secondly, the roots of this project found fertile soil in the equally uncomfortable sense that many of us equate God with mythical figures such as Santa Claus, or the Big Bad Wolf—and rarely find God relevant to anything that we do; that religion is more often than not last in our lives, if at all, and thinking in moral terms will most probably stop us from killing each other, but rarely would it deter us from cheating on our taxes; pilfering items from our jobs, or avoiding all those "little white lies."

I believe in an inherent, inner goodness within the vast majority of human beings; however, that goodness seems to emerge only when coaxed to the surface by atypical events ranging from the somewhat common: helping someone move their overheated car off the road, to the more extraordinary: saving someone's life. Yet, I find this inner goodness lies usually dormant in the everyday, ordinary, uneventful occurrences that cross our paths each day, such as: doing a good job despite the obnoxious boss/the low pay/the lazy co-worker; giving up our seat on a crowded bus for the elderly or infirm; letting the other person have his/her say; putting our concerns on hold while another's more pressing need is accomplished, or simply being pleasant to people outside of our normal, daily experience. I find it sad and disquieting that unless the call is pressing, most of us could care less about others.

I have found that this impassivity has been acquired as a learned response stemming from the emotionally desensitizing effect many of our modern social and cultural practices have had upon individuals. In my opinion, the most culpable of these practices is the diminished moral standard so widespread throughout America today. This is apparent in the increased tendency, especially in the media, to depict as commonplace behavior and/or having an entertainment value, exhibitions of, and references to violence, sexual promiscuity, criminal behavior, drugs, hedonism, deviant behavior, and the like—either actual or contrived. Most relevant here is the fact that it has been widely reported in several behavioral studies over the years, that people exposed to inordinate amounts of stimuli eventually build up levels of tolerance to that stimuli. This finding, known as sensory adaptation, has been noted in both physical and psychological testing procedures. In this sense, as we are further bombarded by much of the antisocial activities stated above, and an entertainment value is often attached to the same, we invariably become conditioned to an internal lessening of our own personal moral evaluations—that is, we tend to express less objection, and/or become increasingly indifferent to those actions and behaviors which we previously found to be offensive, or repulsive simply because we have become used to their appearance. In addition, the included entertainment factor of these actions and behaviors has the augmented effect of attaching a certain amount of pleasure to them, which we then associate with enjoyment. Often without realizing it, once the duality of the frequency of the antisocial activity and its potential entertainment/enjoyment factor become steadily reinforced, we begin to feel little to no objection to these actions and behaviors, and our previous moral evaluations, which included being offended or feeling revulsion, disappear. This phenomenon manifests itself in a continued tolerance of these activities, which results in the desensitizing effect mentioned earlier. Not only do we become further immune to the implications and outcome of these actions, but our sense of moral evaluation becomes confused and progressively stunted. When whole populations experience this effect, their collectively conceived moral field begins to wither. I find this to be the current state of American society.

Within this state, a great many Americans are crying out for orientation, and although many educators, intellectuals, and politicians (primarily members of the liberal camp) proclaim the supremacy of "the separation of church and state"—there are those who feel otherwise. In an appearance on a *Religion and Ethics Newsweekly* broadcast of January 2, 1999, Phyllis Tickle, author and contributing editor of religion for *Publishers Weekly*; Peter Steinfels, of Georgetown University who also writes the "Belief" column for *The New York Times*, and Martin E. Marty, author, professor, and director of the Public Religion Project—all agreed that in light of America's then recent political battles and scandals there is an even greater need for both public and private moral guidance within this country. In fact, there was general agreement among the three that this moral guidance should come from our religious institutions. Here, Tickle specifically stated that the churches must continually revivify their efforts to guide humanity using the "old yardstick" of the Ten Commandments whereby individuals sinned not only against God, but society as well. This thinking is apparently not limited to Tickle, since on June 17, 1999 the House of Representatives voted to allow the Ten Commandments to be displayed in public buildings, which prompted Rep. Robert Aderholt to observe, "it is an important step to promote morality." (Newsday 18 June 1999, A5).

Furthermore, and in contrast to those who support a strict separation of church and state, is the fact that on a *Religion and Ethics Newsweekly* broadcast of September 25, 1999 it was stated that recent polls indicated that 64 percent of Americans think the country's moral and cultural values have changed for the worse since the 1960s. In addition, the remainder of the show explored the rise of "religiosity" and "God-talk" that came from the then current crop of potential presidential candidates which apparently was being made in response to the sentiments expressed in those same polls. Those candidates included George W. Bush, Al Gore, and former presidential contender Elizabeth Dole, and each had sprinkled "God-talk" into their campaign speeches. In commenting on this development, Richard Hutchinson, scholar and presidential historian, and John Green, of the University of Akron, attributed it to the fact that given the social problems and political scandals throughout America today, once again, people feel that in moral terms we are cast adrift.

The purpose of all this is to affirm that there is a hunger in this country for God, religion, and moral orientation that is rarely covered by the traditional media who, in my opinion, promote a liberal agenda devoid of these topics. However, if one steps beyond these traditional sources of information there is apparently quite a difference of opinion among many Americans from all walks of life regarding the exclusion of these topics from the public dialogue. In fact, in an apparent response to the above, the Supreme Court agreed to begin hearings in April 2000 on the subject of prayer within public schools which has been banned for an entire generation of school children since the landmark 1962 Court ruling. (*Newsday* 16 November 1999, A4). Why? Because there have been many cases cropping up across the land where young people today, craving some form of God or religion in their lives, have spontaneously prayed in class or at school functions (e.g. graduation ceremonies and sporting events) and where in a case involving the Supreme Court, student led prayer preceded a Santa Fe High School football game. All of these actions have taken place much to the consternation and protestations of school officials. This of course does not include those teachers and educators who genuinely want, but are forbidden to help nurture the spiritual and moral needs of their students.

This new generation of Americans is apparently fed up with the atheist direction this country has taken, especially since the end of World War II. Their interest in God and religion is made obvious by newspaper reports of, "tens of thousands of young people" in attendance throughout all the stops Pope John Paul II has made in the United States over the last few years, and their "cheering enthusiastically" for his message of sexual responsibility, together with his condemnation of abortion, and assisted suicide. (*New York Post* 28 January 1999, 28). This hunger for God, religion, and moral orientation is apparently also behind Baptist minister William Murray's call for the return of school prayer. (*Newsday* 18 April 1999, A39). What makes Murray's comments significant is that when 17, his objection to school prayer prompted his mother Madalyn Murray O'Hair to file a lawsuit in Maryland that helped end school prayer in this country. William Murray then went on to lead American Atheists Inc., but later renounced atheism and became a Christian.

Regarding spontaneous and voluntary public prayer that is not dictated, encouraged, restrained, censured, sponsored, funded, taught, or promoted by government, or specifically organized by government solely for a religious purpose, it is my opinion that it should be allowed expression as an extension of one's profundity regarding one's religious belief. In this sense, these prayerful gestures in no way violates the secular position of separation of church and state, but rather simply recognizes one's right to religious expression as guaranteed by the Bill of Rights. Nowhere in this country's foundational documents, and neither was it ever decreed since, that gestures of religious expression were to take place behind closed doors, or solely in a private setting. The dangerous precedent here is that, in this case, if young people are banned from offering a spontaneous prayer for the success of their favorite football team, would policing public events follow to assure that no prayers are said? Would people then not be allowed to publicly call upon God for assistance in difficult, stressful, or emotionally wrenching situations? The implications here are profound, and have caused many, including our young, to wonder how and why America evolved into a seemingly atheistic nation.

Indicative of the disgust many have expressed regarding this sentiment is perhaps the reaction to the Clinton sexual scandal which apparently has had a much more profound impact on this country's moral fiber than was at first realized. Here, even the Clinton apology and request for forgiveness from the American public for the scandal was not only met with skepticism among a wide range of Americans regarding the depth of its sincerity, but many expressed exasperation over the distinct possibility that it was more politically than morally motivated. In addition, appearing on the *Religion and Ethics Newsweekly* broadcast of November 20, 1998, Professor Robert Jewett of Garrett Theological Seminary in Evanston, Illinois expressed some of the deeper questions raised with regard to Clinton's broadcast apology. According to Jewett—who represented the views of eighty-five religion scholars who signed "The Declaration Concerning Religion, Ethics, and the Crisis in the Clinton Presidency"—the concept of, "forgiveness...(has) been misunderstood in this circumstance in such a way that it impedes our ability to grapple...with the underlying issue of honesty, fairness and not lying." Here, Jewett goes on to explain that an apology is a secular condition, but forgiveness is between oneself and God. He continued by stating that the public cannot forgive, only God forgives, and in this sense Clinton's broadcast plea for forgiveness was not without political implications. Here, the intention was to influence public opinion. In summary, Jewett stated that: Clinton confessed on camera, but offered no responsibility for his actions, and in doing so promotes the premise that once you confess sins, there are no further consequences. The final conclusion drawn by the scholars Jewett represented is that we have been "seduced" by a false, preposterous, and irresponsible notion of forgiveness of sins which has obscured the underlying moral issue regarding this type of sexual misconduct, and misrepresented the religious position regarding truthfulness and the consequences of lying.

In addition, I have found it interesting to note that the concept of morality never arose in Clinton's explanations and confession regarding his ongoing adulterous sexual dalliances, yet this same concept was raised quite often by Clinton to justify our intervention in Kosovo and the waging of a "moral" war. In fact, appearing in several periodicals were the observations of Benjamin Schwarz, former executive editor of *World Policy Journal,* who in questioning our involvement in Kosovo stated, "Bill Clinton has often spoken of America's moral force as born of this country's 'founding ideals.' " (*Newsday* 20 April 1999, A33). To which I add, then why is this "moral force" behind our "founding ideals" ignored, for example, with regard to the issue of school prayer, or religious involvement in the public forum? Have we become a nation of individuals selectively employing morality for personal purposes, much like a tool to be used in different situations to fit one's particular needs?

It seems part of the answer to this question lies in the sentiments expressed by Michael Kelly in an article entitled "How Clinton Saved Liberalism" (*New York Post* 17 November 1999, 45). Here, Kelly criticizes the Clinton reworking of the liberal Democratic manifesto by rejecting most of liberalism's "least popular features" and embracing many of those associated with the conservative Republican idealism favored by the Ronald Reagan/George H. W. Bush era, such as radical welfare reform, mandatory-minimum drug sentencing, "more cruel" anti-crime measures, a mercantile approach to international relations, balancing the budget, and tax hikes. Furthermore, "as has been noted by political students from both the right and the left...the cumulative effect of Clinton's triangulation has been to fashion a new liberalism (essentially, a sub-urban liberalism) with mainstream appeal." (45).

It is obvious to me that to attain and sustain power, Clinton would have adopted any position and said anything, be it an apology, a public confession, a "moral" stance to war, or the philosophies of others. Clinton knew what Americans wanted and gave it to them even if it meant constantly changing his hat. Therefore, the "new liberalism," Clinton fashioned relegated this country's "moral force" to the back burner by adopting whatever stance Clinton deemed necessary in order to promote those actions favorable to his public position, furthering his political interests, and advancing his philosophical agenda.

Of course, all these developments involving God, school prayer and the moral direction of our society encompass one of the most powerful institutions ever known to humanity: religion. It is an undeniable fact, and one the Founders were acutely aware of, that despite its sublime intentions, religion can, and most certainly has been, used negatively—even abusively. How then can we guard against this possibility? The answer is not that we simply eradicate religious influence from our society by laws and legislation, or relegate it to the fringes of American life by adopting a public posture which suggests a diminishment of its importance. Surely, we would not ban religion just as we would not allow government support of any single religion. Rather, through a united initiative seeking a synthesis of accumulated knowledge and philosophy via, for example, my proposal for the establishment of the National Social Morality Project, America might find a way to: define a general moral code which would satisfy all traditions; find a parallel path upon which government and religion can equally travel, and quite possibly allow religious principles involving right and wrong to regain their place within this country's civil life. If the Founders wanted religion to function only in the private setting they would not have instituted a system of self-government whereby the ultimate power of government changed every four years via the voting process which is based on people's private opinions shaped by, among other things, religious belief.

Still, despite the efforts of so many who continue to deny the importance of religion in American life, there are many individuals and organizations who have already begun to seek a reversal of this trend. For example, as stated earlier, we have the actions of many courageous young people across this country who, in their own way, have sought to return God to our public institutions by simply praying whenever and wherever the need arises.

There are also organizations such as the Josephson Institute of Ethics in Marina Del Ray, California which, through its publications *Ethics in Action* and *Ethics: Easier Said Than Done,* seeks to rebuild our communities upon a structure of ethical and moral values. In addition, through its "Character Counts" initiative, the Institute seeks to teach young people the difference between right and wrong, and the value of personal character via a program which emphasizes, "The Six Pillars of Character: Trustworthiness; Respect; Responsibility; Justice & Fairness; Caring; Civic Virtue & Citizenship."

Two political offerings, neither without controversy, were the Religious Freedom Amendment (RFA) which was reintroduced on September 15, 1999 after being defeated in the House of Representatives on June 4, 1998 for failing to receive the required two-thirds majority. This amendment to the Constitution sought, in essence: to secure one's rights to acknowledge God according to the dictates of conscience; that one's right to pray and to recognize their religious beliefs, heritage, or traditions on public property, including schools, shall not be infringed, and that government cannot require any religious activity, discriminate against religion, or deny equal access to a benefit on account of religion. The second was the Religious Liberty Protection Act (RLPA) which was also introduced to Congress for consideration also in 1999. This act sought to restore the Religious Freedom Restoration Act which was passed in 1993 but was struck down by the Supreme Court in 1997 on the grounds that it was too broad. Over the years since this action, the Court has repeatedly ruled as unconstitutional many religious practices instead of recognizing the free exercise of religion. The RLPA sought to reaffirm government's limits in religious affairs, in that, it required government to have a compelling reason before it could restrict religious practices or consider them unconstitutional, and it also sought to keep the Court accountable to the Constitution. Although the House passed the RLPA on July 15, 1999, both the Religious Freedom Amendment and the Religious Liberty Protection Act languished in limbo during the balance of the Clinton administration.

Of course there are thousands of other examples—the majority going unreported—of people and organizations working to return God to America, and religion into our society. However, this resurgence of religiously oriented activity in America does not contradict my basic contention of a lack of religious principles within the sociopolitical structure of this nation. Here, this activity of the citizenry is being undertaken as a direct reaction to the patently irreligious direction this country has adopted within its policies, legislation, legal arguments, and governance. What we are witnessing is the voice of the people crying out for religion to be included as part of this nation's public life, and for religion to be an integral part of America's public forum. Thankfully, many of America's leaders have been listening.

What is most encouraging in this regard is the agenda undertaken during the just completed first one hundred days of George W. Bush's tenure as President. Within this period many of Bush's initiatives have set the tone for, what I believe is, the future direction of his goals and intentions with regard to the reorientation of this country's moral core. That tone is best characterized in a speech President Bush gave on March 21, 2001 at the White House before a group of Roman Catholic cardinals and bishops. In it he said, "a great awakening is underway in America; people are rediscovering...the inspiration of faith in their lives, and the importance of faith in our society." In addition, the President stated that America would do well to put the teachings of Pope John Paul II into action.

Lest we be lulled into a continued complacency by the mere words that many of our leaders often offer instead of deeds, the following is a sampling of President Bush's efforts during the first few months he has been in office, which I believe exemplifies his deep desire to repair this country's seriously damaged moral core:

A) on January 22, 2001, the twenty-eighth anniversary of the *Roe v. Wade* decision, and the first full day of his presidency, Bush signed an executive order which prohibited the use of American dollars to fund international family planning agencies who promote abortion, or that provide the procedure abroad. (Incidentally, in May 2001 the House voted to preserve this ban.);

B) a new plan was unveiled by Bush in the second month of his presidency which created a White House Office of Faith-Based and Community Initiatives. This office would distribute millions of federal dollars to religious and community groups in order for them to provide social services to the poor; sick; abandoned; victimized; addicted; destitute, and otherwise unfortunate members of our society. On this effort, President Bush spoke repeatedly of the government's solemn responsibility to offer compassion and help to those Americans in need of assistance. He affirmed that, "(t)he indispensable and transforming work of faith-based and other charitable service groups must be encouraged";

C) on several occasions during his first one hundred days in office, President Bush has voiced support for some form of school tuition voucher system which would offer financial assistance to those parents who choose to send their children to parochial schools;

D) on March 23, 2001, President Bush spoke at the dedication ceremony of the Pope John Paul II Cultural Center in Washington, D.C. and repeatedly praised the Pontiff for his "moral authority," and extolled the Pope for spreading God's message of hope, faith, truth, and love throughout the world. In addition, Bush offered one of the most powerful statements to date in support of the sanctity of human life when he declared, "(t)he culture of life is a welcoming culture, never excluding, never dividing, never despairing and always affirming the goodness of life in all its seasons…We must defend in love the innocent child waiting to be born";

E)   in April 2001, the Federal Communications Commission issued a long-awaited policy statement regarding new broadcasting indecency standards. Citing a, "festering problem of indecency on the airwaves," the Commission urged all broadcasters across the nation to work with Congress and President Bush to reinstate a strictly voluntary code of conduct in order to eliminate the, "onslaught of on-air smut";

F)   on April 27, 2001, the House of Representatives voted to make it a federal crime to harm a fetus during an assault on a pregnant woman, and urged further actions be taken on behalf of "unborn victims." Earlier in the week, President Bush issued the following statement which aided in the bill's passage, "(t)he administration supports protection for unborn children and therefore supports House passage." Many believe this bill is the first step toward the government's legal recognition of the fetus as a person.

G)   as of May 2001, with regard to the more current issues involving prayer in public schools, recent reports indicate that the Supreme Court may rule on allowing a representative elected by a school's student body to offer a brief (not to exceed two minutes) statement at a student assembly, graduation, etc. This statement may be religious in nature, but not restricted to only religious themes.

I applaud President George W. Bush, and support the majority of his efforts (with the exception of a federally funded school tuition voucher system for parochial schools which, for obvious reasons, would lead to too much government involvement in religious education programs).

My hope is that, at a minimum, his time in office can undo the damage the Clinton years have done to America's moral and religious foundation. However, I pray that in the long run President Bush's legacy will not only return this country to our moral and religious underpinnings, but also put an end to the scourge of abortion in America.

The overall view outlined here, and throughout this entire book, is one which not only seeks to strengthen this country's internal bonds, but one which also hopes to begin a revitalization of our damaged communities which have been infested with crime, apathy, and other forms of severely antisocial behavior. Although President Bush has set the tone for the nation as a whole, many believe that much of this revitalization must begin on a local level. For example, the Long Island newspaper *Newsday* sought to counteract the "growing sense of isolation from neighbors, government and institutions of all kinds" via their "A Search for Community" project, which published a piece in their "Viewpoints" column entitled "Mix Morality into the Conversation" (*Newsday* 11 October 1999, A29). This piece, written by Richard Koubeck, who is coordinator of the Public Policy Education Network at Catholic Charities of the Diocese of Rockville Centre, stated, "(m)oral vision should be an essential part of community life. Moral conversation is the essence of politics; it is...how free people must order their lives together." (A29).

Others find that all segments of the global community at large are similarly plagued by much of the same problems affecting the United States, and although most seek a more universal solution, the general blame is placed directly on America's doorstep. For example, writing in an issue of *Cross Currents: The Journal of the Association for Religion and Intellectual Life*, Daniel J. Adams, a theologian teaching in Korea, in an article entitled "Toward a Theological Understanding of Postmodernism," stated that the world is in a period of transition as we enter into a era he characterized as an "unsecularization of the world"

(520), that is, the decline of modernism. Here, Adams finds evidence for the rise of traditional religion and the sacred, and one of the major reasons he cites for this era of postmodernism is, "the decline of the West." (520). Adams indicates that: Western philosophy has reached an impasse of linguistic analysis; Western art is lost in abstractions; Western science is suffocating in its own pollution; Western religion is caught in a dilemma of secularism and personal piety—all of which is being challenged through the rejection of Western democratic political theory by many of the remaining world cultures. In addition, Adams goes on to explain that the modern worldview shaped by the "West is best" assumptions of, "the inevitably of progress, the invincibility of science, the desirability of democracy, and the unquestioned rights of the individual" (521), has changed dramatically, as other cultures seek to recover the "fragmented remains" of their cultural heritage, "as well as make certain that Western cultural hegemony comes to an end." (521).

In essence, Adams sees Western culture as a society fragmented by special interest groups based on a variety of issues, which only succeeded in, "paralyz(ing) the political process, destroyed the idea of the common good, and given rise to intense competition for increasingly smaller pieces of the political and economic pie." (522). Again, all of which is being rejected by the balance of world cultures as they work to rebuild their heritage.

From this perch, America vociferously protects, defends, and proclaims the supposed advances made à la the scientific as that ultimate projection of material reality which best orients humanity's future—to the exclusion of all else. In its wake, this projection has spawned and implanted individualistic and liberal philosophies into every aspect of our culture. This has resulted in the destruction of our national community; created confusion in the nature and direction of our common good; turned the majority of our population into self-centered, self-satisfying, selfish individuals; generated a climate which separates God from our consciousness; removed religion from our public lives, and upended any sense of the moral. Consequently, family life is being replaced by widespread divorce; sex and violence in every conceivable form is as available as the closest TV set; our unborn are aborted; our children are abandoned, abused, murdered, or molested; and our young people are taking up weapons and killing or maiming each other in gang related violence or ambushes at the local school—all of which has evoked the ire of much of the rest of the world who not only despise our secular lifestyle and repudiate our conclusions, but firmly resent being viewed as "backward," "primitive," or "ignorant" for not adopting our so-called "advanced" social system.

Many voices both within and outside of our society have decried our secular condition, which Fenton Johnson writing in *Harper's Magazine* described as being set on the cornerstone of money, sex, and power. In reflecting on our technological advances in light of the new millennium, Steve Dunleavy writing in the *New York Post* admonished, "it's time to put the brakes on runaway technology and science that completely ignores the most basic moral standards." (28 December 1999, 3). In his most recent visit to the United States Pope John Paul II, speaking to a crowd of one hundred thousand in St. Louis, called on all Americans to strive for higher morality and to rebuild their family life, for, "(a)s the family goes, so goes the nation!" (*New York Post* 28 January 1999, 16). Writing in *Newsweek* (June 13,1994) in an article entitled "What is Virtue?" Kenneth L. Woodward identifies "virtue" as, "a quality of character by which individuals habitually recognize and *do* (author's emphasis) the right thing" (38), and he links virtuous behavior with moral philosophy. Woodward goes on to advise that within America, "all of the core institutions that once transmitted moral education are in disrepair...yet many Americans are unprepared to recognize any moral authority outside themselves." (39). He concludes that America must continue to encourage good character, and hence virtuous behavior, by, "living in communities—family, neighborhood, religious and civic institutions—where virtue is encouraged and rewarded." (39). And finally, from Harvard Divinity School, in an article entitled "Faith, Politics, And The Common Good," E. J. Dionne, Jr. explains, "the moral crisis Americans are experiencing (has its roots) in a society built on values that steadily cut away the bonds of solidarity, morality, and trust...reform...will require a rebirth and reconstruction of the communities that constitute civil society, democracy being a community of communities." (2-3).

Our human journey has always been one where the underlying truths of our collective condition, that is, the real state of things, are actively sought by employing our intellectual and reasoning abilities through the workings of our secular establishments and from the orientations of our sacred institutions. That this is inexorably and intricately woven throughout all of human history testifies to the universality of this theme and the highly significant position it occupies in the formation, structuring, and perpetuation of human civilization. To do otherwise negates the latter condition which implies a return to a barbarous state. Though those underlying truths often remain elusive, they nonetheless exist and require the strength of our efforts to not only discover and employ, but to adhere to their principles once they are made manifest to us. According to author, scholar, theologian, former Jesuit, and professor, the late Malachi Martin, "(t)o seek...enlightenment from secular sources is...to subject man to this material universe...man has been created by God to be master of, not subject to, the material universe. He must, therefore, have a scale of values, a spirituality, that transcends the universe." (288).

That is quite different from the disturbing analogy Barbara Ehrenreich employed in a *Time* article celebrating "The Real Truth About the Female Body" which likened, "the human sexual impulse, (to) like that of the bonobo (and) is not as tightly coupled to reproduction as certain pro-family moralists like to think." (8 March, 1999: 69). Incidentally, the bonobo is a species of primate, similar to, but smaller than a chimpanzee, who substitutes sex for aggression and who engages in every possible partner combination at any possible time. The link here is that only humans and bonobos engage in sex for something other than reproduction, but I would hope the comparison ends there for the sake of civilized society. What Ehrenreich failed to consider is that the bonobo has never exhibited evidence of possessing a moral code within its simian social structure, and here I fervently hope that the social/cultural context within which the "human sexual impulse" exists still adheres to a moral code. What should be emphasized is that in addition to reproduction, human sexuality is also an expression of love and therefore of a higher ideal than that which the bonobo could ever hope of achieving. If Ehrenreich believes the nature of truth regarding human sexual conduct lies in the more perverse aspects of that conduct, then quite possibly she would similarly consider gluttony to be the dominant reason we eat, and hunger and sustenance simply but minor physical inconveniences. Here, the "real truth" about human sexuality is based primarily on reproduction and love, not promiscuity and substitution of purpose, as Ehrenreich seems to indicate. Just because some humans are capable of perverting the process does not explain the truth of human sexuality or render moral principles regarding its purpose passé. Here, the nature of truth, in this case of human sexuality, cannot be diluted or depicted as otherwise simply because the natural behavior of the bonobo happens to parallel a preternatural behavior in humans.

Therefore, with regard to the human capacity to seek and acknowledge truth, I quite firmly agree with Pope John Paul II when he stated within his encyclical "Veritatis Splendor" (The Splendor of Truth) and reiterated in another entitled "Fides et Ratio" (Faith and Reason), "(a)lthough each individual has a right to be respected in his own journey in search of the truth, there exists a prior moral obligation, and a grave one at that, to seek the truth and to adhere to it once it is known."

It is quite true and obvious from my investigation and made apparent throughout this book, that in the case of the United States of America, the Founders did not initiate a moral system for an immoral people, nor one to be devoid and barren of religious significance, and that this system was not established for the benefit of singular individuals. Rather, it was one so ideally and indefectibly immortalized by Abraham Lincoln in his "Gettysburg Address," that is, "...that this nation, under God, shall have a new birth of freedom; and that government of the people, by the people, for the people, shall not perish from the earth."

Epilogue

We Americans are a robust and resilient conglomeration of races, cultures, beliefs, and ideologies. Despite these sometimes painfully obvious differences, it is through the free nature of our society that we seek to coalesce into a unified people. Here, we find that the desire to attain and continuously experience human freedom—that is, the glue which binds us together—further fosters and allows each American the ability to enjoy the fruits of this freedom.

However, there was one major question I continuously asked myself throughout the writing of this work: Why has this freedom evolved to the point that today's Americans seem to repel from each other rather than draw closer together? As I sought to answer this question, I found mounting evidence for a continuous rise in antisocial behavior amongst Americans in direct correlation to their achievement of greater levels of social and personal freedom. Instead of a strong and growing social unity, Americans have become increasingly self-absorbed, selfish singularities in pursuit of "the next big thing" to satisfy their current need for stimulation.

For today's American, freedom has become more the satisfaction of an immediate personal desire rather than the drive to attain and secure social liberty for the effective governance and wellbeing of every member of the entire society. Sadly, most Americans could care less about the blood spilled in this country over the last two or three centuries in our quest for the achievement of freedom. Even as today's headlines announce some further abuse against human rights in some foreign land, the average American still just doesn't completely "get it." It seems that many Americans equate freedom with acquiring material possessions, and express deep concern over the fact that many foreign cultures don't sell jeans on every other street corner, or that MTV hasn't been piped in to every country on earth. I have found that rarely do most Americans really worry about the level of education within some foreign dictatorship, or the mental health of someone forced to renounce his/her religious beliefs for life, as was the case in the Russia of the recent past and is the case in many totalitarian regimes today.

To my way of thinking, the blood spilled during the American Revolution seemed a sad, but necessary sacrifice if Americans were to some day enjoy freedom from a tyrannical foreign government hell-bent on propagating a policy of social oppression and continuous abuses of basic human rights. The freedom that our Colonial ancestors achieved was first sought for these and many similarly lofty goals, not for their ability to wear the latest fashions from Europe. Although exactly how the trade routes would be affected by declaring the Colonies independent from English rule may have been way back in his mind, I doubt that Thomas Jefferson would have risked the lives of himself, his family, and the ruination of his personal property over being deprived of having the latest wig sent over from England.

However, this focus on the acquisition of personal satisfaction through the attainment of the material seems to be the dominant case amongst Americans today when the issue of freedom is raised. When a new law is being voted upon, our modern citizenry seems primarily concerned over the ultimate effect the new law would have upon one's freedom to achieve expected levels of self-gratification. Beyond that, people are rarely motivated into action. For example, I find that there is some twisted logic at work when many of today's American citizens worry more about how their sex lives are affected if *Roe v. Wade* is overturned, rather than the fact that every single day millions of humans in their fetal stage of development are being deprived of the freedom of life.

So, again I ask: Why has this freedom evolved to the point that today's Americans seem to repel from each other rather than draw closer together? The answer is painfully obvious to me: We are all in an intense competition with our neighbors for the attainment of even greater levels of personally derived self-satisfaction set within a mostly distorted concept of freedom based solely upon the acquisition and experiencing of all things available within the material world, and in all its various manifestations. To ensure the successful outcome of this paramount quest, we have abandoned many of this country's fundamental moral values; have rendered God and religion to the fringes of our social and civil forums; enacted laws which completely contradict the underlying notion of the freedom upon which this country's underpinnings are based, and held up as heroes many individuals in politics, sports, the arts, etc. despite widespread reports of their highly questionable character and behavior.

As a result of this untrammeled pursuit of the satisfaction of the self, we are becoming an increasingly selfish and less unified people, not only further distancing ourselves from each other, but also from the fundamental principles upon which this country was based. We have virtually abandoned the Founding generation's notion of a people united in the pursuit of a common goal for the common good, in favor of the modern notion of people in pursuit of personal goals for their own individual good. This contemporary concept of freedom, so fully embraced by today's American citizenry, is completely antithetical to America's foundational ideals. Therefore, if this trend continues to dominate our society I am compelled to ask: How much longer can we expect to remain together as a people? With this daily assault on the continuance of our national cohesion I again ask: How long can we remain a "United" States?

About the Author

Frank S. Farello belongs to the "Baby Boomer" generation, and first became aware of the positive possibilities of social reformation within this country during the initial promise, and the unfortunate turbulence of the 1960s. Mr. Farello has viewed with dismay how the "Baby Boomers" moved from a young generation who once understood, expressed hope for, and worked toward the betterment of all through a selfless notion of the common good, to a mature generation who has fully embraced a more "me first" oriented concept of social interaction. Along the way, Mr. Farello has found that the loss of a belief in God; the lack of the importance of religion in one's life, and the dominance of a social ethic centering on the philosophy of Epicureanism has further inclined today's Americans to adopt an almost purely egocentric view of society, and an apathetic, selfishness toward each other.

Mr. Farello currently lives with his wife and three children in New York State, and continually hopes and prays for an American society quite the opposite of the above.

Bibliography

BOOKS

Abraham, Henry J., and Barbara A. Perry. *Freedom and the Court: Civil Rights and Liberties in the United States*. 6th ed. New York: Oxford University Press, Inc., 1994.

Alderman, Ellen, and Caroline Kennedy. *In Our Defense: The Bill of Rights in Action*. New York: Avon Books, Inc., 1991.

Alley, Robert S., ed. *James Madison on Religious Liberty*. Buffalo: Prometheus Books, 1985.

Allman, William F. *The Stone Age Present: How Evolution has Shaped Modern Life—From Sex, Violence, and Language to Emotions, Morals, and Communities*. New York: Touchstone, 1995.

Arthur, John, and Amy Shapiro, eds. *Campus Wars: Multiculturalism and the Politics of Difference*. Boulder: Westview Press, Inc., 1995.

Barnet, Richard J., and John Cavanagh. *Global Dreams: Imperial Corporations and the New World Order*. New York: Touchstone, 1994.

Barton, David. *Original Intent: The Courts, the Constitution, and Religion*. Aledo: WallBuilder Press, 1997.

Bellah, Robert, et al. *Habits of the Heart: Individualism and Commitment in American Life*. Updated ed. Berkeley: University of California Press, 1996.

—-. *The Good Society*. New York: Vintage Books, 1992.

Bennett, William J. *The De-Valuing of America: The Fight for Our Culture and Our Children*. New York: Touchstone, 1992.

Berger, Peter L. *The Sacred Canopy: Elements of a Sociological Theory of Religion*. New York: Anchor Books, 1990.

Bernstein, Carl, and Marco Politi. *His Holiness: John Paul II And The History Of Our Time*. New York: Penguin Books, 1996.

Bishop, Jim. *The Birth of the United States*. New York: William Morrow and Company, Inc., 1976.

Bonomi, Patricia U. *Under the Cope of Heaven: Religion, Society, and Politics in Colonial America*. New York: Oxford University Press, Inc., 1986.

Boston, Robert. *Why The Religious Right Is Wrong About Separation of Church & State*. Amherst: Prometheus Books, 1993.

Brinkley, Alan. *Liberalism and Its Discontents*. Cambridge: Harvard University Press, 1998.

Bronowski, J., and Bruce Mazlish. *The Western Intellectual Tradition*. New York: Barnes and Noble Books, 1993.

Bruce, Steve. *Religion in the Modern World: From Cathedrals to Cults.* New York: Oxford University Press, Inc., 1996.

Cahn, Stephen M. *Classics of Western Philosophy.* 4th ed. Indianapolis: Hackett Publishing Company, Inc., 1995.

Carr, Edward Hallett. *What Is History?* New York: Vintage Books, 1961.

Carter, Stephen L. *The Culture of Disbelief: How American Law and Politics Trivialize Religious Devotion.* Updated ed. New York: Anchor Books, 1994.

Chatterjee, Margaret. *Gandhi's Religious Thoughts.* Notre Dame: University of Notre Dame Press, 1983.

Chryssides, George. *The Elements of Unitarianism.* Boston: Element Books, Inc., 1998.

Copleston, Frederick. *A History of Philosophy. Vol. 1 Greece and Rome.* 2nd ed. New York: Image Books, 1993.

Cox, Harvey. *Religion in the Secular City: Toward a Postmodern Theology.* New York: Simon and Schuster, 1984.

Curry, Thomas J. *The First Freedoms: Church and State in America to the Passage of the First Amendment.* New York: Oxford University Press, Inc., 1986.

Daloz, Laurent A. Parks, et al. *Common Fire: Leading Lives of Commitment in a Complex World.* Boston: Beacon Press, 1996.

Derber, Charles. *The Wilding of America: How Greed and Violence are Eroding Our Nation's Character.* New York: St. Martin's Press, Inc., 1996.

Dewey, John. *Liberalism and Social Action.* 6th ed. New York: Capricorn Books, 1963.

Du Bois, W. E. Burghardt. *The Souls of Black Folk.* Signet ed. New York: Penguin Books, 1995.

Eck, Diana L. *Encountering God: A Spiritual Journey from Bozeman to Banaras.* Boston: Beacon Press, 1993.

Englehardt, Elaine E., and Donald D. Schmeltekopt. *Ethics and Life: An Interdisciplinary Approach to Moral Problems.* Dubuque: Wm. C. Brown Publishers, 1992.

Etzioni, Amitai. *The New Golden Rule: Community and Morality in a Democratic Society.* New York: BasicBooks, 1996.

—-. *The Spirit of Community: The Reinvention of American Society.* New York: Touchstone, 1994.

Evans, M. Stanton. *The Theme Is Freedom: Religion, Politics, and the American Tradition.* Washington: Regnery Publishing, Inc., 1994.

Fackre, Gabriel, ed. *Judgment Day at the White House: A Critical Declaration Exploring Moral Issues and the Political Use and Abuse of Religion.* Grand Rapids: William B. Eerdmans Publishing Company, 1999.

Feldman, Robert S. *Understanding Psychology.* 4th ed. New York: McGraw-Hill, Inc., 1996.

Finke, Roger, and Rodney Stark. *The Churching of America, 1776-1990: Winners and Losers in Our Religious Economy*. 3rd printing. New Brunswick: Rutgers University Press, 1997.

Fremantle, Anne. Introduction and Commentary. *The Age of Belief: The Medieval Philosophers*. New York: Mentor Books, 1954.

Friedman, Ellen G., and Corinne Squire. *Morality USA*. Minneapolis: University of Minnesota Press, 1998.

Frost, S. E., Jr. *Basic Teachings of the Great Philosophers: A Survey of Their Basic Ideas*. Rev. ed. New York: Anchor Books, 1962.

Glasser, Ira. *Visions of Liberty: The Bill of Rights for All Americans*. New York: Arcade Publishing, Inc., 1991.

Glendon, Mary Ann. *Rights Talk: The Impoverishment of Political Discourse*. New York: The Free Press, 1991.

Glenn, Msgr. Paul J. *A Tour of the Summa*. 5th printing. Rockford: Tan Books and Publishers, Inc., 1978.

Herman, Edward S., and Noam Chomsky. *Manufacturing Consent: The Political Economy of the Mass Media*. New York: Pantheon Books, 1988.

Higgins, Rev. Thomas J. *Man as Man: The Science and Art of Ethics*. Rev. ed. Rockford: Tan Books and Publishers, Inc., 1992.

Hochschild, Jennifer L. *Facing Up to the American Dream: Race, Class, and the Soul of the Nation*. Princeton: Princeton University Press, 1995.

Jamieson, Kathleen Hall, and Karlyn Kohrs Campbell. *The Interplay of Influence: News, Advertising, Politics, and the Mass Media.* 4th ed. Belmont: Wadsworth Publishing Company, 1997.

Kammen, Michael. *A Machine That Would Go of Itself: The Constitution in American Culture.* New York: St. Martin's Press, Inc., 1994.

Kekes, John. *Against Liberalism.* Ithaca: Cornell University Press, 1997.

Kramnick, Isaac, and R. Laurence Moore. *The Godless Constitution: The Case Against Religious Correctness.* New York: W. W. Norton & Company, Inc., 1997.

Kreeft, Peter. *A Shorter Summa: The Most Essential Philosophical Passages of St. Thomas Aquinas' Summa Theologica.* San Francisco: Ignatius Press, 1993.

Ladd, Everett Carll. *The Ladd Report.* New York: The Free Press, 1999.

Lasch, Christopher. *The Culture of Narcissism: American Life in an Age of Diminishing Expectations.* New York: W. W. Norton & Company, Inc., 1991.

Lewy, Guenter. *Why America Needs Religion: Secular Modernity and its Discontents.* Grand Rapids: Wm. B. Eerdmans Publishing Co., 1996.

Lind, Michael. *The Next American Nation: The New Nationalism and the Fourth American Revolution.* New York: Free Press Paperbacks, 1996.

Lipset, Seymour Martin. *American Exceptionalism: A Double-Edged Sword*. New York: W. W. Norton & Company, Inc., 1997.

Lowi, Theodore J. *The End of Liberalism: The Second Republic of the United States*. 2nd ed. New York: W. W. Norton & Company, Inc., 1979.

MacIntyre, Alasdair. *Three Rival Versions of Moral Enquiry: Encyclopaedia, Genealogy, and Tradition*. Notre Dame: University of Notre Dame Press, 1990.

MacLeod, Jay. *Ain't No Makin' It: Aspirations and Attainment in a Low-Income Neighborhood*. Boulder: Westview Press, 1995.

Maier, Pauline. *American Scripture: Making the Declaration of Independence*. New York: Alfred A. Knopf, Inc., 1997.

Martin, Malachi. *The Decline and Fall of the Roman Church*. New York: G. P. Putnam's Sons, 1981.

Marty, Martin E. *The One and the Many: America's Struggle for the Common Good*. Cambridge: Harvard University Press, 1997.

May, William E. *An Introduction to Moral Theology*. Rev. ed. Huntington: Sunday Visitor, 1994.

McConnell, Campbell R., and Stanley L. Brue. *Economics: Principles, Problems, and Policies*. 13th ed. New York: McGraw-Hill, Inc., 1996.

Morris, Richard B., ed. *Encyclopedia of American History*. New York: Harper & Brothers, 1953.

Murdoch, Iris. *Metaphysics as a Guide to Morals*. London: Penguin Books, 1993.

Peterson, Merrill D., ed. *The Portable Thomas Jefferson*. New York: Penguin Books, 1975.

Rakove, Jack N. *Original Meanings: Politics and Ideas in the Making of the Constitution*. 4th ed. New York: Alfred A. Knopf, Inc., 1997.

Robertson, Ian. *Sociology*. 3rd ed. New York: Worth Publishers, Inc., 1987.

Samuelson, Robert J. *The Good Life and Its Discontents: The American Dream in the Age of Entitlement 1945—1995*. New York: Vintage Books, 1997.

Sandel, Michael J. *Democracy's Discontent: America in Search of a Public Philosophy*. Cambridge: The Belknap Press of Harvard University Press, 1996.

—-. *Liberalism and the Limits of Justice*. 2nd ed. New York: Cambridge University Press, 1998.

Scheffler, Samuel. *Human Morality*. New York: Oxford University Press, Inc., 1992.

Schlesinger, Arthur M., Jr. *The Disuniting of America: Reflections on a Multicultural Society*. New York: W. W. Norton & Company, Inc., 1993.

Schmalleger, Frank. *Criminal Justice Today: An Introductory Text for the Twenty-First Century*. Third ed. Englewood Cliffs: Prentice Hall Career & Technology, 1995.

Schor, Juliet B. *The Overworked American: The Unexpected Decline of Leisure.* New York: BasicBooks, 1992.

—-. *The Overworked American: Why We Want What We Don't Need.* New York: Harper Perennial, 1998.

Sennett, Richard. *The Fall of Public Man.* New York: W. W. Norton & Company, Inc., 1992.

Shapiro, Martin., ed. *The Constitution of the United States and Related Documents.* Wheeling: Harlan Davidson, Inc., 1973.

Sharp, Ansel M., Charles A. Register, and Paul W. Grimes. *Economics of Social Issues.* 13th ed. Boston: Irwin/McGraw-Hill, 1998.

Shklar, Judith N. *Ordinary Vices.* Cambridge: The Belknap Press of Harvard University Press, 1984.

Smith, Huston. *The World's Religions: Our Great Wisdom Traditions.* Rev. and Updated ed. San Francisco: Harper Collins Publishers, 1991.

Smith, Page. *Rediscovering Christianity: A History of Modern Democracy and the Christian Ethic.* New York: St. Martin's Press, Inc., 1994.

Stark, Rodney, and William Sims Bainbridge. *The Future of Religion: Secularization, Revival, and Cult Formation.* Berkeley: University of California Press, 1985.

Stone, Lynda, ed. *The Education Feminism Reader.* New York: Routledge, 1994.

Sullivan, Daniel J. *An Introduction to Philosophy: The Perennial Principles of the Classical Realist Tradition.* Rockford: Tan Books and Publishers, Inc., 1992.

Taylor, Charles. *Sources of the Self: The Making of the Modern Identity.* 8th ed. Cambridge: Harvard University Press, 1996.

Thiemann, Ronald F. *Religion in Public Life: A Dilemma for Democracy.* Washington: Georgetown University Press, 1996.

Tocqueville, Alexis de. *Democracy in America.* Ed. J. P. Mayer. New York: Harper Perennial, 1988.

Twitchell, James B. *Lead Us Into Temptation: The Triumph of American Materialism.* New York: Columbia University Press, 1999.

Weinreb, Lloyd L. *Natural Law and Justice.* 4th printing. Cambridge: Harvard University Press, 1997.

Westbrook, Robert B. *John Dewey and American Democracy.* Ithaca: Cornell University Press, 1991.

Wilson, James Q. *The Moral Sense.* New York: Free Press Paperbacks, 1997.

Wolfe, Alan. *One Nation, After All.* New York: Viking Penguin, 1998.

Zinn, Howard. *The Politics of History.* 2nd ed. Urbana: University of Illinois Press, 1990.

JOURNALS IN ENTIRETY

Cross Currents: The Journal of the Association for Religion and Intellectual Life. New Rochelle: College of New Rochelle, issue: Volume 47, Number 4, Winter 1997/1998.

Ethics: An International Journal of Social, Political and Legal Philosophy. Chicago: The University of Chicago, issue: October 1997.

Ethics: Easier Said than Done. Marina Del Rey: The Josephson Institute of Ethics, issue: #29, May 1995.

Religion and Values in Public Life. Cambridge: The Center for the Study of Values in Public Life at Harvard Divinity School, issue: Volume 6, Number 4, Summer 1998.

SELECTED ARTICLES FROM JOURNALS

From *Cross Currents: The Journal of the Association for Religion and Intellectual Life.* New Rochelle: College of New Rochelle.
—-Goulet, Denis. "Tasks and Methods in Development Ethics." (Summer 1988): 146-163.
—-Incandela, Joseph M. "Playing God: Divine Activity, Human Activity, and Christian Ethics." (Spring 1996): 59-76.
—-Kolbenschlag, Madonna. "The American Economy, Religious Values, and a New Moral Imperative." (Summer 1984): 153-170.
—-Levinas, Emanuel. "Ethics and Infinity." (Summer 1984): 191-214.
—-Raines, John C. "Toward a Relational Theory of Justice." (Summer 1989): 129-160.

From *Ethics: Social Issues Resources Series*. Boca Raton: SIRS Social/Critical Issues, issue: Volume 4.

—-Buchan, David. "Laying Down a Code of Honor." Article 30.

—-Goodstein, David. "What Do We Mean When We Use The Term 'Science Fraud'?" Article 12.

—-Leopold, A. Carl. "The Science Community is Starved for Ethical Standards." Article 2.

—-Macklin, Ruth. "Choice or Control?" Article 44.

—-Yenkin, Jonathan. "Ethics Officers Manage Companies' Morals." Article 17.

From *The Journal of American History*. Bloomington: Organization of American Historians, issue: Volume 84, Number 1, June 1997.

—-Breen, T. H. "Ideology and Nationalism on the Eve of the American Revolution: Revisions Once More in Need of Revising." 13-39.

—-Desrochers, Robert E., Jr. "'Not Fade Away': The Narrative of Venture Smith, an African American in the Early Republic." 40-66.

—-McGreevy, John T. "Thinking on One's Own: Catholicism in the American Intellectual Imagination, 1928-1960." 97-131.

From *The Wilson Quarterly*. Washington: Woodrow Wilson International Center for Scholars, issue: Volume XXII, Number 4, Autumn 1998.

—-De Long, J. Bradford, et al. "The Promise and Perils of the New Economy." 13-53.

—-Miller, Stephen. "A Note on the Banality of Evil." 54-59.

MISCELLANEOUS

Adams, Daniel J. "Toward a Theological Understanding of Postmodernism." *Cross Currents: The Journal of the Association for*

Religion and Intellectual Life. issue: Volume 47, Number 4, Winter 1997/1998: 518-530.

Alvarez, Maria. "Pope ends visit with plea for a higher morality." *New York Post* 28 Jan. 1999: 16.

Bader, Michael. "Selfishness and the Politics of Meaning." *Tikkun* 13.5 (1998): 10-11.

Bennett, William J. "President's Lying Under Oath Simply Cannot Be Tolerated." *Human Events* 9 Oct. 1998: 16-17.

—-. "Does Honor Have a Future?" *Imprimis* Dec. 1998: 1-8.

—-. "Neuroscience and the Human Spirit." *National Review* 31 Dec. 1998: 32-35.

—-. "What We've Learned." *The Wall Street Journal* 10 Feb. 1999: A22.

"Bowling with Government." *Wilson Quarterly* Spring, 1998: 132.

Cloud, John. "Law On Bended Knee." *Time* 13 Sept. 1999: 32-33.

Dionne, E. J., Jr. "Faith, Politics, And The Common Good." *Religion & Values in Public Life:The Center for the Study of Values in Public Life at Harvard Divinity School* issue: Volume 6, Number 2/3, Winter/Spring 1998: 1-8.

Dunleavy, Steve. "Technology run amok has no morality." *New York Post* 28 Dec. 1998: 3.

Durkin, Barbara J. "Former Atheist Makes Case For School Prayer: Now minister, wants religious renewal." *Newsday* 18 Apr. 1999: A39.

Ehrenreich, Barbara. "The Real Truth About The Female Body." *Time* 8 Mar. 1999: 56-71.

Gallagher, Kathleen M. "Law Must Bar Assaults on Unborn." *Newsday* 20 Apr, 2000: A53.

Galtung, Johan. "Religions, Hard and Soft." *Cross Currents: The Journal of the Association for Religious and Intellectual Life.* issue: Volume 47, Number 4, Winter 1997/1998: 437-450.

Goodman, Peter. "FCC Issues Smut Policy: Response to an 'onslaught.'" *Newsday* 7 Apr. 2001: PA6.

Greeley, Andrew, "Habits of the Head." *Society* May/June, 1992: 74-81.

Greider, William. "Global Economy." *The Nation* 15 Dec. 1997: 11-16.

"House Votes to Criminalize Assault on 'Unborn Victims.'" *Newsday* 27 Apr. 2001: A26.

John Paul II. "Faith and Reason." *Encyclical 13* 15 Oct. 1998.

—-. "The Splendor of Truth." *Encyclical 9* 6 Aug. 1993.

Johnson, Fenton. "Beyond Belief: A Skeptic Searches for an American Faith." *Harper's Magazine* Sept. 1998: 39-54.

Kelly, Michael. "How Clinton Saved Liberalism." *New York Post* 17 Nov. 1999: 45.

Koubek, Richard. "Mix Morality Into the Conversation." *Newsday* 11 Oct. 1999: A29.

Limbaugh, Rush. "My Conversation with Bill Bennett." *The Limbaugh Letter* Oct. 1996: 6-8.

Lincoln, Abraham. "Gettysburg Address." Dedication of the National Soldiers' Cemetery. Cemetery Hill. Gettysburg, Pennsylvania. 19 Nov. 1863.

Lipset, Seymour Martin. "Much Obliged." *The Washington Post* 9 Nov. 1998: 33.

McClay, William M. "Fifty Years of The Lonely Crowd." *Wilson Quarterly* Summer, 1998: 34-42.

Putnam, Robert D. "The Prosperous Community: Social Capital and Public Life." *The American Prospect* 13 Spring, 1993: 35-42.

—-. "Bowling Alone: America's Declining Social Capital." *Journal of Democracy* 6:1 January, 1995: 65-78.

—-. "The Strange Disappearance of Civic America." *The American Prospect* 24 Winter, 1996: 34-48.

Quayle, Dan. "No More Pro-Abortion Justices." *Human Events* 2 Oct. 1998: 12.

Schwarz, Benjamin. "Beware the Risk of Waging 'Moral War.'" *Newsday* 29 Apr. 1999: A33.

Shaw, Gaylord. "Prayer Case to Court: Justices to review ban of Texas student ceremony." *Newsday* 16 Nov. 1999: A4.

"The Pope and the Young." *New York Post* 28 Jan. 1999: 28.

Toedtman, James. "Reply to Violence: House would let schools display Commandments." *Newsday* 18 June 1999: A5.

Woodward, Kenneth L. "What Is Virtue?" *Newsweek* 13 June 1994: 38-39.

INTERNET WEB SITES

Douglass: Archives of American Public Address. Evanston: Northwestern University School of Speech—Department of Communication Studies,
http://douglass.speech.nwu.edu/wils_b06.htm
26 Apr. 1999.

Religious Freedom Amendment: The Text. Washington: Office of Congressman Istook, U.S. House of Representatives,
http://religiousfreedom.house.gov/text.htm
09 Nov. 1998.

Religious Freedom Amendment: Legal Review and Analysis. Washington: Office of Congressman Istook, U.S. House of Representatives,
http://religiousfreedom.house.gov/rlegal.htm
09 Nov. 1998.

Separation of Church and State. Gilbert: Christian Answers Network,
http://www.christiananswers.net/q-wall/wal-g004.html

09 Nov. 1998.

Separation of Church and State Home Page: Responding to the Religious Right, The Basic Arguments. Louisville: University of Louisville,
http://www.louisville.edu/~tnpete01/church/argidx.htm
09 Nov. 1998.

State of the First Amendment: Religion. Arlington: The Freedom Forum Online,
http://www.freedomforum.org/newsstand/reports/sofa/chap03.asp
09 Nov. 1998.

Thomas Jefferson on Politics and Government. Charlottesville: University of Virginia,
http://etext.virginia.edu/jefferson/quotations/
04 May 1999.

The Virtual Community: Homesteading on the Electronic Frontier.— Rhiengold, Howard. Sausalito: The Well, LLC., (also: New York: Harper Perennial, 1993.)
http://www.well.com/user/hlr/vcbook
13 Nov. 1999.

Virtual Communities: Abort, Retry, Failure?—Fernback, Jan, and Brad Thompson. Sausalito: The Well, LLC.,
http://www.well.com/user/hlr/texts/vccivil.html
13 Nov. 1999.

Virtuality and its Discontents: Searching for Community in Cyberspace.—Turkle, Shirley. Boston: The American Prospect 24, Winter 1996: 50-57.
http://www.prospect.org/archives/24/24turk.html
13 Nov. 1999.

TELEVISION PROGRAMS

Religion and Ethics Newsweekly. PBS. WNET, New York.
Pertinent broadcast dates: 21 November, 1998; 20 December, 1998; 2 January, 1999; 30 January, 1999; 28 February, 1999; 17 April, 1999; 24 April, 1999; 26 June, 1999; 17 July, 1999; 25 September, 1999; 6 November, 1999; 24 March, 2001; 14 April, 2001.

Pope John Paul II. The History Channel, New York.
Broadcast date: 16 December, 1999.

Name Index

Lewy, Guenter, 25, 39, 42, 62, 69, 88, 89

Lind, Michael, 80

Lipset, Seymour Martin, xxxv, 16, 17, 36, 37, 44, 53, 54, 59, 61, 69, 73, 140, 147

Lincoln, Abraham, xv, 196

Locke, John, xx, xxi, xxiii, xxiv, xxv, 52, 72,74

Lowi, Theodore J., 77, 78

Luther, Martin, 35, 36, 37, 64

MacLeod, Jay, 129

Madison, James, xxv, 9, 11, 12, 13, 27, 28, 113, 116, 117, 118

Maier, Pauline, 6

Martin, Malachi, 194

Marty, Martin E., 46, 47, 49, 68, 89, 134, 155, 168, 181

Marx, Karl, 76, 77, 78, 105, 137

Mary (Mother of Jesus), 92

Mason, George, 6

May, William E., xix

Mazlish, Bruce, 136

McCarthy, Joseph, 166

Mill, John Stuart, xxi, 74

Moore, R. Laurence, xxxix, 27

Murdoch, Iris, xxiv, 112, 113

Murray, William, 183

Neuhaus, Richard John, 173

Nietzsche, Friedrich Wilhelm, 21

O'Hair, Madalyn Murray, 183

Pain, Thomas, xxii

Peterson, Merrill D., 11, 28, 30, 32, 115, 117, 119

Plato, xx

Putnam, Robert D., 155, 156, 157, 158, 159, 162

Rakove, Jack N., xxvi, 5, 10, 12, 13, 116, 117, 118

Reagan, Ronald W., 185

Reed, Stanley F., 30

Rhiengold, Howard, 158

Robertson, Ian, xxxii

Roosevelt, Franklin D., 75

Rousseau, Jean-Jacques, xxi, xxiii

Russell, Bertrand, 167

Rutherford, James, 69

Samuelson, Robert J., 22, 74

Sandel, Michael J., 70, 81, 85

Saperstein, David, 174

Sartre, Jean-Paul, 105

Scheffler, Samuel, 61

Schlesinger, Arthur M., Jr., 154, 155, 160

Schmalleger, Frank, xix, 113

Schmeltekopft, David D., 104

Schor, Juliet B., 138, 139, 142, 143, 144

Schwarz, Benjamin, 185